RECLAIMING FAIR USE

Reclaiming Fair Use

HOW TO PUT BALANCE BACK IN COPYRIGHT

Patricia Aufderheide and Peter Jaszi

THE UNIVERSITY OF CHICAGO PRESS · Chicago and London

Patricia Aufderheide is University Professor in the School of Communication at American University and director of the Center for Social Media. She is the author of, most recently, *Documentary: A Very Short Introduction.*

Peter Jaszi is professor of domestic and international copyright law at the Washington College of Law, American University, where he directs the Glushko-Samuelson Intellectual Property Law Clinic. He is the coeditor of *Making and Unmaking Intellectual Property,* also published by the University of Chicago Press.

The University of Chicago Press, Chicago 60637
The University of Chicago Press, Ltd., London
© 2011 by The University of Chicago
All rights reserved. Published 2011.
Printed in the United States of America

20 19 18 17 16 15 14 13   3 4 5

ISBN-13: 978-0-226-03227-6 (cloth)
ISBN-10: 0-226-03227-2 (cloth)
ISBN-13: 978-0-226-03228-3 (paper)
ISBN-10: 0-226-03228-0 (paper)

Library of Congress Cataloging-in-Publication Data
Aufderheide, Patricia.
      Reclaiming fair use : how to put balance back in copyright /
   Patricia Aufderheide and Peter Jaszi.
          p. cm.
      Includes bibliographical references and index.
      ISBN-13: 978-0-226-03227-6 (cloth : alk. paper)
      ISBN-10: 0-226-03227-2 (cloth : alk. paper)
      ISBN-13: 978-0-226-03228-3 (pbk. : alk. paper)
      ISBN-10: 0-226-03228-0 (pbk. : alk. paper) 1. Fair use
   (Copyright)—United States. 2. Copyright infringement—
   United States. I. Jaszi, Peter. II. Title.
   KF3020.A944 2011
   346.7304'82—dc22
                                                    2010053817

CONTENTS

ACKNOWLEDGMENTS

We are grateful to the many people in the communities of practice we have been privileged to work with, who shared with us their stories and concerns. We thank our program officers at the Ford Foundation, the Rockefeller Foundation, the Haas Family Trusts, the Hewlett Foundation, the John D. and Catherine T. MacArthur Foundation, and the Andrew Wood Mellon Foundation for encouragement, critique, and funding to pursue the projects that led to this book. We are grateful for the conscientious and supportive work of our editor, David Morrow, and our manuscript editor, Carol Saller. We also thank anonymous readers and editors, as well as colleagues who graciously read this book in progress, including Barbara Abrash, Tarleton Gillespie, and Jessica Clark. American University has offered longstanding support; and we are particularly grateful to School of Communication dean Larry Kirkman for liberal use of course releases to conduct this work and to Washington College of Law dean Claudio Grossman. We owe a debt to our students, who have followed us so enthusiastically in this work, particularly Katie Bieze, Claire Darby, Genna Duberstein, Ashley Gordon, Matt Gordon, Jessica Mickelsen, Colleen Mulcrone, Winn Phillips, and Maura Ugarte. Our staffs at the Center for Social Media—especially Agnes Varnum, Alison Hanold, and Angelica Das—and at the Program on Information Justice and Intellectual Property—especially Sean Flynn and Stacey Jackson-Roberts—deserve special mention. We have benefited from a national informal network of scholars and lawyers who have selflessly helped us shape the tools for fair-use advocacy, including Jonathan Band, Jamie Bischoff, Brandon Butler, Robert Clarida, Kenneth Crews, Michael Donaldson, Lewis Hyde, Anthony Falzone, Bill Herman, Mizuko Ito, Henry Jenkins, Rob Kasunic, Jack Lerner, Corynne McSherry, Michael Madison, Virginia Rutledge, Pamela

Samuelson, Jason Schultz, Gigi Sohn, Rebecca Tushnet, Jennifer Urban, Fred von Lohmann, and Bruce Williams. The many staffers and board members at professional associations and organizations with whom we have worked to shape fair-use tools have been extraordinarily generous. We have been privileged to benefit from the dedication and advocacy of many creative community members and advocates who have taken up the cause of expanding access to fair use, among them Steve Anderson, Sheila Curran Bernard, Chris Boulton, Katy Chevigny, Kate Coles, Jon Else, Marjorie Heins, Bill Herman, Renee Hobbs, Byron Hurt, Dean Jansen, Barbara Kopple, Kembrew McLeod, Ben Moskowitz, Gordon Quinn, Libby Smigel, David van Taylor, and Lindsey Weeramuni. And of course we are grateful to our loved ones, who share our pragmatic idealism.

INTRODUCTION

In every cry of every Man,
In every Infants cry of fear,
In every voice; in every ban,
The mind-forg'd manacles I hear

WILLIAM BLAKE, *London*

This book will help you understand how to think about and use copyright, and especially your right to use copyrighted material without permission or payment when you make a work—whether a blog entry, a song, a mashup, a poem, a documentary, a magazine article, a lesson plan, a scholarly archive, a slide show, a technical manual, a scrapbook, a collage, or a brochure. That right to use unlicensed material is called fair use. This book also gives you strategies to deal with some copyright policy problems right here and now. Finally, it reframes the debate about copyright issues, revaluing copyright's role in encouraging future creators.

Copyright conversations have become like a battleground between two worldviews. One is that of the mass-media corporations fighting for control of what they understand to be their enclosed garden, generating fruit to be sold by the harvested bushel. They have pushed for and won long and strong copyright—copyright policies that heavily privilege the rights of copyright owners. The other is that of people who make new cultural works—often artists, remixers, appropriators, self-styled pirates—who understand the cultural landscape from which they draw to be a common field, ready for grazing and the creation of new, zesty products redolent of the past yet promising the future. These people's perspective often is that copyright is bunk.

Their conflict is an unwinnable and unnecessary battle—and it's bad for the rest of us, who are neither big copyright holders nor bomb-throwers. At this point, most of us make cultural products at some point in our days and weeks. People do it at work, in community groups, and at home. Whether it is a Sunday school presentation or higher-ed curriculum, a slide show for your uncle's birthday or for the board meeting, an adorable exchange between two cousins at the reunion, documentation of a rough moment in the town council meeting, a fashion assembly on the DIY designer site Polyvore, a blog post, or a teaser for an important report on YouTube—people are encountering copyright issues in their daily lives. They want more choices than seem to be available in the "war of words" that pits big business against copyright anarchists. They would like to know that when they create something—even when it is not for money—they have some rights over it. And they would also like to be able to make work that references the world around us without getting into trouble.

We believe that on top of the problems people have with an ill-fitting copyright law today, they also often bind themselves with "mind-forg'd manacles" (as the poet William Blake once put it, surveying the misery of industrial London). This book was written in the hopes of loosening those manacles. It is designed to free you not only from unnecessary strictures of copyright but from the disempowering structure of a "copyright wars" way of thinking about how to use the culture at your fingertips.

It gives you a way to see copyright as a set of policies that govern how we collectively manage our cultural heritage and how we nurture cultural production—a policy in the public interest. It provides you with the historical and legal background that can give you confidence in your decision making. It provides a proven, workable method for people to reclaim the constitutional and human rights they have as creators under copyright. It gives you tools to change both practice and policy.

Over the last few years, we have worked with filmmakers, online video makers, dancers, creators of open-access university courseware, media literacy teachers, and librarians. They all had one common problem. They needed to quote copyrighted material in order to do their work well, and the licensing arrangements that work perfectly well for highly professional media operations such as Hollywood studios just didn't fit their needs. In fact, they sometimes could not get anyone at a studio or music company or archives house to answer their e-mails or calls, because there was so little money in the licensing deals.

We were able to work with them to create codes of best practices in fair use—the right to use copyrighted material without permission or payment, in some circumstances. By creating these codes and then widely disseminating them, these communities not only liberated themselves to do the best work they could do—without hurting their own rights as copyright holders or those of others—they also set in motion a trend of people reclaiming their rights under the law.

As we worked with these communities, we understood ever more clearly the consequences of a deformed and shrunken understanding of copyright policy and its purpose. We saw that when people do not understand the law, when they are constantly afraid that they might get caught for referring to copyrighted culture—whether an image, or a phrase of a song, or a popular cartoon character—they can't do their best work. Their work as well as their imaginations shrink down to what they think might be possible. Deciding to just go ahead and "do it" is no solution for all the people who worry that taking a risk may put their assets or family's stability at risk, and who in any case are just trying to do the right thing.

We came to see how this misunderstanding cripples creativity at its base and deforms the growth and development of our own culture. We saw that it was happening in ways mostly invisible to people, who often were quietly convincing themselves that some things were simply too hard to imagine doing, under the circumstances. We also saw how much change people could bring about in their own lives and that of their creative communities when they applied a better understanding of copyright to their own practices.

We introduce you to communities who are making fair use more useable, and invite you to do the same, whatever it is you want to create. Fair use is a tool of creative freedom for the purposes you choose.

But fair use becomes real only when people actually use it; like a muscle, it can shrink with disuse. Too few people today understand how it meets the needs of copyright policy as well as their personal creative needs.

We came to this work differently. Pat Aufderheide, as a historical and communications scholar as well as a film critic, had long worked on the problem of how grassroots and dissident cultural expression enters and circulates in the culture. She had spent decades working with the documentary film community. Peter Jaszi, as a lawyer and scholar of international intellectual property law, had long studied the evolution of law in the context of custom and culture. He had worked extensively with librarians, film scholars, and others on their specific copyright issues.

We met at a conference Peter organized at American University's law school, Washington College of Law, to create a copyright research agenda. A variety of legal scholars demonstrated with skill and logic how copyright constrained media makers. They showed that extended copyright, default copyright, and intimidation tactics by large media companies limited the choices of new creators of culture. They lacked, however, anything other than purely anecdotal evidence from any creative practices.

Something bothered Pat and some creators in the room about this conversation: The creative voice was not present. "They need to convince musicians of this," Jenny Toomey, then the director of the Future of Music Coalition whispered to Pat. The filmmakers Pat knew also would not recognize the description of copyright's problems; they never complained about this aspect of copyright. They complained about the welter of licenses they had to get. They complained that someone had ripped off a scene or an archival sequence or an image from their movie and put it into another. They were afraid of losing distribution money to downloaders. But they didn't complain about why they couldn't do their work because of copyright problems. The worldview of many legal scholars—copyright is stifling creativity—didn't match up with that of musicians or filmmakers, who at the time were mostly asking, How can I protect my copyright more securely? This, it turned out, was a question that bothered the legal scholars too. The conference started a discussion between Peter and Pat: How could copyright research contribute to crossing the gap between the legal scholars and the creators?

The answer to how these worldviews could coexist without connecting lay in the problem of shrunken imagination—the "mind-forg'd manacles." If artists did not even see that they were avoiding certain creative opportunities and failing even to imagine that they might undertake others, then they would not feel the loss that the legal scholars kept pointing to but could not document. Together we decided to explore the minds of documentarians, to see if we could actually find those mental manacles.

Why documentary filmmakers? Because Pat knew a lot of them, and they are people who need to access copyrighted material in the course of their work, and finally because most documentary filmmakers work alone or in small teams, where they themselves are making the hard choices and can identify those choices. This project, which resulted in a study of documentary filmmakers' creative choices in light of their understanding of copyright, began the process that launched this generation's seizing of their fair-use rights in the United States.

We never thought, when we began this simple academic research project—the result of a question nagging at both of us—that we would be part of a process that has changed business practices, helped to inspire new kinds of cultural creation, and contributed to a change in the way culture-makers look at copyright. In fact, we were thrilled to receive a grant from the John D. and Catherine T. MacArthur Foundation to hold a conference on documentarians' rights problems and a grant from the Rockefeller Foundation to execute in-depth research on documentarians' experience with copyright. We imagined ending the research within a few months. Instead, six years later we have facilitated a clutch of codes

Fair Use: You Be the Judge >> PTA Flyer

You're making a flyer for the PTA's book fair. You'd like to reproduce some book covers to decorate it, and you expect to send this flyer around the e-mail list and also post it on the school website. Is that copyrighted material? If it is, do you have the right to reproduce it? What kind of trouble can you get into? Is the copyright situation any different for the web than for the paper version?

Answers at the back, and more at http://centerforsocialmedia.org/fair-use.

of best practices in fair use, advised school districts, policymakers, and trade associations on positions and practices, and watched an international trend grow. We have watched people change from self-perceived victims to unafraid creators and even vigorous civic actors.

For inspiration, we have drawn differently from our backgrounds, although with a common conviction in the capacity of people from many walks of life to make appropriate and reasonable decisions about their creative choices, if they have the understanding they need. Pat has anchored her analysis of culture and society in Raymond Williams's and Pierre Bourdieu's cultural production work, and her understanding of the connection between communication and public action in the work and lives of John Dewey, Stuart Hall, and her mentor James Weinstein, founder of *In These Times* newspaper. Peter has drawn on the rich heritage left by copyright historians and theorists such as Benjamin Kaplan and L. Ray Patterson and on the work of the scholars who contributed to the "critique of authorship" in law and literature from Barthes and Foucault onward, especially Peter's frequent collaborator Martha Woodmansee.

We share a commitment to the notion that with the right information and education, people can and should make their own decisions about their creative and cultural choices. We both believe that copyright has for far too long been a lawyer's preserve, and that copyright decisions, particularly about reuse of others' copyrighted work, can and must be made by creators if we are to get the best culture we can. We also have a commitment to an open society, one where a wide range of viewpoints can flourish, power can be held to account, new ideas can be explored, and big problems addressed. We think understanding the need for a balance in copyright between owners and those who use their material to make and analyze culture will be a crucial part of building an open society for tomorrow.

A note on notes: We drew on many resources to create this book, but decided against using footnotes, in the interest of readability. We have provided a reference list with some of the most important texts that we drew from, and that we think will help others who want to plunge deeper into this material.

In addition to this book, we have created a website that provides more background and examples, as well as discussion scenarios, information on litigation, and current fair-use news: http://centerforsocialmedia.org /fair-use. We welcome your comments and stories there.

1 The Culture of Fear and Doubt, and How to Leave It

Gordon Quinn, for forty years a professional filmmaker, including as executive producer on the award-winning film *Hoop Dreams*, was working on a public television program in 2001. *New Americans* is about the lives of new immigrants to the United States. In one scene, Israel Nwidor, a Nigerian immigrant trained as a chemical engineer and now working as a cab driver, is listening to a George Strait song in his car when a white guy on a motorcycle pulls alongside and gives him the evil eye. It's one of those little moments that reveal a lot.

Twenty years before, Gordon wouldn't have given the song playing on the speakers another thought. But over the last two decades, he had become hyperconscious of the copyrighted material in documentaries. Broadcasters and insurers had become hypervigilant, demanding assurances that he had licensed every stray bit of copyrighted material. Did the reunited family sing "Happy Birthday"? License it. Were the middle-school girls on a sleepover listening to pop songs? License them. Did the little autistic boy love "Puff the Magic Dragon" as a comfort song? License it. And what about those posters on the walls? The books on the shelf?

As a result, Gordon didn't doubt that he would need to license the George Strait song that Israel was nodding along to. Only he knew from experience that he probably wouldn't get an answer to an e-mail sent to the music company. The amount of money involved would be so trivial that the music company's licensing executives wouldn't even respond.

So Gordon cut out the scene. Nobody watching it even knew they were missing anything. It was one of a thousand little cuts that nobody knew they were missing, each one of them a silent erasure of a piece of reality.

Cyndy Scheibe, a psychology professor at Ithaca College and director of Project Look Sharp, a media literacy initiative, uses comic strips from newspapers and other pieces of popular culture—clips from documentaries, popular films, and print advertisements—in her classes to teach about point of view and representation. Her team at Project Look Sharp has created online curriculum materials about the media's representation of the Middle East, featuring among other things a clip from the Disney film *Aladdin*.

Could Cyndy's teaching materials safely be shared with other teachers? Did she dare to put it on an open website? The Ithaca College legal experts and administrators were divided, and finally demanded that both Cyndy and her colleague Chris Sperry personally pledge their willingness to go to court to defend themselves should their use of unlicensed copyrighted material be litigated.

Cyndy and Chris gambled, and let the site go up. They erred on the side of caution where they could. For one exercise that involved comparisons of covers of the magazine *Newsweek*, they tried to license the covers from the news corporation. But the company would not license them for an appropriate fee, and furthermore, the company told them, Cyndy and Chris would also have had to negotiate with the subjects of the covers. The company spokesperson was actually talking about two kinds of rights: the company's copyright, and the celebrities' right of publicity. Cyndy and Chris believed, correctly, that they did not need to get permission from the likes of Osama bin Laden, since they had a First Amendment right that overrode any publicity claims he could make. As for the copyright claims, they decided to use the magazine covers under fair use; they and their university counsel believed there was no question that they had a right to do so.

Even when they were sure they were within the law, though, Cyndy and Chris were given pause by what they'd heard in the rumor mill. That little clip from *Aladdin*—did that put them in jeopardy from the Disney Corporation? They'd heard that Disney was wildly litigious. They finally added that clip to the website, and held their breaths.

They were relieved to see Project Look Sharp be widely used, and even more relieved as the threat of litigation failed to emerge. They had pledged if necessary to loot their 401(k)s for legal funds to defend their rights to reference their own culture, and—for now—they thought they didn't have to.

Stephanie Lenz, proud mother of thirteen-month-old Holden in State College, Pennsylvania, posted one of those hilarious-for-family videos of Holden jiggling up and down in the kitchen, dancing to the beat of a

Prince song. Unlike media professionals, she never once thought about copyright as she did so. But no sooner had she let friends and family know about the video than it was gone. YouTube had obeyed a request from Universal to take down the video for copyright infringement.

Stephanie did what most YouTube posters don't. She went to the Electronic Frontier Foundation, which in 2007 sued Universal for abusing the Digital Millennium Copyright Act. (The DMCA requires Internet service providers like Verizon and YouTube to take down works that copyright holders claim infringe on their copyright.) EFF seized on the chance to work with Stephanie; the lawyers there wanted a good case to establish that frivolous takedown notices could be costly. They sued Universal for bad faith in issuing the takedown notice.

By 2010, Holden had progressed to jungle gyms, and Universal was still stalling. The company had tried to argue that even if Stephanie's use was fair, it was also infringing (yes, that made no sense). Then it argued that it was unreasonable to have to consider fair use before issuing takedowns. None of this worked with the judge, and neither did Universal's claim that Stephanie and EFF were in bad faith themselves. A 2010 summary judgment on some of the charges went against Universal, with the trial continuing.

Whatever their rights to use the copyrighted material they employed in these works, Gordon, Cyndy, Chris, and Stephanie all were trapped within a culture of fear and doubt. They didn't necessarily participate in it, but they faced gatekeepers who were also enmeshed in the same culture, and who enforced it (sometimes willy-nilly). Ultimately, each of these people challenged that culture, in a way that gatekeepers could hear and, in some cases, even listen to. These are just a few of the people who are changing their own stories and showing the way for the rest of us.

Gordon Quinn had been trained by the last two decades of producing for television to know that he needed to show insurers a license for every last smidgen of copyrighted material he built into a film. He knew that, in theory, he had the right to refer to that George Strait song, under what is known as the fair-use doctrine of copyright law. That doctrine says that, under some circumstances (broadly, when social benefit is larger than individual owners' loss), people can quote copyrighted work without permission or payment. But insurers would probably have challenged his claim, because they avoided risk wherever they could. Without a grounded understanding of filmmakers' interpretation of fair use, the insurers would not know how much risk they were taking. If they did challenge it, Gordon probably couldn't get his work on television. He faced censorship via the insurers' reluctance to employ fair use.

In the next film he made, Gordon Quinn was in a far different position. By that time he had participated in the creation of a pioneering document, the *Documentary Filmmakers' Statement of Best Practices in Fair Use*. This document, built on the experience and judgment of many veteran filmmakers, made it extremely easy for any maker—professional or not—to decide whether their use of copyrighted material met the standards of the law. The statement was soon part of the backpack of any documentarian, and even insurers began to use it, including with films from Gordon's company, Kartemquin Films.

Cyndy and her colleague Chris put up with months of agonizing scrutiny from university lawyers and administrators, even pledging their own savings to back their gamble that they had the fair-use right to quote news, public affairs, and popular culture in order to analyze it. After that experience, Cyndy and Chris also acted to change their fate. Seeing how effective education had been for filmmakers, they worked with other educators to create the *Code of Best Practices in Fair Use for Media Literacy Education*. This code turned out to be helpful not only to teachers but also to librarians and even administrators.

Stephanie Lenz discovered that even when you make your own video and upload it for free to the Internet, there are gatekeepers who participate in the culture of fear and doubt. She found out that under the DMCA, YouTube as an Internet service provider is free of responsibility for YouTube users' copyright choices under law—but only if it honors any copyright holder's request to "take down" an offending video without question. A user has the right, after that, to demand that YouTube put it back up again, although the user will receive a message saying that the user could be sued individually by the complainer. You have to be sure you know you're within the law to be the person who clicks that button.

Most individual YouTube users who suffer from takedown notices, even when they are not valid, simply assume that perhaps they did infringe a copyright, and that even if they didn't, they shouldn't risk trouble by challenging a big corporation. Stephanie instead chose to team up with the Electronic Frontier Foundation in order to put a spotlight on an ugly spot in today's legislation. She found out that she had the right to post her material, under fair use, and that she had the right to a countertakedown. She decided, with EFF's help, to get a court to affirmatively declare that her use was fair. "This case mattered a lot to Stephanie," said Jason Schultz, the lawyer who initiated the case. "When Universal told her she had done something wrong, she felt terrible. Now she's stood up for her rights, and that feels good." Schultz thinks the case will show copyright holders that they can't just issue blanket takedown notices.

Meanwhile, other online video enthusiasts, including lawyers and cultural studies experts, had created the *Code of Best Practices in Fair Use for Online Video*, which made clear that Stephanie's use of the video was entirely within the law. Thus, Stephanie's challenge to a fear-based status quo was bulwarked by a strong statement of community practice.

None of these people wanted to overturn copyright law. Indeed, Gordon, Cyndy, and Chris are all people who hold copyrights themselves and value the limited monopoly rights they hold. Stephanie Lenz simply didn't want to take down a cute family video. But they all saw opportunities to assert rights that already exist, and to challenge behaviors that intimidate new makers of culture.

The key to challenging the culture of fear and doubt is knowledge. Knowledge unlocks the door to action, which lets you join the culture of creativity.

Why We All Care about Copyright

You might ask, Do I really have to know that much about copyright law, especially if I'm someone who just wants to write a blog, make a video, put together a slide show, build a class lesson, teach a Sunday school class? Not really. You just need to know the right stuff—most importantly, that you have rights. And then you need to know the real risks you take when you exercise your rights.

You then might ask, Shouldn't we really leave legal questions in the hands of lawyers? You can, but that's a big decision. It's a decision that leaves you powerless to make creative decisions on your own, and it is unlike other decisions in life. You don't expect to consult lawyers when you speak in public, even though incautious remarks might trigger actions for defamation. If you are attacked on a dark street, you don't stop to call a lawyer to see if you have the right to self-defense. There's nothing so difficult about the decisions people have to make about reusing copyrighted material that requires you to keep a lawyer at hand as you work.

And then you might ask: How often, really, do these arcane questions of copyright come up for non–copyright experts anyway? More and more, both at home and at work. That is not only because people have more and more tools with which to make and distribute their own digital work. It is also because over the last century, copyright became both

Answers at the back, and more at http://centerforsocialmedia.org/fair-use.

Fair Use: You Be the Judge >> Blogging

You are a citizen journalist with a particular interest in food safety. These issues regularly surface in the news—recalls, E coli outbreaks, panics over particular additives. Many people visit your website to get up-to-the-minute coverage of food safety. You would like to post TV news clips that cover the topic on your website, retiring them after they are no longer topical. You'll scrupulously credit all the sources. Do you need permission from the TV stations?

Answers at the back, and more at http://centerforsocialmedia.org/fair-use.

long and strong. These days, it sometimes seems as if our whole culture is copyrighted.

This was not always to case. But since 1978, in the United States all expression that ends up in a fixed medium (and that means everything—your shopping list, the interoffice memo, your kid's homework) is copyrighted by default. There is virtually no chance that you will make even a home video that is not littered with copyrighted material, including your kindergartner's adorable picture of Mom (yes, that kid does own the copyright).

Copyrights did not always last forever, either. And they don't now, but for most ordinary purposes they might as well. Copyrights now last generations beyond the life of the author. That means that almost all of current culture—*X-Men, Star Trek, Saturday Night Live* routines, or Jay-Z or Stevie Wonder's songs—is likely to be off limits until after not only all the participants but all the people who ever heard of them are dead.

Big media companies and their trade associations, such as the Recording Industry Association of America (RIAA) and the Motion Picture Association of America (MPAA), were not always huffing and puffing about copyright infringement, other than commercial-scale bootlegging. But they are now, and they have been ever since digital technology made it easy to make copies. They have been watching their business models change without seeing workable new ones emerge. Their resort has been both to leverage intellectual property ownership into ever greater control over their "assets," and to scare people into thinking that ownership rights are even more far-reaching than they actually are.

Furthermore, scare tactics in one area of practice scare people in another. When the RIAA sues P2P downloaders, people who are repurposing bits of copyrighted culture to comment upon it get frightened. When Fox asserts a dubious claim in the slogan "fair and balanced," people erroneously believe this is a copyright problem—rather than trademark overreaching. Problems that big media companies have with massive commercial piracy in China and elsewhere are confused with individual acts of copying. People are far more alarmed, in general, than they need to be, and they rarely understand exactly what is worth getting alarmed about or why.

None of that would matter that much if we were not becoming a nation of makers and sharers, not just consumers of other people's copyrighted material. We are rediscovering the participatory, collaborative cultural practices that many of us forgot during the peak era for mass media. We create birthday slide shows and scrapbooks, mix CDs and files, mashups and remixes, websites and self-published books. We expect programs such as GarageBand and Windows MovieMaker to come preinstalled on our new computers, and we turn to Flickr and Facebook for other people's memories to fill in when ours comes up short.

For centuries, no one much thought about copyright in daily life. Now, we don't have a choice. We are both consumers and creators every day, and we need to use our rights to draw on our own culture as well as claim rights to our own productions. We need to reclaim the conversation about copyright as something that belongs to all of us.

But what if we are just producing work for love, not money? Do we still need to think about copyright then? Sadly, yes. It is true that strictly "educational" work benefits from some special exemptions. And in some situations, noncommercial work does get a break under fair use. But what qualifies is difficult to assess, in part because the term "noncommercial" has no clear legal definition, and so there is no guarantee that your idea of the noncommercial is the same as someone else's—especially since even the most personal work often is made public over for-profit platforms. Thus you would not want to rest a case for fair use entirely on noncommerciality.

Whatever you produce, you are likely to face gatekeepers who want to know that you have a solid justification for your fair use. Of course, if work never leaves the four walls of a bedroom, a classroom, or a boardroom, there is no need to worry, for the simple reason that nobody will know. But rarely these days do we want to produce work that stays within four walls. And when we go beyond those walls, we use intermediary services that have copyright standards. For instance, if you take material to a duplicating service so that a slide show can be a holiday present for the extended family, or because you want to share a work presentation with colleagues, the duplicator may balk at reproducing work with copyrighted material in it. Only if you have a fair use justification may it be possible to override the duplicator's concern. The duplicator is only one example of gatekeepers whose institutional need to control risk may impinge on our rights as users—others include insurers, Internet service providers, and sometimes even teachers and librarians (who often are reluctant gatekeepers).

Although this book will give you a solid framework to make your own fair use decisions, it will not do some other things. If you are downloading copyrighted work for free because you want to enjoy it and do not feel like paying for it, this book will not help you out. We're not here to tell you that the major media companies' resistance to twenty-first-century distribution mechanisms is rational or smart. We agree with smart lawyers like William Patry and Fred von Lohmann and savvy digerati like Cory Doctorow and Tim O'Reilly who censure the big media companies for turning their customers into their enemies. Like most of the rest of you, we are waiting for the day when business models in the entertainment industry catch up with the technologies that people prefer to use on a daily basis. But we are pretty sure that the basic notion that copyright holders deserve, if they choose, to be paid for work is not going to be challenged usefully anytime soon. Besides, we note that people who make new works of any kind are copyright owners. Some of them really do not care how their work gets used, or whether they get recognition or get paid. But many of these people—possibly including you—may want to benefit from the limited monopoly rights of copyright owners.

Fair use is not a universal solvent. When you want to reuse material and recirculate it for its original purpose, especially in its entirety or in significant part, fair use may not cover your activity. For instance, suppose you would like to use a popular song as the soundtrack for a commercial slide show. Or you are making a biographical portrait film of a political figure and want to use large chunks of an earlier film about that figure. Or you would like to repost the entire school play—your kid was a mushroom in one scene—on YouTube. Or you want to photocopy a manual for a new video camera, scan it, and put it on an open user's forum to make it easy for all your students to access. You then have to seek out licensing options.

This book will not help you license work, but help is available from others. You might turn to Susan Bielstein's excellent, unpretentious guide, *Permissions: A Survival Guide*, for step by step advice on how to license graphic material. For audiovisual work, you might want to use Michael Donaldson's *Clearance and Copyright: Everything You Need to Know for Film and Television*. If you are podcasting, you can consult the Podcasting Legal Guide; bloggers can turn to EFF's Legal Guide for Bloggers. (Don't expect much help on fair use from the last document, which was written before the resurgence of fair use.) And for a good solid overview of copyright in general you can turn to Bruce Keller and Jeffrey Cunard's *Copyright Law: A Practitioner's Guide*.

Fair Use within the Copyright Critique

Fair use was in eclipse for decades, with judges, lawyers, legal scholars, and many creators unsure of its interpretation and convinced of its unreliability. Since the late 1990s, fair use has resurfaced strongly and has become a sturdy tool for a wide range of creators and users. This transformation has been remarkable; we discuss it in detail in Chapter 5, and provide highlights here.

It happened in part because of changing scholarship. A generation of legal scholars has developed arguments for fair use as they have analyzed the doctrine's history and examined contemporary copyright's effect on cultural expression. At the same time, cultural studies scholars have showcased the relevance of fair use to their work, which often involves analyzing popular culture. Teachers and scholars are beginning to take up the fair-use banner, publicly using their rights and encouraging their students to do the same.

Established communities of creators, administrators, and users—filmmakers, teachers of English and visual art, librarians, makers of open courseware, poets, and dance archivists—have identified fair use as a necessary tool to achieve their missions. They have turned to the sturdy tool of consensus interpretation by making codes of best practices in fair use through their professional associations.

Members of these communities have become active advocates for fair use. Their organizations and representatives have appeared before the Copyright Office to testify about the way that the DMCA, which makes illegal the breaking of encryption on DVDs, limits their ability to employ fair use in their work. As a result, the Librarian of Congress has granted both documentary filmmakers and college teachers exemptions that support their fair-use rights.

Remix artists of all kinds, working online, have come to adopt the claim of fair use as an anticorporate banner. They trade information on fair use in conferences and conventions. When they receive takedown notices on YouTube, they issue counternotices and explain why their uses are fair. Recently, remixers won exemptions from the Librarian of Congress to permit them to make their highly personal and often socially critical work.

New businesses have flourished employing fair use, and their trade associations have supported them. Google, the Consumer Electronics Association, and the Computer & Communications Industry Association have all advocated for fair use. Legal and professional services for communities of practice such as lawyers and web developers have built their fair-use expertise to serve their clients better.

Think tanks and advocacy organizations have promoted fair use. The Electronic Frontier Foundation, Public Knowledge, the American Civil Liberties Union, Duke University's Center for the Study of the Public Domain, and the Stanford Fair Use Project have all taken action on fair use. The Organization for Transformative Works was founded in part to help remixers use their fair-use rights more effectively.

Between the scholars, creators, artists, and organizations, fair use is emerging out of a twilight existence in which, for decades, it had languished. During those decades, many professionals and especially professionals in the corporate media environment—whether broadcast journalism, cable documentary, or newspapers—routinely and extensively employed fair use. But if you were not a professional, you might not even have heard of it. That has changed.

The various actors in this resurgence of fair use differ in their goals. Some simply want to assert their rights to improve their work, lower their costs, and start or grow new businesses. Some want to expand the sphere of freedom of expression so that copyrighted culture does not become off-limits for new work. Some believe that an expansion of fair-use rights is imperative both to protect fair use as copyright policy is tinkered with, and to maintain the crucial principle of balance between owners' rights and the society's investment in new cultural creation. Some believe that fair use, exercised to the maximum, will provide concrete experience of the limitations of today's copyright law, and point to more effective change. They all share a common understanding that individual and community action simply to assert their rights has an immediate and long-range effect on markets and policy.

The resurgence of fair use, the topic of this book, forms part of a much greater discourse in the United States and worldwide, critiquing the most stifling, confining features of copyright practice today. That discourse is variously called copyright reform, copyfighting, the copyleft, and advocacy for a cultural/creative/intellectual commons, depending on your angle of entry. Some people call it a movement, though it still lacks evidence of broad social mobilization of the kind that Patrick Burkart has noted for the fair use of music. The people in this discourse share an acute awareness that copyright policy and practice are tilted unfairly toward ownership rights, in a way that prejudices the health and growth of culture. This broader discourse is evident in many ways besides the efforts to make fair use more useable: proposals for copyright law revision, efforts to create legally sanctioned copyright-light or copyright-free zones or to expand the public domain, and civil disobedience.

Some propose copyright reform to shrink the monopoly claims of owners. Among legal scholars, Jessica Litman and Pamela Samuelson have led in proposing a start-from-scratch reconceptualization of copyright law. They imagine a simpler, shorter copyright law, grounded in principles rather than the "obese Frankenstein monster" it has become through stakeholder pressure and endless tinkering. Neil Netanel has proposed a range of tweaks to pull back the extent of copyright protection, such as limiting copyright length and dropping protection against the preparation of derivative work, so that less licensing is needed. Lawrence Lessig also has argued for simplifying and minimizing copyright protection for owners.

Some legal scholars offer suggestions to improve the efficiency of licensing, which today is messy, clumsy, and frustrating. David Lange, for instance, proposed increased use of statutory (or compulsory) licensing schemes, such as those that allow today for the retransmission of TV signals by cable and satellite systems. Others have suggested new voluntary digital platforms through which users could make "micropayments" for each individual access to copyrighted material offered commercially. William Fisher has proposed a voluntary collective administration system, akin to those that today enable public performances and broadcasts of music, which would collect licensing payments through Internet service providers and distribute them to copyright owners and artists whose material is used online. Some copyright owners, including the Association of Commercial Stock Images Licensors, are even toying with how to restructure their own licensing schemes, to eliminate archaisms such as regional rights in a transnational Internet age.

The ideas and projects all respond to the real problem that copyright law now fits ever more poorly the way people are actually making culture. They may well take some time to become useful, though. The big stumbling block both to fundamental copyright reform and to licensing

Fair Use? Creative Commons? Which Is Best?

People who are well aware of how copyright ownership weighs on new creators often confuse fair use with efforts to recover and recreate the public domain, or material not (or no longer) bound by copyright ownership. Sometimes they even think these efforts are in competition. In fact, they are complementary ways to address the same general problem, as David Bollier has noted.

Furthermore, enthusiasm for public domain work sometimes leads people to believe that fair use is not as useful as it is. This is because they have been drawn to public domain work by their frustration with copyright ownership restrictions, and have associated all of copyright with copyright ownership. They have not yet become aware of the flexibility and power of the fair-use doctrine, and they see one side of copyright as the only side. Sometimes they simply do not have faith that copyright imbalance can be righted.

Creative Commons (CC) is possibly the best publicized of the efforts to create an artificial public domain through contracts, to compensate for the badly eroded zone of copyright-free work. It was launched by legal scholar Lawrence Lessig, who at the time indeed was dismissive, even contemptuous, of the potential of fair use to address copyright imbalance. However, CC was not an attempt to supplant or be better than fair use. Rather it was an attempt to solve a different problem: how to allow people to give away or condition their long and strong copyright. CC licenses use the strength of owners' rights to allow owners the leeway to release their works.

So CC creates a zone inside copyright ownership for owners who want to be generous and give their works away. All CC licenses impose some conditions, and some impose more than others. (Some users of CC material ignore this; owners of CC licenses sometimes complain that people do not honor the conditions.) The conditions people put on use of their work makes CC a copyright-light zone rather than copyright-free zone, and of course it does nothing (and doesn't pretend to) to loosen long and strong copyright policy.

A CC license, intended to promote circulation of work, may limit it to the alternative CC world it was born into. This is precisely because it is designed to be an alternative to rather than a feature of the copyrighted environment. CC licenses forbid the use of digital rights management (DRM), which is standard to all commercial DVD contracts. Thus, a CC license may kill a commercial distribution deal.

Even people who depend upon CC licenses, such as the makers of open educational resources—scholarly materials of all kinds, available

(continued)

free on the web—still sometimes need fair use. That is because most new work refers to existing culture. When that happens, people need to exercise their right of fair use, because most work is not in the copyright-light, fenced-in zone.

reform is that large copyright holders—key stakeholders in any change in licensing schemes—are not able to agree on what they would like to do. They do not know what business models will be most relevant in a few years, so living with a lumbering, archaic licensing system with a lot of holes in it looks better to them than change that might have unanticipated downsides. As major stakeholders in any legislative reform, they will stall, derail, or rewrite legislation in the same unbalanced direction as today, until their interests shift with shifting business models. As major actors in licensing, they will collaborate on new methods of licensing when they understand how emerging business models favor their interests.

Another part of this broad copyright critique is a range of efforts to expand copyright-free and copyright-light zones, efforts discussed in detail by David Bollier and by James Boyle. People in this arena often invoke the phrases "the public domain," "open access," and "Creative Commons." Projects such as open-source software (collaboratively created and freely offered software), open-source (free and accessible to all) academic and scientific journals and databases, and OpenCourseWare (freely available curriculum materials) offer such alternative zones. The various Creative Commons licenses contribute to this alternative zone by offering a way for creators to give their work away more easily, although with conditions, by labeling it appropriately.

These efforts have indeed created significant copyright-light zones, as well as creating enormous enthusiasm for a more flexible copyright policy. They work well for people who want to share their work without economic reward. They also work for follow-on creators who are looking for material of a particular kind (such as a photograph of a certain landmark or background music) rather than seeking to critique or build upon specific artifacts (such as a popular movie, TV show, or popular song). A pool of noncommercial works now exists, but it is tiny compared with the field of copyrighted and often commercial work. Viacom and News Corp will continue to copyright their holdings and treat them as assets.

The existence of copyright-light zones, however large, does not address the frequent need that people have to access mass commercial culture to make new cultural expression.

Finally, copyright critique is seen in opposition and resistance, such as giddy, open flouting of copyright law by "culture jammers," pranksters, and appropriation artists. Burkart describes this work as part of the incipient and still inchoate cyber-liberties social movement, taking up "the politics of symbolic action," typically "weapons of the weak." These people and groups—Negativland, the Yes Men, *Adbusters* magazine and others—position themselves on the margins of official culture and see themselves as reclaiming culture one image or gesture at a time. They also see themselves as challenging the terms of long and strong copyright. Ironically, many of the ways they incorporate or refer to copyrighted material are actually completely legal fair uses.

This broad and diverse discourse calling for changes in long and strong copyright thus has many faces and approaches, each with opportunities and limitations. They add up to a broad public awareness of trouble around long and strong copyright. Within this discourse, efforts to make fair use more useable stand out because they can be done now, by people in many walks of life; they can be publicized and celebrated, thus spreading the word; and because using this right expands its range of uses.

Fair use is not necessarily a popular phrase for all in this broader collection of copyright critics. Some regard it as hopelessly compromised because of technologies such as encryption, which override a user's will to excerpt. Some believe that exemptions are good but that fair use is too murky or unclear to be a helpful exemption. Some believe that fair use partakes too much of the status quo, and that another copyright-free world is possible. One way that concern is expressed is to argue that it is too limited a doctrine, and that therefore we need to reach beyond it to accomplish our goals.

In fact, under the current interpretation, fair use does apply in a wide variety of situations. These range from making viewing copies of TV programs on our DVRs to creating digitally annotated critical texts to making an archive of the worst music videos ever to making relevant curriculum digitally available to students. Fair use has evolved, having different functions at different moments in US history. Today it has an ever-growing importance and value within copyright, as a primary vehicle to restore copyright to its constitutional purpose, and the transformativeness standard assists in creating that value. Fair use is like a muscle; unused, it atrophies, while exercise makes it grow. Its future is open; vigorous exercise will not break fair use.

Fair use will continue to be important, no matter what the success of other kinds of long and strong copyright protests and proposals. Even if we could wave a magic wand and execute a reform of copyright policy that rolls back some of its longest, strongest terms, fair use would still be an important tool to free up recent culture for referencing in new work. Even if licensing were much easier than it is today, it would never address all the needs people have for use of copyrighted material. Even if copyright-light zones vastly expanded, the need to access the copyrighted material existing outside those zones without permission or payment would still remain. Sometimes people need to use materials that the copyright owner simply will not license to them. Fair use will be important to anyone working in the cultural mainstream. Culture jamming can be fun, although some culture jammers are actually just employing their fair-use rights without knowing it. But most creators, teachers, learners, and sharers of information do not see themselves as criminals or pirates, and they don't want to.

Reclaiming fair use plays a particular and powerful role in the broader range of activities that evidence the poor fit between today's copyright policy and today's creative practices. In a world where the public domain has shrunk drastically, it creates a highly valuable, contextually defined, "floating" public domain. The assertion of fair use is part of a larger project of reclaiming the full meaning of copyright policy—not merely protection for owners, but the nurturing of creativity, learning, expression. Asserting and defending fair-use rights are a crucial part of constructing saner copyright policy.

2 Long and Strong Copyright

WHY FAIR USE IS SO IMPORTANT

Overprotecting intellectual property is just as harmful as underprotecting it.... Overprotection stifles the very creative processes it's supposed to nurture.
ALEX KOZINSKI, judge of the US Court of Appeals, Ninth Circuit

Copyright policy and practice today are lopsided in favor of copyright owners. That destabilized copyright situation depends on two poisonous notions: that copyright exists only to protect owners, and that creators of new work deserve total protection because they have created it all by themselves (or perhaps with divine inspiration). The two concepts reinforce each other, and they are both wrong.

Ask your friends what copyright is, and they will tell you with confidence that it is the right that creators have to their own work. But this is only a piece of the story. Copyright policy is the collection of ways that a government provides incentives to create culture. And we mean culture broadly—building, aggregating, and sharing knowledge. Progress is grounded, as policymakers know, in the growth of culture. Your friends are partly right; the best-known way to motivate the creation of culture is to reward creators (or the people they sell or give their copyright to) by giving them a limited monopoly over the use of their work. They can charge for the use of it, and they can use the law to punish people who don't use it in the way that they authorize.

But rewarding creators is just one tactic, and one that, as is universally recognized, must be limited to protect the larger goal of encouraging creation of culture. As Judge Alex Kozinski, a veteran judge of the Appeals Court of the Ninth Circuit (a court that hears many copyright cases) notes, overprotecting copyright holders has its own problems. If you do not limit the control that copyright owners have over their work, owners become chiefs of private fiefdoms of culture, and private censors of future culture. A collection of private fiefdoms provides local security, but not a peaceable kingdom, much less a thriving economy and culture. The chieftains' guardianship of their work can become not a way to en-

> **Examples of Special Exemptions**
> - Copying by libraries and archives
> - Educational uses such as classroom use of entire videos
> - Charitable performances where the money returns to the charity or no admission is charged, and copyright holders have not previously objected
> - Retransmission of broadcast signals by small businesses such as bars
> - Music performed and displays exhibited in the course of religious services
> - Performances at annual nonprofit agricultural or horticultural fairs
> - Performances and reproductions for the print-disabled

courage expression, but a way to discourage it. They become culture misers, hoarding their own pile of it.

Copyright policies provide ways to get unlicensed access to copyrighted material in part to encourage new creators, who inevitably need to access culture as they add to it. In US law, some people in special categories—teachers inside four walls of a classroom, for example—have ample rights to use copyrighted material without permission or payment. So, for that matter (but for very different reasons), do small businesses who want to supply their customers with background music. But these are often highly specialized and limited exemptions, usually created as small "carve-outs" to serve a narrowly defined public interest or pacify a stakeholder in the policymaking process.

But some limitations on owners' rights apply to everyone. For instance, everyone who has bought a copy of a book or a film or a music recording can resell or give away that copy to anyone he or she likes without paying an additional fee; this is called the "first sale doctrine." (For computer program discs and recordings such as CDs, rental is prohibited; other media objects, such as DVDs and books, may be rented under the "first sale doctrine.") Users also have wide latitude to use cultural products in their personal lives. We are all free to sing a Beatles or Beyoncé song in the shower or at a party or on a camping trip with college buddies, because the only performances that are regulated by copyright are public ones. We are all free to take facts and ideas from other people's work, since copyright does not protect facts or ideas, only expression—that is, the detailed manner in which those ideas are worked out.

The biggest, most important exemption from a copyright owner's monopoly control today is fair use. Everyone in the United States, in any medium, has the right of fair use—although most people don't know it. Fair use is an exemption that applies to all of a copyright owner's monopoly rights, including the owner's right to control adaptation, distribution, and performance. It is a bold demonstration of the need to share culture in order to get more of it. Part of US law for more than 150 years, in recent decades fair use has become a crucially important part of copyright policy. It is a core right, part of your basic package of freedom-of-speech rights. And it is widely used, sometimes in situations where those who rely on it do not even realize they are doing so. In copyright litigation, your first chance to formally invoke fair use comes only when someone accuses you of infringement; in terms of court procedure, therefore, it is classified as an "affirmative defense." In everyday practice, however, fair use functions as a reliable, full-fledged right, of which we are all free to take advantage. In this respect, it is a lot like the doctrine of self-defense, which we do not claim until after we have resisted an attack and been sued for assault as a result.

There are actually two kinds of fair use. One is your right to do with copyrighted material what you will for personal purposes. Some scholars think this should not even be considered as within the scope of copyright at all, but should be seen as merely unregulated private activity. Either way, you can take notes on and/or take excerpts from a book you read, for study purposes, whether you photocopy them, digitally copy, or scan them. You can watch a TV show you copied earlier on your digital video recorder. You can copy a chapter from a library book to study at home.

That kind of fair use was taken for granted for many years, partly because no copyright holder could easily monitor or cash in on personal copying. It has become more controversial as digital culture has started zooming around the Internet, and large copyright holders have gotten more worried about how copying cuts into their profits. Copyright law has not gotten more stringent about personal fair use, but content companies have worked hard to keep their products from circulating for free. Restrictive licensing deals with libraries, shrink-wrap consumer licenses, monitoring programs that keep track of consumer uses, digital rights management, such as the CSS (Content Scramble System) anticopying code on DVDs—these are some of the ways that private businesses have taken action to limit private fair-use rights. As we will discuss, they have even secured new legislation, such as the DMCA, to help them do that work.

What this private or "passive" fair use will look like as we digitize all cultural expression is unclear right now. Content industry companies argue furiously that the very notion of private fair use disappears on the Internet; in one 2009 case, Cartoon Networks, Disney, Paramount, and other companies sued Cablevision over its plan to offer customers a remote version of a DVR. The Supreme Court's Sony decision had established that suppliers can provide consumers with personal recording devices (such as VCRs) to exercise their fair-use rights to time-shift programming. Content companies want to say that where the virtual equivalent of a VCR is concerned, this principle no longer applies. They lost that lawsuit, but will not be letting go of the campaign to restrict the exercise of fair use in the online environment anytime soon.

Consumer behavior may influence what happens here, too. Consumers have mightily resisted digital rights management and shown desire for format-shifting; business practices have shifted to accommodate them. But consumers also love their iPods and iPads, which are designed to be endpoints, not sharing points, even though some enterprising consumers are diligently trying to hack them to open them up. Since so much of the pressure to limit personal fair use comes from business practice, the continued resistance of consumers to limiting their personal fair use will continue to be important.

The other kind of fair use is when you reuse copyrighted material in the process of making something else. Publisher and copyright scholar Leon Seltzer called this "productive" fair use. Legal scholar Pamela Samuelson has suggested creating three categories of fair use: transformative (by which she means something like parody and satire); productive (for instance, quoting for illustrative purposes); and orthogonal (using the material in ways different in purpose from the original). Legal scholar Michael Madison has noted that these kinds of fair use are all being discussed today as under the umbrella of "transformative" use (simply, doing something different with the material).

This kind of fair use is very common, but it is hidden unless you know where to look. Fair use is exercised every day in every television news program. Broadcasters are very comfortable with their fair-use rights; they often think they get them because they are journalists, but they actually are just vigorously using the rights everyone else has. They know they cannot report on, say, the death of Michael Jackson, without running an image of the celebrity and playing a bit of his music—and perhaps showing footage that illustrates his style of dancing. And they don't stop to license it, either. You also see fair use in academic texts, where scholars feel free to quote other scholars; they are scrupulous, of course, about giving them credit. You see it online when bloggers quote relevant sections (not the whole thing) of a newspaper article, and when shopping websites give you a picture of what you might purchase. You see it every day in remixes and mashups on YouTube. Some of those remixers think they are violating the law, but most of them are probably just exercising their fair-use rights without knowing it.

Fair use is in play whenever you have the right to take copyrighted material without getting (or even asking for) permission from copyright holders or their agents. In practice, fair use is simple to apply. There is no fair-use approval board, and no one needs to authorize your decision. You simply take material and reuse it. You only need to exercise your fair-use right affirmatively in the unlikely event of a challenge.

Fair use makes quoting existing culture easy in other ways too. One attractive feature of fair use is that it can cover all copyright claims involved in a work. For instance, musical recordings may have several different copyrights, one for the song and another for the recording itself. Video recordings may involve different sound and image copyrights and copyright in materials such as a painting or sculpture shown in a scene. Where it applies, fair use also has another advantage over licensing. A video may well be encumbered by contractual arrangements with talent, from famous actors or on-air news presenters to studio musicians. These obligations will be passed along with a copyright license. But when material is fairly used, the contracts that the copyright holder has made with others do not carry over. Celebrities' so-called "publicity" rights (designed to prevent simple commercial free-riding on others' fame) are rarely triggered by a transformative (or productive) fair use: state laws exempt uses for documentation or discussion or critique from publicity rights. If they did not, there would be a collision with the US Constitution's First Amendment.

Copyright in Collaborative Culture

Copyright today heavily emphasizes individual authors, individual works, and the notion that creativity is an individual act—a notion that emerged only recently. That is a truly unfortunate distortion of reality, and one that increasingly conflicts with experiences we all have every day.

Participatory digital culture has generated a huge body of work done by people who just love to do it and share it. Online video platforms, blogs, Flickr pages, and Facebook are full of impromptu and elaborate cultural expression, done not for profit but for the love of it. Legal scholar Rebecca

Tushnet studies people who make all kinds of fan fiction, mixing up and reclaiming popular culture narratives such as *Star Trek*. She reminds us that creators of all kinds say that they create because they want, even need to, no matter what the economic reward. Tushnet quotes the writer Anne Lamott, who says that writing a felt truth "is a little like milking a cow: the milk is so rich and delicious, and the cow is so glad you did it." Much of this work, especially remixes and mashups, is done within a collaborative network, and draws widely on existing culture.

Often this work is celebrated by digerati as embodying the liberation of personal creativity by technology. We believe that this way of thinking about the phenomenon participates a little too much in the Romantic notion of the genius-creator that has given such a boost to the notion of cultural production as property, pure and simple. Remixers demonstrate every day the basic notion that creativity is a social phenomenon more than the individual expression of any individual or individuals. That used to be taken for granted. Indeed, the notion of authorship as an act of individual genius is a fairly new concept, and its primacy in copyright law has always had an awkward connection with the realities of creativity.

Everyone makes work on the basis of, and in reference and relationship to, existing work. We stand, as Isaac Newton and many people before him said, on the shoulders of giants. (This phrase refers to an ancient Greek myth, a fact that demonstrates the antiquity of the phrase itself). Scientists have meticulously mapped the "emergent" quality of creativity as a product of social interaction; the most fundamental processes of brain development depend on collaboration and sociability. Folk culture from time immemorial was a frankly collaborative process. Epic poetry survived by a process of transmission through repetition and subtle variation. At the beginnings of the novel form in the eighteenth century, as Elizabeth Judge has shown, readers felt entitled to reimagine and project the lives of fictional characters in unauthorized sequels, the fan fiction of their day.

As Peter Jaszi and Martha Woodmansee have noted, the now-entrenched notion that creative expression is a unique individual act grew up with the evolution of the Enlightenment concept of individual rights and identity. Enlightenment values linked social agency to ownership. The political scientist C. B. MacPherson well described the political and economic significance of "possessive individualism," which is the notion of self-realization through ownership of the self, extending then to ownership as a core feature of economy and culture. Individualizing creativity permitted the assigning of rights to creative work as property—a

Fair Use: You Be the Judge >> TV Program

You are planning to make a series of cable TV programs on the evolution of Greek myths and epics. To show how different the originals were
from today's ideas of the same stories, you plan to quote from Hollywood films. For instance, in an episode devoted to the hero Jason, you
would open with a scene from the 1963 version of *Jason and the Argo-
nauts*, in which Jason confronts one of Harry Harryhausen's terrifying
monsters. For a discussion of *The Iliad*, you would like to start with a
battle scene from *Troy*, including a close-up of Brad Pitt as Achilles. In
each of these cases, you would be choosing a clip that contrasts sharply
with what you've found out about the "real" Greek tales. In addition,
you would like to make entertaining montages showing the importance
of Greek myths in modern movies. Woody Allen's *Mighty Aphrodite*, Pier
Paolo Pasolini's *Medea*, and the Disney animated film *Hercules* might feature in such a montage, using evocative short clips to make the point of
the continuing importance of Greek culture in general.

Do you have a fair-use right to use the introductory clips contrasting
with your research results? Can you claim fair use for montages of clips
from popular films to make a general point about the pervasiveness of
these references in films today? Would it be better to stay away from the
scenes that feature celebrities?

Answers at the back, and more at http://centerforsocialmedia.org/fair-use.

distortion of experience and practice. Among other consequences, copyright was assigned to original works of authorship. In the Romantic era,
in the late eighteenth and early nineteenth century, poets and philoso-
phers celebrated the role of the individual, conquering or refusing the
restraints of convention. This put clothes on the concept of the genius-
creator, and fed today's stereotype of the artist. Old systems of meaning,
especially those dictated by church and Crown, had eroded; a faith in the
capacity of people to discover truths was burgeoning; and the social actor
charged with making sense of it all was the genius-creator. Increasingly,
as Thomas Streeter describes in the context of tracking the evolution of
Internet culture, the creator was given an almost mystical role in society,
as a meaning-creator and meaning-giver.

The individualistic or Romantic notion of creation, which ignores
social relationships and historical frameworks, has been broadly critiqued by legal scholars, including James Boyle, who notes its distorting
effect on copyright policy. Rebecca Tushnet has argued that all creativity

should be understood as "hybrid," or a mix of individual, historic, and social activity. Legal scholar Jessica Litman goes so far as to call the very notion of originality "a legal fiction." She notes:

> Because authors necessarily reshape the prior works of others, a vision of authorship as original creation from nothing—and of authors as casting up truly new creations from their innermost being—is both flawed and misleading. If we took this vision seriously, we could not grant authors copyrights without first dissecting their creative processes to pare elements adapted from the works of others from the later authors' recasting of them. This dissection would be both impossible and unwelcome. If we eschewed this vision but nonetheless adhered unswervingly to the concept of originality, we would have to allow the author of almost any work to be enjoined by the owner of the copyright in another.

She concludes, "Nurturing authorship is not necessarily the same thing as nurturing authors."

Today's copyright law requires that somebody (or several somebodies) be the author(s) of a copyrighted work. There is no place for truly collective authorship based on notions of group work. This insistence on authorship by individuals (Franklin Smithers) rather than collectives (The Davenport Community Foundation) has had some peculiar consequences. Paradoxically, it supports a weird legal fiction, the "work for hire" doctrine, which gives employers rights to the work of employees. It also puts the cultural work of genuine collectives, such as folklore and traditional arts of indigenous peoples, at a legal disadvantage. It fits poorly, for instance, with the group creation of quilts in contemporary communities such as the African American women of Gee's Bend, as legal scholar Victoria Phillips has documented.

Many invocations of the genius-creator today are mere gambits. Music, publishing, and movie executives constantly invoke the genius-creator with piety, even when their own artists demonstrate the need and will to collaborate widely and even though their own businesses return relatively little to most creators. They put celebrities out in front to celebrate the Romantic notion of the creator, while they depend on crude economic calculation to lay claim to works for hire, done on their time and with their supplies. Hypocrisy aside, however, the basic notion that individual creative authorship deserves all the protection the law can afford remains widespread. It cripples thinking about copyright, because it encourages policies that favor whoever owns the works of the past, rather than the makers of tomorrow's culture.

On the other hand, the existence of fair use is bold legal recognition of the social nature of the creative process. It is a part of copyright law that reminds us that the purpose of the law is to promote creation, not to protect owners. People who use fair use need not feel guilty because they have taken another's work. That person also, implicitly or explicitly, built on his or her own culture. This is how culture endures, by being used and ultimately transformed.

Interpreting Fair Use

The basic fair-use calculation—whether social benefit is greater than private loss—is framed in law with deliberate vagueness. Fair use is always a case-by-case decision, like decisions about the appropriate and necessary in speech generally, keeping in mind certain basic principles and calculations. The Copyright Act builds in several examples of ways to reason about fair use. The statute requires, at a minimum, considering the *character* of the use (what are you doing with the material?), the *nature of the original* work (is it mainly factual reportage, or an imaginative production?), the *amount* taken (and whether it's the central part of the work), and the effect of taking on the *market value* of the work.

These are often called the "four factors." Sadly, since they became part of the law in 1978, the four factors have been as much hindrance as help to making fair use useable, partly because they mean very little without an understanding of the customary practices and habits around the kind of use in question, and partly because people nevertheless endow them with a false autonomy. Each of these concerns—and the law explicitly says they don't have to be the only concerns—may have a different weight in different situations, and certainly has had at different times in legal history.

Fortunately, as a result of litigation in which judges have, implicitly or explicitly, considered custom and practice, there is an easier way. A typical fair-use calculation today can be distilled into three questions:

- Was the use of copyrighted material for a different purpose, rather than just reuse for the original purpose and for the same audience? (If so, it probably adds something new to the cultural pool.)
- Was the amount of material taken appropriate to the purpose of the use? (Can the purpose be clearly articulated? Was the amount taken proportional? Or was it too much?)
- Was it reasonable within the field or discipline it was made in?

(Standards and practices documents, such as the kind TV networks created for their news divisions, and codes of best practices in fair use from various creator and user communities, do a good job of making clear what normally acceptable practice is. In fields that lack such norm-setting documents, creators—and potentially judges and juries—have a harder time assessing what could be considered normal.) Sometimes courts also consider whether the user acted in "good faith." While the concept is vague, it can be partly addressed by demonstrations of having thought through the first two questions (for instance, by leaving a written record of one's reasons for selecting the material). In addition, providing attribution or credit is a wise choice, indicating awareness that the work selected belongs to others.

If the answer to these basic questions is yes, then a court these days— if ever asked—would likely find a use fair. And because that is true, such use is unlikely to be challenged in the first place. The vast majority of fair uses are never challenged, of course. But when they are, judges and juries have overwhelmingly rejected claims of infringement and supported fair users when they carefully employed this reasoning to make their decisions. And this is hardly surprising, given the long history of the fair-use doctrine and its strong constitutional roots.

How Fair Use Evolved

Fair use has evolved as a solution to particular problems in copyright, and it—like the rest of copyright policy—is always capable of more change. Tinkering never stops with any policy that matters to people, because all policies are valuable assets to some, chafing irritations to others, and irrelevant to still others (who may as circumstances change suddenly find themselves affected). Stakeholders gather around governments to shape the policies that will be good for them, and of course everyone always claims that their preferred approach also will be good for everybody else, especially for the one stakeholder who rarely makes a personal appearance in the discussion—"the public."

In legal and policy decision making, the interests of society are represented in the phrase "the public interest." This is not only, as one Reagan-era FCC commissioner put it, merely "what the public is interested in," but what is needed for a society to exist and grow within the values that people in the society share. In the United States, democratic participation, cultural pluralism, freedom of expression, and equality of opportunity are all examples of values that inform the society. Fair use is an example of a policy in the public interest. Fair use does not protect the interests of any one individual or group so much as it protects freedom of expression and the capacity of the culture to develop.

Fair use was not an explicit part of the earliest copyright law, because it was not needed. That is because copyright law until recently was very limited. There was no copyright law, as we know it, in ancient times or in the European Middle Ages. In the premodern era, patronage from the church, the state, or wealthy individuals was the main driver of high-end cultural production—although a faint hint of the future was heard in sixteenth-century Venice, when the doges and council began occasionally to grant favored writers and artists "privileges" in their works.

The copyright policies we depend upon today began, as legal scholar Benjamin Kaplan explained, when London-based publishers lost their royal monopoly on printing in the late seventeenth century, and began to cast around for other ways to secure their commercial advantage against upstart competitors. They proposed that Parliament create a legal monopoly on publishing texts, which could be enforced in English courts of general jurisdiction. This meant they could sue competitors who weren't members of their guild.

Parliament pushed back. For one thing, its members chose to vest many of the rights it recognized in authors, rather than publishers. (In practice, those rights remained the property of publishers, who published authors only if they agreed to hand over their copyrights; it would take generations for this feature of the law to assume much real importance.) More significantly, as legal historian Ronan Deazley recently has shown, Parliament's approach to copyright policy had elements of balance, even then, recognizing the benefit of limiting owners' rights in order to promote public ends, including the circulation of print culture in a society where literacy was rapidly growing. That is why, among other things, the first copyright law, the Statute of Anne of 1710, imposed strict limits on the duration of protection (fourteen years for some works, with a possible renewal for an additional fourteen, and a straight twenty-one years for others) and included rules against predatory book pricing. The limitations built into the Statute of Anne were part of a deeper understanding of cultural expression as belonging to the people as a whole, and benefiting all.

The clash of private power and public purpose informed the Statute of Anne and continued to fuel debate. As literary scholar Lewis Hyde has noted, in eighteenth-century England, skeptics—of which there were many—saw copyright as a private privilege granted to a favored few. They saw monopolies as opposed to the commonwealth, or public good. Ideas that would benefit society by circulating were trapped by monopoly privileges. As a result, books cost more than they should, and opportunities for cultural participation were foreclosed.

The antimonopolistic imperatives at work back in 1710 surfaced again later in the century. In a 1774 conflict, the House of Lords (acting as the highest court of appeal) rejected perpetual copyright. An Edinburgh printer challenged the British publishing monopoly and offered cheap reprints of modern classics throughout the kingdom, even in London. British publishers claimed they had traditional perpetual claims on the work they published—claims they asserted had survived the enactment of the Statute of Anne—but the House of Lords definitively rejected their claim. This reinforced the antimonopolist principles that had been embedded in the statute.

The theme of public interest became even more prominent when British copyright made the transatlantic crossing. The commitment that drove our government's copyright policy, from the start, was not to protect owners—big or small—but to generate new culture.

Thomas Jefferson fiercely resisted the notion of having any recognition of copyright in the US Constitution. In general, Jefferson was opposed to monopolies of all kinds. Specifically, he believed that binding cultural expression by law would violate its essence, as he wrote in 1813:

> He who receives an idea from me, receives instruction himself without lessening mine; as he who lites his taper at mine, receives light without darkening me. That ideas should freely spread from one to another over the globe, for the moral and mutual instruction of man, and improvement of his condition, seems to have been peculiarly and benevolently designed by nature, when she made them, like fire, expansible over all space, without lessening their density at any point, and like the air in which we breathe, move, and have our physical being, incapable of confinement, or exclusive appropriation.

James Madison agreed that monopolies were "justly classed as among the greatest nuisances in Government," but he also thought that in the case of cultural expression some highly limited monopoly rights would provide a healthy incentive to make and circulate creative works. George Washington thought a limited monopoly would encourage learning. Jefferson finally assented under Madison's pressure to a highly limited monopoly of a few years (for both patent and copyright).

What they all agreed about, as Hyde has shown, is that monopolies were an expensive choice for a government to make, the sacrifice of the many for the few, and that such monopolies needed limitations to achieve the policy's objective. In the end, the Constitution granted Congress power to legislate intellectual property law for one purpose and goal: to "Promote the progress of Science and useful Arts." In the early years of the new republic, in cases such as the 1834 *Wheaton v. Peters*—a case involving the competing claims of two Supreme Court reporters—the Justices came down strongly on the side of a copyright law that was aimed at promoting the public good rather than private interest.

In the first half of the nineteenth century, the reach of copyright was still so limited that the need for fair use (or something like it) simply did not arise. The public domain was a wide-open space in early American copyright policy. Most reuses of cultural material were free for the making; copyright was short, and applied to only a few kinds of works (domestic American literary texts, fine art, prints and maps, and a bit later, music). Much of the culture simply was not copyrighted. Moreover, even protected works were protected only against literal or near-literal copying of large chunks.

Even so, by the mid-nineteenth century American businesses came to have ever deeper investments in cultural expression, and competition in the publishing industry led to conflicts. This was the origin of fair use. The case that started it all was decided in 1841. The issue in *Folsom v. Marsh* was whether a new biography of George Washington could use letters that had been collected by an earlier biographer. Justice Joseph Story, building on British precedents, ruled that the new biography had infringed on the copyright of the earlier one, and in the process asserted the standard that ultimately would become the modern four-factor test. As it turned out, the plaintiff triumphed, largely because the follow-on biographer had taken so much material for such a similar purpose. In its own time, the decision could have been seen as restrictive in effect. Where most things were permitted, the Court actually placed limits on permissible unlicensed quotation. By the modern era, as we shall see, the tables were turned; fair use had become a key safety valve from a vastly expanded regime of copyright control.

But it would be some time before fair use came into its own—thanks to the limitations built into copyright doctrine itself. Consider a lawsuit that concerned *Uncle Tom's Cabin*. Harriet Beecher Stowe's book was extraordinarily popular; indeed, it was a pop cultural phenomenon. It generated twenty-seven unauthorized copycat novels (many taking a proslavery

---

Fair Use: You Be the Judge >> Fan Site

You were an avid fan of the television series *Lost* and built a fan website, where you have created graphics using screen captures of many copyrighted images from the program. You also showcased some of your favorite videos that celebrate the characters and themes of *Lost*. You are now part of a network of people creating alternative endings to the television series, which involves analyzing the trajectory of the narrative. You've just found one of your favorite episodes on a file-sharing site, and would love to post it to your site and explain why you think this is a pivotal episode, and possibly one of the best to build an alternative ending upon. Your fan site is completely noncommercial as well as wildly popular. Is your use of copyrighted images to celebrate the show fair use or copyright infringement? In that context, would uploading your favorite episode be fair use?

Answers at the back, and more at http://centerforsocialmedia.org/fair-use.

---

perspective), as well as unlicensed minstrel shows, plays, songs, candies, Uncle Tom statues, jugs, and board games. Stowe may not have earned much in the way of licensing income, but she did earn record-breaking royalties. Hundreds of thousands of copies were sold in the United States and even more in Europe (the European ones all unauthorized), as Terrence Maxwell has noted.

Then someone published an unauthorized German translation of the book in the United States. At the time, Germans were overwhelmingly the largest immigrant group, and German-speakers composed between a third and a half of the population of northern American cities. The translation, like the English original, was immensely popular. Harriet Beecher Stowe sued for infringement of her copyright. In the 1853 *Stowe v. Thomas*, the Court ruled—amazingly, from our perspective today—that the translator had not infringed, because the translation was not a "copy" of the original.

In the Court's view, Mrs. Stowe's actual words were entitled to protection, but only those words:

By the publication of Mrs. Stowe's book, the creations of the genius and imagination of the author have become as much public property as those of Homer and Cervantes. . . . All her conceptions and inventions may be used and abused by imitators, playwrights and poetasters. . . . All that now remains is the copyright in her book: the exclusive right to print, reprint, and vend it, and those only can be called infringers of her rights, or pirates of her property, who are guilty of printing, publishing, importing or vending without her license, "copies of her book." A translation may, in loose phraseology, be called a transcript or copy of her thoughts or conceptions, but in no correct sense can it be called a copy of her book.

No one needed to invoke a right of fair use or any other copyright exception, because there had been no arguable infringement. A translation was outside Stowe's claim to copyright. All Harriet Beecher Stowe owned was her actual words in sequence.

The next half century brought profound changes, including extensions of the term of copyright and expansions of its coverage. Perhaps the first harbinger of the changes to come was the language of another mid-nineteenth-century dispute about a seller of polka sheet music who produced work suspiciously similar to another work, "The Serious Family Polka." The language of the decision, *Jollie v. Jacques*, pointed to the future (though the complaint was dismissed for other reasons). The judge said that the question was whether the defendant was "engaged in selling any polka which is similar in plan or matter to, or is a substantial copy of that published by the plaintiff." Ultimately (in a trend that took decades to materialize) this approach to thinking about infringement would give a lot more leeway to copyright holders than the judge had given to Stowe, who got to protect only her own words in her own language. That way of thinking about the issue opened the door to much more expansive copyright—and to modern conceptions of copyright authority over adaptations (or to use the legal jargon, "derivative works").

In a related development, the expansion of copyright to more and more different kinds of materials was signaled with a sloppy run-of-the-mill circus poster. It was then commonly understood that copyright was for "serious" culture. By contrast, this case was about ephemeral and generic advertisements. At the beginning of the twentieth century, one of the popular entertainments was the circus. There were many companies, and regional competition could be fierce. One circus company brought suit against a printer that had printed a poster for another circus company, not by any means identical but clearly cribbed from its own. Neither poster was much to look at.

The case eventually went to the Supreme Court. In 1903, the Supreme Court, in *Bleistein v. Donaldson Lithographing Co.*, decided that the poster did deserve protection. Justice Oliver Wendell Holmes's answer was clear. Quality, he wrote, has nothing to do with copyrightability, and the meanest commercial productions are entitled to the same protection as the most refined examples of the fine arts: "If [pictures] command the interest of any public, they have a commercial value—it would be bold to say that they have not an aesthetic and educational value—and the taste of the public is not to be treated with contempt." You might congratulate Justice Holmes on his respect for popular culture and his wish not to have lawyers pass aesthetic judgment. But the negative effect of the decision was that the doors of copyright swung wide open to every kind of work.

Cultural Death Grip

One could not have guessed from the polka decision or the circus poster case how profoundly the copyright landscape would change. Today, copyright material is ubiquitous and unavoidable, permeating the fabric of daily life, as many current authors on copyright have noted. The story of how it happened is in chapter 4. Here we sketch the magnitude of the difference in the scope of copyright law between the mid-nineteenth century and today.

In the aftermath of *Bleistein*, almost every imaginable form of fine and commercial art can qualify for copyright, as well as other work such as computer programs and even ephemera such as shopping lists. Over time, copyright holders have come to be protected against more and more different unauthorized uses of their state-created "property." The growth in use of the "adaptation" right (also called the right to prepare "derivative works"), which took off shortly after the *Uncle Tom's Cabin* case, has been dramatic. Today, everything from translations of fictional narratives to video games based on hit movies is controlled by the copyright holder. Those plays, minstrel shows, and copycat novels that *Uncle Tom's Cabin* spurred could not happen today without Stowe's permission. The "reproduction right" now applies to copying parts—even fairly small ones—of a work. Any "public performance" or "public display" of a protected work (even one made without a profit motive—like a school group's dramatization of a popular children's book) is regulated as well.

Not only that, but this protection lasts ever longer. The first US copyright statute, in 1790, granted an initial term of fourteen years for qualifying works, with the potential for an additional fourteen-year renewal—if the work proved to have a long shelf life. In 1831, the initial term was extended to twenty-eight years, though the renewal stayed at fourteen. In 1909, Congress extended the renewal term to match the initial one—for a total potential of twenty-eight years of protection. In 1976, copyright terms were extended as of 1978 to the life of the author plus fifty years after his or her death. In 1990, renewal (which you formerly had to request) became automatic. And in 1998, the Sonny Bono Copyright Term Extension Act (CTEA) handed almost everyone with a copyright another twenty years of protection. Now, a book created in 2011 by a thirty-year-old man with a normal life expectancy will still be protected in the year 2130, 119 years later. If we had the same copyright terms and rules as we had in 1977, that thirty-year-old's 2011 copyright would be up in 2039, when he was fifty-eight, and then he would have to renew it or allow it to lapse.

Making the imbalance much more severe in practice is the growth in the risks that we run when we go up against copyright—intentionally or otherwise. Copyright holders who have formally registered their copyrights before an arguable infringement occurred can choose to receive so-called "statutory damages" instead of damages related to their losses or infringers' profits. This is true even where those actual damages are small or nonexistent, and whether or not the infringer had any commercial objective. Statutory damages always have been part of the US copyright system; for most of copyright history these have been pegged at modest levels. But in recent decades, with pressure from content industries, the ordinary minimum is $750 for each work infringed, up to a potential maximum of $150,000—thirty times what the 1909 act allowed. Even though the higher figures are extremely unlikely, the potential maximum—a figure widely publicized by large copyright holders—has a chilling effect.

Statutory damages scare people away from assuming even small risks in using copyrighted material. And the number of people facing that potential risk is also expanding. Courts have expanded what is known as "secondary liability," a sharing of responsibility for infringement. For example, a landlord who hosts a flea market where infringing works are sold could end up holding the bag for his fly-by-night tenants' activities. A teacher whose assignment leads her students to produce work that incorporates protected content without permission could also be liable for copyright infringement—and face the threat (though very unlikely ever to be a reality) of $150,000 in statutory damages, potentially multiplied many times over (if multiple copyrights were involved).

So the overwhelming majority of content we run into—and certainly almost all of the commercially produced stuff—is protected by copyright, unless we can identify it positively as a work in the public domain. If it is not a work published before 1923, if it was not made by a US government employee at the job, or if it is not at least seventy years after the death of all the authors, there is a good chance it is still copyrighted. Of course, in the pre-1992 days when renewal was required, the copyright holder might have forgotten or decided not to renew it. That is especially true if the material did not have commercial value to someone at the time (most high-profile commercial mass-culture work is zealously renewed, though more obscure books and movies are another matter). To find out whether a copyright had been renewed, you would have to check with the Copyright Office. (Note that Google Book Search has aggregated renewal records, and http://centerforsocialmedia.org/fair-use provides a table that allows you to assess whether works fall into the public domain.) Copyright has become long and strong. With each of those changes, current owners have gained more power over future creators and the culture, and fair use has become more important in freeing future creators from the death grip of the past.

3 The Decline and Rise of Fair Use

THE BACK-ROOM STORY

This isn't just about a bunch of kids stealing music. It's about an assault on everything that constitutes the cultural expression of our society. If we fail to protect and preserve our intellectual property system, the culture will atrophy.

RICHARD PARSONS, CEO of Time Warner

Until the 1960s, everyone interested in copyright law (not a large community) more or less agreed about the goals of the system: copyright was all about promoting cultural production through providing, as Benjamin Kaplan put it, an "incentive or 'headstart'" for "releasing the energies of creative workers." This concept depended on having a range of limitations on the already limited monopoly of owners, such as special exemptions and broad policies like first sale and fair use. It also depended on limits to copyright's scope, which left much material in the owner-free zone of the public domain.

From the 1960s to the 1990s, though, this consensus came under increasing pressure from a number of different sources. One of the consequences was that in the general population, confidence in the importance of fair use was shaken (though not among media companies, which continued to employ it). Copyright became even longer and stronger, as well as generally meaner, during the last four decades, and public awareness of fair use suffered as a result. It did not begin to revive until the turn of the millennium. How that happened is key to understanding how important that revival is.

Fair Use in Retreat

In 1955, a Los Angeles federal district court judge articulated a boldly different philosophy of copyright and fair use than the one expressed by Kaplan and the copyright community in general. The case, *Benny v. Loew's*, involved a young medium, television, and a perennially young comedian, Jack Benny. The controversy was around the planned broadcast of "Autolight," a takeoff on a popular movie, *Gaslight*, about a nefarious husband who schemes to drive his wife insane. Benny had performed an earlier version on radio, which had led to an inconclusive skirmish over copyright with the movie studio. When the TV version was announced, the copyright holder, Loew's, sued to stop it.

Judge James M. Carter, a Truman appointee who formerly had run the Los Angeles motor vehicles bureau, had no copyright expertise. He just treated all quoting as stealing: "[P]arodized or burlesque taking is to be treated no differently from any other appropriation; . . . If it is determined that there was a substantial taking, infringement exists." He also wrote, "The mere absence of competition or injurious effect upon the copyrighted work will not make a use fair. The right of a copyright proprietor to exclude others is absolute and if it has been violated the fact that the infringement will not affect the sale or exploitation of the work or pecuniarily damage him is immaterial." In other words, copyright owners should control not only the actual markets for their works, but all potential markets as well. This was a startling setback for fair use as a defense against attacks on cultural repurposing.

Judge Carter concluded—in striking contrast to longstanding legal tradition—that the copyright owner has more or less complete sovereignty over uses that are more than trivial in quantity or quality. Worse, his decision was affirmed by an appeals court notorious for its friendliness to copyright owners, the Ninth Circuit. That court, in a narrowly divided opinion, relegated fair use to "compilations, listings, digests, and the like." The divided Supreme Court also affirmed, without opinion, and thus avoided making Judge Carter's ruling the law of the land. But the fact that this crabbed economic interpretation of fair use, issued by a nonexpert in copyright law, had been able to march unimpeded that far was an early demonstration of a shift in thinking, indeed a shift in the framework around the concept of fair use. It was also pioneering. Increasingly it became acceptable to slight the public-interest importance of fair use—its value in protecting future cultural expression—in favor of the economic protection of current owners.

The 1976 Copyright Act

The next development in the story of fair use came as the result of legislation that extensively rewrote the Copyright Act, mostly in the service of large copyright holders. These mass-media businesses had become, with the growth of film, broadcasting, and popular publishing, major economic actors both nationally and internationally. They depended on copyright ownership, especially for their ever-expanding archives. In the early 1960s, these businesses began pressuring Congress to make copyright law match with modern technology and practice. Congress began revamping the copyright statute—not just patching gaps, but rebuilding the copyright law from the bottom up. By the time the bill passed in 1976, Congress was also responding to calls for the United States to assert an international presence on copyright policy, providing a counterpressure to the influence of developing nations in the United Nations forums for policy debate.

The effects were profound and far-ranging. The law, which took effect in 1978, reflected the interests of the major media corporations in longer, stronger protection. The final bill looked like a gift to them, including (among others) the protection of all works from the moment of creation; a single copyright term for all new works, instead of the old two-term system with optional copyright renewal; confirmation of the 1972 extension of copyright to sound recordings; the relaxation of copyright formalities such as the need to use a copyright notice; clarification of copyright's application to derivative works and new media; and the provision of new, harsher penalties for infringement.

These changes added up to a tectonic shift in copyright thinking. What had begun 250 years before as a limited set of rules governing only books (not even magazines or newspapers) had become a source of generalized protection for a class of newly valuable market commodities: "works." Legal scholar L. Ray Patterson perceptively recognized that the 1976 act marked a shift away from a "regulatory" approach to copyright, in favor of one based on property rights, pure and simple.

When "works" were property above all, then their economic value always came first. The legislation had given a big stamp of approval to a shift in business thinking that had been underway for some time. It also provided a way to revalue assets. Increasingly, copyrights were showing up on account books as long-term assets, and company backlists were becoming archives.

Legislators did not lose sight altogether of the cultural mission of copyright. Indeed, they singled out fair use for protection. A compelling 1960 historical study by legal scholar Alan Latman, commissioned by the Senate Judiciary Committee, showed the importance of fair use as a safety valve in the US copyright system over the past century. In Patterson's view, the legislators "realized that, without a statement regarding fair use, the combined weight of the other changes constituted a very real threat to the constitutional purpose of copyright—the promotion of learning."

Educators and librarians, not always powerful in the stakeholder scrum, in this case had pushed successfully for an acknowledgment of fair use. They were acutely aware of its value. Photocopying technology

True Stories of Fair Use: Sut Jhally

Media studies professor Sut Jhally runs the Media Education Foundation, and through it distributes videos that critique popular culture and
current politics. His films all make extensive and confident use of fair
use. He explained to us how it started:

> In the late 1980s I developed some materials for a large lecture course
> I taught at the University of Massachusetts. At first it was just ex-
> cerpts from music videos, showing stereotyping and misogynistic
> views of women. Over the course of several years, I gradually devel-
> oped it into a stand-alone piece and by 1990, I thought it would be
> nice to share it with other educators. So I sent out a small mailing for
> the video *Dreamworlds*, and promptly got a cease-and-desist letter
> from MTV, both to me and the university.
>
> I was quite convinced that I was covered by fair use, and said
> that to MTV; they never even got back to me. The university, though,
> thought I should just shut up. I said, Are you crazy? This was a great
> opportunity to make a statement about fair use and academic free-
> dom. So that's when they told me that if I did speak up, I wouldn't be
> covered by university lawyers. I decided to go ahead with a press re-
> lease, and launched the Media Education Foundation to distance my-
> self from the university. We got great coverage for the event, as a free
> speech issue. MTV didn't want to be near the story—it ran against
> their branding.
>
> By now we've done 50 or 60 films; we use fair use the way it's sup-
> posed to be used. It's what the law allows. We also license stuff which
> we don't think is fair use. When we saw the codes of best practices
> come out, we felt reinforced in our judgments.

In only one case has MEF received a challenge to its fair uses. When
MEF distributed *Price of Pleasure: Pornography, Sexuality & Relationships*,
two pornographic film distributors contacted MEF to complain that
their work had been used without permission. In both cases, Jhally
wrote back to inform them that their work had been used under the
doctrine of fair use, but that he would welcome a lawsuit. He believed,
he wrote, that a lawsuit on freedom of expression issues, in which the
pornography industry took an anti–free speech role, would be interesting indeed. Both backed off immediately.

"I used to believe that we would be the best test case for fair use litigation, but we may be unsueable," Jhally said wryly. "I guess the best
thing we can do is to continue doing what we're doing, using fair use
fully and publicly."

was a boon to their missions, while publishers regarded it as a threat to their bottom line. A 1974 Supreme Court case, *Williams & Wilkins*, in which libraries at the National Institutes of Health claimed a fair-use right to photocopy copyrighted materials for research use, resulted in a split decision that amounted to a victory for the libraries and a defeat for publishers. If unlicensed library and educational photocopying were to continue, it would have to be on the basis of fair use.

The challenge was introducing fair use into the statute in a way that would not rouse the ire of zealous content industry stakeholders. Legislators sympathetic to the claims of librarians and educators knew that new language might rile the content industries. (Especially important was Democratic Rep. Robert Kastenmeier, who led the reform process as chair of the House intellectual property subcommittee.) So they used a variant of language that had 125 years of history in the courts: the factors Justice Story had written about back in 1841. With this tactic, they safely slid fair use into the 1976 act, without too much controversy.

The little clause was to have a big effect. It enabled large institutions—not just nonprofits such as libraries and museums, but major mass-media companies—to exploit fair use consistently and quietly over the ensuing years, getting their work done more efficiently and lowering costs. These businesses were able to do so without controversy, partly because they successfully internalized the newly codified legal standard—often through standards-and-practices guides written by experts committed to making the law work for them and drawing heavily on past industry practice.

But the codification of fair use also had a sting in its tail, emphasizing protection of the current market over the promotion of future culture in one key phrase. Back in 1843, Justice Story had directed courts to look at how a use "may prejudice the sale, or diminish the profits, or supersede the objects," of the copyrighted work. The reform legislation refers instead to "the effect of the use upon the *potential market for or value of* the copyrighted work." But if (for example) foregone licensing fees constitute a legally relevant kind of economic loss, then fair use would often (or always) be off-limits. Would the courts treat this language as an excuse to deny fair use wherever there was money at stake? Or would they find a way to limit its potentially sweeping effect?

The Economic Turn in Scholarship and Law

The priority of potential markets in the law raised new issues about how to interpret fair use and threatened to weaken it drastically. For instance, if owners could figure out a way to license traditionally fair uses, would that in itself turn fair use into infringement? The proposition seemed absurd given longstanding practice. For instance, critics traditionally quote sections of a work in reviewing it. If publishers made it easier to license such quotes, would that eliminate the fair-use claim for them? An emerging way of thinking, however, challenged longstanding practice.

By the late 1970s, microeconomic analysis was coming to have an enormous influence in legal thinking, especially after the publication of seminal articles by economist Ronald Coase and legal scholar Guido Calabresi in 1961. The law-and-economics school of thought argues that efficient outcomes (that is, with low transaction costs) are preferable and that free markets promote efficiency by allocating goods—or rights—to those who value them the most. This law-and-economics approach simply does not work when noneconomic values are important; it never really touched human rights law, for instance. But it did affect copyright and fair use. In 1982, for example, legal scholar Wendy Gordon wrote an influential article, "Fair Use as Market Failure." The complexities of her argument were often reduced, in legal debate, to the argument that where there is a smoothly functioning market in rights clearances, fair use might not be applicable.

The economic focus of fair-use analysis prevailed as well, in the famous 1984 *Sony Betamax* lawsuit. That case, about whether VCRs, with their built-in copying capacity, unlawfully contributed to infringement, demonstrated how copyright had become a field of battle for big economic interests. Media companies forecast the end of entertainment as they knew it if the VCR went viral. They wrapped themselves in the American flag and called for protection because of their importance to the US economy. The MPAA lobbyist Jack Valenti shamelessly invoked a jingoistic fear of Japanese overtaking US industry, in incidents discussed by both Lawrence Lessig and William Patry.

The Supreme Court's decision turned on the question of whether copying for "time-shifting" purposes could be considered fair use; if so, the machines had important lawful function, and electronics companies couldn't be tagged with secondary liability for selling them. In their analysis, the Justices took the fourth factor seriously, placing considerable weight on the fact that the movie companies hadn't demonstrated any present economic harm (or risk of future harm) to them from consumers' use of the new technology. For once, at least, the economic turn in fair-use analysis actually helped to bolster a fair-use claim.

Unexpectedly, another kind of market-based analysis also came to the aid of the VCR and its users—and thus, indirectly, the consumer electronics industry. In addition to parsing the fourth factor, the majority of the Justices also interpreted the first factor—the purpose of the use—with an economic gloss. Time-shifting, they noted, was noncommercial, and therefore likely to be fair.

Of course, the *Betamax* decision was a boon to technology companies selling all kinds of electronic gear with playback functions. More generally, the Court's decision to put a thumb on the scale where noncommercial uses were involved could benefit not only consumers but also educators, libraries, and other institutional users. But there was a downside. In his majority opinion, Justice Stevens specifically asserted that commercial uses had "a much weaker claim" to fair use. This unfortunate judicial aside threatened some of the most important applications of the fair-use doctrine. Much culture-making is, actually or potentially, commercial. In many areas of overtly commercial production, including publishing, filmmaking, and music, fair use had long been critically important to creative work, as it would quietly continue to be. Indeed, most of the cases in which fair use had prevailed in court over the years before and after 1984 involved commercial uses—by trade publishers, newspapers, movie companies, and others. (Lawsuits usually are lodged against entities with assets.) Paradoxically, the Justices' diminished respect for "commercial" fair use may have had the greatest dampening effect on individual creative professionals and on new businesses. The approach that saved the VCR, its manufacturers, and its users threatened to hobble other kinds of fair use.

The law-and-economics framework came to be widely reflected in judges' opinions. Two cases illustrate the prevalence of that framework in judicial reasoning about fair use. In 1985, the Supreme Court decided a case, *Harper & Row*, in which *The Nation* published small but crucial excerpts from ex-president Gerald Ford's memoirs. *Time* magazine then backed out of a contract to publish excerpts. The book's publisher then sued *The Nation*, which argued unsuccessfully that it had a right to fair use for those excerpts. It didn't help their cause that the manuscript apparently had been stolen in the first place. But the bigger problem for *The Nation* was that the Court's ruling strongly reflected the then-current emphasis on economic rights and economic harms. Significantly, on its way to a conclusion favoring the copyright owners, the Court opined that the effect on the market "is undoubtedly the single most important element of fair use."

The creative consequences were evident from an appeals court decision in 1992 favoring a photographer whose potential market might have been invaded by a sculptor whose work the Court found distastefully commercial. The defendant was Jeff Koons, a flamboyant artist whose work typically comments on the banality of commercial and popular culture. He had designed a bizarre, larger-than-life sculpture based on the plaintiff photographer Art Rogers's intimate shot of a human couple holding a large litter of puppies. Koons's fair-use defense failed, in large part, because Judge Richard Cardamone was fixated on the twin facts that he had made a good deal of money, and that the photographer might conceivably have lost some:

> It is obviously not implausible that another artist, who would be willing to purchase the rights from Rogers, would want to produce a sculpture like Rogers' photo and, with Koons' work extant, such market is reduced. Similarly, defendants could take and sell photos of "String of Puppies," which would prejudice Rogers' potential market for the sale of the "Puppies" notecards, in addition to any other derivative use he might plan.

What made Judge Cardamone speculate so wildly? The judge had decided that the fourth (potential market) factor was the "most important, and indeed, central fair use factor," according to the Supreme Court's *Nation* decision, and he cited *Betamax* for the proposition that (in the judge's own words) "where the use is intended for commercial gain some meaningful likelihood of future harm is presumed." The economic turn in fair-use analysis was turning into a serious liability for emerging culture.

Fair Use and Free Trade

Turning cultural expression into simple property matched up nicely with the government's mandate at the time to improve international trade conditions. In the 1980s, with strong federal mandates for deregulation and expanded international trade, any policy that helped an economic trade advantage won out. Large copyright holders immediately argued that they needed even more copyright protection for commercially produced culture—an important part of US international trade, with all those movies, TV shows, and music CDs being sold around the world. New and emerging cultural expression often starts out noncommercially, and noncommercial expression did not have well-heeled stakeholder representation. The economic mandate obscured the cultural mandate. Fair use was not so much specifically attacked in the new discourse of copyright and international trade as it was simply ignored and sometimes overridden.

In 1984, content industry organizations formed the International Intellectual Property Alliance, including publishers groups and associations of the music and movie industries, to "improve international protection and enforcement of copyrighted materials and open up foreign markets closed by piracy and other market access barriers." They were not the first to raise this banner. That distinction probably belongs to the MPAA, which by the early 1980s had established "film security offices" in major cities around the globe. But the IIPA took a lead role in changing copyright from a cultural to an economic policy. Software businesses soon joined in, through a new umbrella organization, the Business Software Alliance, organized in 1988. These groups benefited from the creation of the Joint Anti-Piracy Intelligence Group, founded in 1984 as a counterpart to Interpol.

The marriage of convenience between large corporate copyright holders and government diplomats was immediately visible in the 1984 Caribbean Basin Initiative, a Reagan-era plan to create a new economic Monroe Doctrine. The goal was to tie weaker countries of the region to the United States through trade preferences. At the time, Jamaican entrepreneurs were pirating TV signals without any penalties from their government. Arguing that lax copyright enforcement was, in effect, a kind of covert government subsidy to local businesses, the IIPA prevailed on US negotiators to offer trade agreements that would favor Caribbean nations if they would crack down on the stealing of US commercial media. In addition, in the early 1980s drug companies worked with the administration to get extended protection for their products during international trade negotiations. This set the stage for a much larger role for intellectual property forces in international treaty-making. A decade later, in 1994, the *Agreement on Trade-Related Aspects of Intellectual Property Rights* (usually known as *TRIPS*) bound signatories to a long list of promises to provide strong protection to foreign IP—including, of course, US copyrights encountered in other countries. Agreeing to honor those terms is now a requirement for much-coveted participation in the World Trade Organization.

Domestic policy also pushed fair use and other culturally grounded copyright doctrines to the margin. This was driven by mass-media companies' terror of emerging digital distribution. With the expansion of digital technology and the growth of Internet use, digital copying also became digital distribution. People had always been able to share their books with friends, play their music at a party, share sheet music with their choir mate—their passive fair-use rights, or possibly their rights outside of copyright altogether. Large copyright holders had been able to live with that level of sharing. But digital transmission made it way too easy to share; digital sharing fundamentally jeopardized their business model. Copyright was their best weapon, and they set out to hone it. Time Warner CEO Richard Parsons thundered, "Artists will have no incentive to create. Worst-case scenario: The country will end up in a sort of cultural Dark Ages."

In 1995, the content industry stakeholders' all-commerce-all-the-time approach to copyright was put neatly between covers when a new Clinton administration report emerged. Clinton had been elected with strong support from Hollywood and the recording industry. His czar for those issues was veteran copyright lawyer Bruce Lehman, the undersecretary of commerce for intellectual property. Lehman's Working Group on Intellectual Property Rights produced a policy paper on intellectual property—especially about copyright: *Intellectual Property and the National Information Infrastructure.*

Lehman recommended extending the regime of copyright to make the Internet a safe place for copyright holders to distribute their work. That report included the first draft of the legislation that three years later emerged as the DMCA. The report called for anticircumvention rules to make it illegal to override digital encryption. That those rules would then override users' fair-use rights didn't faze the report's drafters, who (in an interesting twist of economic rhetoric) referred to fair use as a "tax" on copyright owners. The *White Paper* called for the liability of Internet service providers for their subscribers' copyright infringements, hoping to make ISPs design and police their services to discourage infringement (and, in the process, chill the rights of fair users). It also urged public education to make sure that young people understood that all copying without permission was stealing, even though some copying was clearly legal. The report was written as if all unauthorized use of copyrighted material were a threat to the body economic and politic.

The language of the *White Paper* was purely and exclusively that of information commerce. Exemptions were not balancing features in the service of new culture, but simply impositions on rights holders. Thus, a university using fair-use rights is just seeking "subsidization" from rights holders. The report demonstrates how a rigorously economic emphasis downplays the importance of fair use and obscures the real objectives of the copyright system.

There was a prompt and loud reaction from familiar advocates of the public interest in copyright, such as libraries, and from scholars, including Pamela Samuelson and Peter Jaszi. They joined with businesses that depend on fair use in the Digital Future Coalition (DFC). The coalition

Fair Use: You Be the Judge >> Public Radio News

You are a reporter for public radio. You are doing a story on a fifteen-second commercial that employs material from your station as fuel for a political campaign and in the process critiques public radio as dangerously liberal. You have been told that you can use up to 10 percent of copyrighted material, even if you are not commenting directly on it. But in this case, you think you need to run the whole commercial. What can you do?

Answers at the back, and more at http://centerforsocialmedia.org/fair-use.

and its allies—including consumer electronics manufacturers, telecommunications companies, and other Internet service providers—managed to block the administration's first push to create legislation based on the *White Paper*. When the administration took the same issues into the international arena in 1996, a wide range of civil society organizations, including the DFC, successfully lobbied the World Intellectual Property Organization to soften the treaty terms that content industry stakeholders sought on issues like "circumvention." Furthermore, these public interest advocates helped to assure that the new WIPO Copyright Treaty (and its companion, the WIPO Treaty on Performances and Phonograms) included unprecedented language asserting the importance of balance in copyright and access to culture.

Internationally, corporate copyright holders won only a watered-down form of the *White Paper's* proposals to protect digital content. But the administration eagerly followed up on the chance to interpret those proposals. It again proposed legislation focused on creating new civil and criminal penalties for breaking industry-designed "digital rights management." This bill, which eventually became the DMCA in 1998, made it illegal among other things to break such code and also to distribute code-breaking tools, under most circumstances. Significantly, circumvention for fair use was not among the short list of proposed exceptions to this new technological regime.

The political fight was furious, and the copyright-as-property ideological frame was a powerful one. Content industries strongly argued that such legislation was essential to international trade, and indeed to the security of the nation. As Tarleton Gillespie has recounted, the MPAA's Jack Valenti freely associated downloading, hard-copy piracy, and terrorism. Civil society organizations, including libraries, educators, and the

DFC, argued for the vision of copyright that Benjamin Kaplan and other scholars had so elegantly espoused, one that nurtured the future of culture as well as protecting current owners. They worked with key commercial allies, including Internet service providers (who wanted to avoid being entangled in responsibility for their users' choices) and equipment manufacturers (who wanted their users to be able to use hardware freely).

During the brutal stakeholder battles, inevitably alliances changed. Internet service providers dropped their opposition once they secured protection from shared responsibility for acts of their users on their systems. In return, they had to remove promptly any material a copyright holder objected to, while also giving the poster an opportunity to contest the takedown. Equipment manufacturers won a clause saying that they did not need to redesign equipment to recognize digital copy controls. The open-access software community secured important statutory exemptions for reverse engineering. And the cultural-vision advocates ended up with small but significant victories. Their concerns were partially acknowledged in a provision allowing fair users to seek exceptions to the anticircumvention provisions where their ability to make "noninfringing" uses (including their fair-use rights) were "adversely affected."

Overall, the passage of the DMCA in 1998 was a dark moment for fair use. But the DMCA was also a turning point. In the stakeholder slugfests, the civil society stakeholders loudly and often made clear that fair use was an essential feature of copyright law, and that marginalizing it would have serious cultural and economic costs. This work did not reclaim the potential of fair use at the time. But it made the concept something to fight over, and gave it new visibility.

Meanwhile, economic tunnel vision continued to dominate policymaking. It culminated in term-extension legislation, which finally passed (after a decade of pressure by corporate copyright holders) as the Sonny Bono Copyright Term Extension Act of 1998. Both Hollywood and the music publishing industry were its champions. The music publishing industry, a particularly vocal stakeholder, was protecting rights in musical perennials, such as the catalogue controlled by Irving Berlin's estate.

Now the corporate copyright holders and the international trade supporters had what they wanted. Copyright policies were longer and stronger on behalf of owners than ever before. They were now Internet-ready— they thought. They believed they had the audience back in the box. They were wrong, of course. Their business-model problems were only beginning.

But in the process, legislation had redrawn the copyright landscape.

It had created unprecedented breadth and depth of rights for copyright owners, and slighted all others. Now that enormous damage had been done to their rights, consumers and users began to wake up. They were beginning to use their newfound digital freedoms; they were buying laptops; they were experimenting with unprecedented services such as Napster, designed in 1999; and they were bumping up against unforeseen problems. Digerati and professors, some of them mere spectators during civil society stakeholders' desperate legislative skirmishes with corporate stakeholders, also decided to take action.

Lawrence Lessig decided to challenge the all-economics-all-the-time environment with a lawsuit. He teamed up with an electronic publisher, Eric Eldred, whose publishing of public-domain books was hurt by copyright extension, and Eldred was joined by other publishers. In 2003 Lessig took *Eldred v. Ashcroft* to the Supreme Court, arguing that copyright extension was unconstitutional because the Constitution mandated "limited terms." Current terms—though technically limited—were so long that they might as well be forever for the uses people make of the public domain. The Supreme Court eventually ruled against that argument, saying that the terms, though long, were in fact limited. Moreover, they protected US copyright holders who wanted to distribute work internationally, since European law denied extended copyright protection to nationals of any country that did not honor Europe's long copyright terms. The Supreme Court acted in line with the economic-protection thinking that had metastasized over the previous fifty years. The one ray of light in the decision was the Court's note that extended terms did not violate constitutional First Amendment rights because of doctrines that limited the scope of owners' authorship —including fair use.

By 2003, owners' copyrights applied to nearly everything a person could create; they applied to many of the works people could make out of those original works; they were automatic, created along with the work; and they lasted, effectively, forever. There was still one escape hatch: fair use. Lawyers and judges knew it, and so did people who worked in mass-media organizations and in libraries. From the early 1990s there was a dramatic shift toward judicial enthusiasm for fair use, which was in part a reaction to the tightening copyright net. Fair use was being rediscovered by everyone from remixers to elementary school teachers. But it now faced another serious challenge: a bad image. Both copyright holders and copyright critics contributed to that.

4   The Decline and Rise of Fair Use

THE PUBLIC CAMPAIGNS

Our world is different.   JOHN PERRY BARLOW

As copyright became an ever more relevant issue in digital culture, both content industry groups and activists for a less restrictive approach to copyright—often designating themselves as copyleftists or free-culture activists—began to reach out to the general public. In this battle for the hearts and minds of digital-culture users, fair use ended up a casualty. This was more accidental than by design. Content industry groups were largely concerned with asserting maximum control in the new, uncertain digital environment. Free-culture activists, including many legal and cultural studies scholars, trumpeted the dream of a vastly expanded public domain, as part of a romantic rhetoric of free or open-source culture. The clash of these two extreme agendas effectively sidelined the concept of balance in copyright law.

Content industry rhetoricians called unlicensed use theft, criminality, and piracy. Free-culture activists called copyright holders greedy corporate thugs, and called for a culture of free sharing. As several scholars (especially Tarleton Gillespie, John Logie, and William Patry) have noted, this was not a helpful way to frame a public policy discussion. Patry has characterized the polarized discourse as an example of a moral panic. Copyright was treated not as a multifunctional tool to promote culture, but as a shield by some and a cage by others.

The content industry circulated a few simple concepts: Copyright is just another kind of property. Unauthorized copying is stealing. Stealing hurts artists. Asking permission is always the right thing. They represented copyright as all about property ownership, and raised the specter of lost jobs and ballooning trade imbalances when owners' rights were violated.

In their role as public intellectuals (as contrasted with their profes-

sional and academic positions), legal and cultural studies scholars popu-
larized the vision of an "information commons" (by analogy to physical
public spaces open to all). These scholars accepted unbalanced copyright
as a brutal but unmoving fact. Since copyright's version of the commons,
"the public domain," had been effectively plundered, the best hope was to
act around the law to expand uncopyrighted zones where owners would
not rule. Enlightened creators, they argued, could use their copyright authority to opt out of the system. Meanwhile free-culture activists, mostly
tech-nerds, students, and artists, portrayed copyright as the villain of
their story, in the process representing the law as irretrievably all about
the owners. Together, whether intentionally or not, they ceded the crucial ground of the public interest *within* copyright; they effectively capit-
ulated to a property vision of copyright, hoping to find a world elsewhere.
As Niva Elkin-Koren has noted, the Romantic-era notion of the genius-
author pervaded the discussion.

Meanwhile, the sturdy, utilitarian doctrine of fair use—the main element of copyright law that could be used to restore balance—went ignored. While content industry lawyers talked about fair use as shadowy,
dangerous business, self-styled copyleftists treated it with a mixture of
contempt and pity.

Content Industries and Criminal Copying

This wasn't the first time that content industry executives had lectured
their customers about the dangers of copying. Indeed, when the movie
industry faced the prospect of the copy-friendly VCR—a machine that
eventually saved Hollywood—its lead lobbyist Jack Valenti thundered
that "the VCR is to the American film producer and the American public
as the Boston Strangler is to the woman home alone." He vividly crimi-
nalized the act of copying and portrayed the American public as a help-
less victim. Valenti was the pope of moralistic rhetoric, referring to the
"sanctity" of copyright owners' rights, and associating all copying with
fear-laden words such as "outlaw," "terrorist" and "pirate."

The perceived threat of peer-to-peer file sharing precipitated new
levels of cross-industry coordination around publicity and education
campaigns. The efforts reached down into every level of the school system, and reached any young person who went to popular gaming and entertainment websites. It fostered a language of transgression, and even
criminality, around copying.

Starting in 2000 in the wake of enthusiastic reception to Napster, the first widespread online music file-sharing service, trade associations began campaigning for the hearts and minds of young people. As Tarleton Gillespie has shown, they worked through public service advertising campaigns, in schools and school-based media, and directly with consumers. The Business Software Alliance (BSA), the Recording Industry Association of America (RIAA) and the Canadian Recording Industry Association, the American Society of Composers, Authors and Publishers (ASCAP), the Copyright Alliance, and the Motion Picture Association of America all launched campaigns. TV ads, posters, comic books, game-based websites, Boy Scout merit badges, themes in sitcoms, teachers' guides, and free school curricula were all part of the effort. Trade associations sometimes got government organizations such as the US Copyright Office and the UN's World Intellectual Property Organization to echo their campaigns.

The trade associations focused, in these early twenty-first-century campaigns, on discouraging downloading, but they carried lots of other messages too. Most importantly for fair use, they represented all of copyright policy as being about protection of copyright holders' monopolies. All unlicensed taking was stealing, or "piracy." Paying copyright holders was a moral act—the only right thing to do. The only way to "respect" copyright, in these lessons, was to pay for all access to copyrighted material. Copying was represented not only as wrong but as immoral. A teacher's guide for instance suggested kicking off discussion with this: "Has anyone ever copied your homework or stolen your ideas? How did this make you feel?" An RIAA poster said, "NEVER copy someone else's creative work without permission from the copyright holder."

When these "educational" materials actually addressed fair use, they often exaggerated and sometimes were outright wrong:

> Students are allowed to copy short passages of copyrighted text, individual copyrighted images, and excerpts from other copyrighted material in their school work, as long as they credit their sources. This is called 'fair use.' *But no one is allowed to copy copyrighted material outside the classroom for any reason without getting permission.* [emphasis added]

When mentioned at all, fair use was typically described as dangerous: "Unless you are absolutely sure, relying on the doctrine of 'Fair Use' to avoid seeking Permission to copy a work is risky. The best course of action is simply to seek permission for all copied material you intend to use."

The idea of "copyright education" has caught on. In some places, the efforts that began with the trade associations' voluntary campaigns are even being made mandatory. In 2006, the State of California required school districts to develop a curriculum on "Internet safety, the manner in which to avoid committing plagiarism, the concept, purpose, and significance of copyright" so that students could understand "the implications of illegal peer-to-peer file sharing." In 2009, the federal government began demanding evidence that universities were educating their students about legal and illegal downloading. Inevitably, students who receive this instruction carry their fears and confusions with them, ready to pass them on either as prescription or as resistance attitude. Their teachers and librarians internalize and transmit the sacred-property version of copyright. In case they happened to stumble across the glancing references to fair use, the content industries' campaigns have taught them that it is a marginal, occasional, and undependable doctrine.

Scholars and the Public Domain

Some legal and cultural studies scholars who acted as public intellectuals, communicating far beyond the academy, also played a powerful role in shaping a larger public understanding about copyright. In the late 1990s and early 2000s they worked together, meeting to coordinate rhetoric and to plan conferences. Unfortunately, they too settled upon a message that implied that copyright was all about owners. This was because their core message—that drastic new measures were needed to expand the "commons"—implied that the current copyrighted environment was entirely locked up by those owners.

For some time, liberal scholars, especially legal scholars but also literary scholars and anthropologists, had been concerned by the radical changes in copyright policy. An international group who met in Bellagio, Italy, in 1993, convened by Peter Jaszi and Martha Woodmansee, concluded with a manifesto declaring that intellectual property policies that overly privilege individual authors prejudice the public interest. The Bellagio scholars noted that collaborative work of all kinds, from folklore to agricultural innovation, was routinely denied protection while individuals—often in more affluent Northern countries—could poach the results. Each intellectual property right, they wrote, "fences off some portion of the public domain," the shared resource from which future culture could draw. Calling for broader public participation in intellectual property policymaking, they stated, "In general, we favor an increased recognition and protection of the public domain by means of expansive fair use protections, compulsory licensing, and narrower initial coverage of property rights"—in other words, a balanced, non-absolutist approach to implementing the public interest *within* the general framework of intellectual property law. Their vision of the public domain embraced not only material that was free of all ownership claims, but also copyright rules that promoted public access to protected material. A different understanding was soon to emerge among the community of copyleft activists.

The Bellagio Declaration alerted many in the legal scholarly community to the problem of unbalanced copyright. The concerns voiced in it grew, after the 1994 *TRIPS* agreement, the 1998 copyright extension legislation, and the DMCA. Unfortunately, with the passage of time many critics of intellectual property overreach came to ignore the question of how balance within copyright can be implemented by using the tools, such as fair use, that the system itself provides.

Writing on the issue, two legal scholars quickly rose to prominence in the United States: James Boyle and Lawrence Lessig. James Boyle, in 1996, wrote *Shamans, Software and Spleens*, about the encroachment of copyright policy on cultural expression in the service of content companies. It summarized the core insights of the Bellagio conference, which Boyle attended, and decried the absence of wide public debate and outcry on the social and cultural implications of these policies. He argued that the copyright-free zone had shrunk dramatically and needed to be both increased and protected by government regulation from depredations by economic actors. He pointed to an entitlement rhetoric around copyright ownership as a fundamentally flawed conceptualization, and urged different ways of thinking about the social role of information itself. Boyle went on to cofound the Center for the Study of the Public Domain at Duke University, with the help of funds from the Red Hat Foundation, then the nonprofit arm of the same company that facilitates use of open-source Linux software products.

Lawrence Lessig burst into public attention, complete with catchy slide show presentations, with his first book, *Code: And Other Laws of Cyberspace* (1999). The book noted that as digital commerce increased, particularly with digital monitoring and control of user action, traditionally free cultural uses of copyrighted material were curtailed. Instead of resisting corporate aggrandizement of cultural space in the digital era, he noted, copyright law had facilitated it. The technical designers of digital commercial culture were setting the rules, with no pushback from policy. Cultural expression was endangered. Among other things, technologies were pre-empting fair use by making copying difficult through encryption. Laws reinforced that obstacle by punishing people who broke the encryption.

Other legal scholars also contributed to the discussion. Disillusioned in the wake of the DMCA debacle, Jessica Litman addressed a more general public with her book *Digital Copyright* (2001). In it, she charted the gap between copyright policy and actual digital practice. It was a despairing cry for attention to the issue. She wrote that she had been made cynical by the marginalization of public interest advocates in DMCA policy formation, and put her faith for change in the general public's failure to comply with the terms of copyright law.

Legal scholars held private convenings, backed by major foundations including the Ford Foundation and the John D. and Catherine T. MacArthur Foundation, discussing how to publicize the problems posed by long and strong copyright. They discussed how to develop rhetoric that could move people outside the scholarly circle to an awareness of claustrophobic copyright policy. At the start of the new century, the Red Hat Foundation created the short-term project Center for the Public Domain, led by nonprofit entrepreneur Laurie Racine, which also held urgent meetings. Looking for an equivalent to the umbrella term "environmentalism" to describe their movement, they turned to the phrase "the commons," referring to a public domain zone. The information commons at the moment, they noted, was sparse and barren. And yet it was the source of tomorrow's creative work. Fair use was not even considered in these discussions, although it has the potential to function as a situational public domain, providing creators with much of the access to copyright culture that it requires.

Working with concepts about the layers of activity and control in digital production put forward by another legal scholar, Yochai Benkler, Lessig extended this argument with an even more reader-friendly format in his 2001 *Future of Ideas*. He painted a dire picture of a future Dark Ages controlled by digital moguls whose monitoring and control of all user action—sanctioned by law—would stifle creativity. He called for a wide range of legal changes, including the rewriting of copyright law to drastically roll back the length of copyright. He began to link the words "free culture" with "commons." He spoke widely, and passionately, on the problem. His Center for Internet and Society at Stanford Law School took on challenges such as a lawsuit against the grandson of James Joyce for keeping Joyce family letters from the critical scholars—and, thus, from the public. Ironically, the basis of this suit was scholarly fair use. As Lessig refined his message, he became ever more impatient with the staid and sturdy qualities of fair use. He wanted, he told popularizer David Bollier, to "rename the social practice" and ultimately build a new "legal and technical infrastructure of freedom." He called for the reimagining of the entire legal and cultural framework.

Boyle, Lessig, Benkler (whose *Wealth of Networks* eventually synthesized his elegant argument for participatory culture and policies to support it), and others also participated in a growing think-tank interest in the commons, promoting the concept both to inside-the-Beltway policy wonks and to the general public. Bollier synthesized the commons arguments in two reports published by the New America Foundation (the latter cosponsored by the think tank Public Knowledge), launched at a well-attended conference. Bollier summarized the theme in four words: "Public domain under siege." He leaned heavily on environmental language: "Just as companies today cannot pollute the air and water as if it were a free and unlimited resource, so the public domain should not continue to be 'used up' without serious consequences."

Creative Commons emerged from this way of thinking. At a Center for the Public Domain conference, Lessig highlighted the General Public License, created by software programmer Richard Stallman in 1983. Stallman had pioneered the code that eventually was built into Linux and in 1989 developed the GPL. Stallman, who grew up in hacker culture in a pioneering moment for networked computing, believed that openness, anonymity, and freedom were crucial moral values to keep that open culture alive. He found copyright far more irksome than helpful, and the GPL was a way, he thought, to subvert it. The GPL uses the strong rights that now belong to owners to assert that the owner's material is and must remain free and open for anyone to use. His solution—which basically took strong copyright's strength and used it to sabotage the idea of ownership—became the first blow in the struggle to create a "free software" movement. People began applying the term "copyleft" to this kind of licensing. Lessig also had other conversations, including one with MIT's Hal Abelson, about the idea of a "land trust" for public domain material. (Abelson had pioneered MIT's OpenCourseWare, free curriculum material on the web.) Soon a virtual network of scholars was shaping the idea that became Creative Commons, with Red Hat Foundation money infusing its creation.

Creative Commons licenses use the power copyright gives authors to allow creators simply to give their work away under a range of conditions. Eventually Stallman harshly critiqued the Creative Commons licenses for creating such a variety of conditions, since this weakened the capacity of work with a CC license to fully participate in the pool of public domain culture. Others, including Niva Elkin-Koren, have suggested that such licenses, in the absence of a common standard for freedom of information, can create more uncertainty around the terms of contracts, and ironically more barriers to access. But Creative Commons licenses quickly became a badge of participation in the global copyright counterculture for culture-makers of all kinds. They have not, however, become prevalent enough in any particular field of creative expression to carve out a new, distinctive, and vital cultural realm—in other words, a true functioning "commons," in the sense in which that term originally was understood. Nor have Creative Commons licenses been able to form the basis of economically viable business models. As Stallman foresaw, Creative Commons' need to accommodate a range of creator preferences has meant that many works subject to its licenses are not really generally available—as they would be if they were part of a genuine public domain or subject to fair use.

The commons rhetoric is a vivid way of portraying the problem of long and strong copyright (and other policies, such as patent, trademark, and telecommunications regulation, that constrain expression). It celebrates a particular vision of the public domain as a space entirely free of intellectual property constraint, while either ignoring or slighting exemptions and balancing features that limit copyright owners' monopoly control. In general, the commons advocates shared an alarmist vision of cultural strangulation by copyright. They often placed their hopes on radical (and probably unlikely) changes in legislation, hoping that their work would mobilize enough public opinion to create a stakeholder position for "free culture," or the commons. Finally, they shared a David versus Goliath view of cultural expression, with individual, isolated users pitted against corporate behemoths. They celebrated the insouciant renegades who challenged and critiqued popular culture and flouted copyright. This approach did not depend upon the notion of balance within copyright; rather it backhandedly accepted the copyright owner maximalist interpretation of the law and aspired to expand the arenas of culture that exist beyond copyright, no matter how difficult that project might be to accomplish.

Actually expanding the public domain would require either persuading significant numbers of individuals to voluntarily donate material into it by renouncing copyright altogether, or—arguably the more likely of the two—changing the law itself. By design, the commons rhetoric does not address many of the practical problems of negotiating the ins and outs of copyright law today in order to accomplish creative projects. Instead, it was ultimately designed to rally people so indignant about the state of things that they would demand change from legislators and force such change by refusing to obey current rules.

These passionate efforts by public intellectuals succeeded in creating a broad anti-copyright sentiment, especially among college students, geeks, some digital artists, and other techno-activists. They also had the sometimes unintended effect, however, of diminishing public awareness of and confidence in the tools available today to balance copyright—especially fair use.

Scholars and Resistance

Cultural studies scholars, acting as public intellectuals, also shaped anti-copyright sentiment that incidentally slighted the power of fair use. Soon upon the release of the first pro-culture volleys by legal scholars, cultural studies scholars joined them in sounding the alarm about shrinking cultural opportunities, often with flair and even flamboyance. Cultural studies scholars often focus on popular culture, and especially how people use and respond to it. They typically ask, in the tradition of John Fiske and others, how people reuse, rework, and resist the messages of popular culture (especially advertising and implicit consumerist messages). The question of how people did and could resist the strictures of long and strong copyright was like candy to them.

The cultural studies scholars took the arguments beyond policy wonkism. They used a language of resistance drawn from their own disciplinary study of responses to popular culture. Siva Vaidhyanathan, an ex-journalist and media studies professor, wrote a widely read academic book, *Copyrights and Copywrongs* (2001), which used the by then familiar structure of pitting corporate-led government policy against the public interest to imagine expansion of copyright-light and copyright-free zones. In his 2004 *The Anarchist in the Library* Vaidhyanathan deliberately reduced complexity further and painted the copyright landscape with a very broad brush. On one side were siloed, hoarding entities (content companies, software companies, governments) and on the other were forces of decentralization and connection. Along the way, he lumped together international business pirates, downloading students, and fair users. He argued that policymakers needed to learn from the "anarchists" to foment grassroots cultural expression. Vaidhyanathan became a widely published and quoted pundit on intellectual property. As a sought-after public speaker, he became a vocal critic of fair use, repeatedly saying that fair use was not clear enough to be useable by nonlawyers. He believed that even codes of best practices in fair use—documents revealing a community of practice's sense of normal application of the doctrine—were too hard for most people to follow, and advocated reform legislation to introduce specific exemptions, more in the mold of other countries' approaches to copyright limitations and exceptions. (Consult chapter 10 for more on how these issues are handled in the Commonwealth and Continental legal traditions).

Kembrew McLeod, a cultural studies professor and prankster, both wrote and performed self-described provocations to strong copyright and trademark, without distinguishing the two. McLeod's work was witty, arresting, and funny, brilliantly employing humor, ridicule, and satire to dramatize the overreaching of intellectual property policies. He embraced the language of crime, for instance, describing the Robert Greenwald film *Outfoxed* as "media piracy," an act of defying copyright control freaks. Actually, Greenwald had worked with pro bono lawyers and Lawrence Lessig to ensure that every use of Fox material in the film was legal under fair use. McLeod celebrated culture jammers such as the Yes Men, pranksters who have pretended to be representatives from Dow Chemical apologizing for Bhopal, developed fake editions of the *New York Times* and *Post*, and designed a fake website for the World Trade Organization. The Yes Men regularly copied trademarks, but barely touched copyright issues. But McLeod was interested in challenging the legitimacy of all intellectual property regulation, more than addressing specific problems. McLeod treated the entire range of intellectual property issues as symptomatic of the same general problem, and treated all kinds of protest, dissent, and rejection as part of the same general reaction. His portrayal synthesized a range of rejectionist attitudes and made it easier for people to generate outrage—but potentially harder for people to address more immediate and pragmatic solutions. This was partly because the pranksterism and the broad-brush attacks were more visible than his recurrent and reasonable call for creators to employ fair use more aggressively.

Cultural studies work importantly drew attention to the heretofore marginal, even subterranean, cultures critiquing and playing upon commercial culture, including fan culture. Scholars often participated in the spirit of critique and play, using scorn and contempt as tools. In the process they often conflated—much as corporate education programs did—copyright, trademark, and other regulatory systems, creating a broadly oppositional rhetoric of resistance. Extremist language flourished, and fair use was treated as a weak, poorly defined, hard-to-use part of the law. Laws bad enough to discredit were not the place one looked for a tool for change.

This copyright alarmism was at some distance from the approach of Henry Jenkins, a leading scholar of US cultural studies. He had documented the cutting edge of creative popular culture. Fan fiction, machinima, participation in reality TV—do-it-yourself culture had been his material for decades. His careful and detailed documentation of fan-culture practices became a resource for many. His work stressed not the suppression but the burgeoning of do-it-yourself culture-making. He stressed the continuity between this new DIY world and creative practices in the old; he critiqued the notion that digital practices demanded new rules. Rather, he argued, the society needed to encourage DIY culture and permit online what was permissible in a pen-and-paper world. While noting the conflicts that this participatory culture had with copyright, he advocated more flexible interpretations of fair use. For instance, he was frustrated by the way professional communities more easily employed fair use than amateurs, who were often intimidated.

Geeks, Artists, and Students

Although scholars and policy wonks found the general public clueless about intellectual property issues, they entered a field already quite alive with activity loosely identified with the terms "free culture" and "open source." These were people who had no patience for copyright restrictions of any kind: software developers. This was, as scholar Adrian Johns notes, a group that had long roots in an antiregulatory attitude, going back to ham radio. Most geeks worked in formal or informal teams, solving problems iteratively as many individuals worked on the same problem and shared results. Usually employed by a business, they often worked across corporate lines to solve each other's problems. They had all seen how important it was to build from a base of existing knowledge, how helpful it was when many folks independently tried to solve the same problem, and how knowledgeable the community was. The answer was always somewhere, if you could connect with enough people. Many had seen a move from open software to proprietary software in their communities after the 1976 Copyright Act. Richard Stallman's creation of the GPL gave them not only a tool but a banner.

Free software, or open-source software—available for any purposes for anyone, so long as people labeled at which point their own proprietary work had diverged from the community project—was a highly successful mode of production. It enabled a variety of commercial and semi-commercial ventures, including Red Hat and Mozilla, and was the center of a growing romantic vision of cultural creation with software designers at its center, as Streeter chronicles. It was captured in Michael and Ronda Hauben's 1997 book *Netizens*, which described collaborative and freely shared models as morally virtuous.

Free software's voice was amplified in the later 1990s by the Electronic Frontier Foundation, started with money derived from founder Mitch Kapor's widely used Lotus software programs. EFF was the project of three men who knew each other from the early Internet bulletin board the Well: Grateful Dead songwriter and cattleman John Perry Barlow, software developer and activist John Gilmore, and Kapor. They counted as friends countercultural allies including Stewart Brand (founder of *The Whole Earth Catalog*), who is credited with first saying "information wants to be free." Free software's voice was also amplified by *Wired* magazine, which on its debut in 1993 miraculously made geek culture look cool. *Wired* reached a far broader audience than geeks, becoming a consumer magazine that created an identity for people not just adopting digital machinery and toys but creating digital expression.

It was in *Wired* that John Perry Barlow wrote his 1994 "The Economy of Ideas," in which he imagined that "those who are part of the problem will simply quarantine themselves in court, while those who are part of the solution will create a new society based, at first, on piracy and freebooting. It may well be that when the current system of intellectual property law has collapsed, as seems inevitable, that no new legal structure will arise in its place." He even put a timetable on it: "these towers of outmoded boilerplate will be a smoking heap sometime in the next decade."

It was widely circulated among copyright critics. Then came his manifesto, "A Declaration of the Independence of Cyberspace," in response to the 1996 Telecommunications Act, which largely concerned itself with telephony and cable regulation in ways that slighted the Internet. His manifesto had many of the traits of later copyright activism. He boldly announced contempt for the existing order, and announced effectively that he and his cyberfriends were seceding:

> I declare the global social space we are building to be naturally independent of the tyrannies you seek to impose on us. . . . Your legal concepts of property, expression, identity, movement, and context do not apply to us. They are based on matter. There is no matter here. . . . We are forming our own Social Contract. This governance will arise according to the conditions of our world, not yours. Our world is different.

Barlow described this culture as one that was sharing and giving, unlike the grasping, hoarding world of the copyrightists: "The only law that all our constituent cultures would generally recognize is the Golden Rule." It would all happen on the new frontier: cyberspace.

This vision had great advantages, especially for geeks tucked away in salaried and unpatrolled cubicles throughout the new digital economy, for idealistic students, for utopian artists, for nonprofit organization staffers, and for other people who lived and worked outside the traditional economy—as well as some within in. Indeed, even the Yale gathering of scholars that James Boyle organized to brainstorm the commons concept took its title from Barlow's manifesto. The vision was captivating. It was insouciant; Barlow was shrugging off the old world without even a revolutionary challenge. It was generous; it imagined an anarchic informational Garden of Eden, with self-generated abundance. It imagined information for good, not for profit. It appropriated the language of the Evil Empire—piracy, freebooting—and made piracy the act of good guys. It participated in the Romantic ethos of the heroic creator breaking free of convention.

Of course, as Lessig noted, this idealistic portrayal of an open Internet was already a fiction in 1996. Even more fundamentally, Barlow's agenda had the disadvantages of any secessionist program. It had no way to engage the current reality—not a problem for those not confronting it, but a great one for anyone in the traditional economy. It rejected political engagement. If you're going to create the new world elsewhere, who needs to deal with the messy politics of the old? The vision presented copyright itself, not strong copyright or unbalanced copyright, as the problem. It valorized transgression and, effectively, demanded that anyone who wanted to join pull up stakes and light out for the Territory.

Although progressive legal scholars sometimes criticized the radical utopianism of this vision, they nevertheless intersected with it. Their own vision of the commons also described a commerce-free zone of sharing, and their own prescriptions for policy actions promoted that vision. Together, they imagined a fabulous alternative that actually mirrored the maximalist vision of imperial copyright—one in which owners were dis-

---

Fair Use: You Be the Judge >> Orphaned Material

You're making a movie that is part documentary and part fiction, using the photos and letters of a now deceased man found in a photo album discovered in a second-hand store. You have been unable to locate the copyright owner through a cursory Internet search. Can you use this material under fair use? Is the unpublished photo album even copyrighted?

Answers at the back, and more at http://centerforsocialmedia.org/fair-use.

empowered and sharers ruled, one in which nonprofit moralism took the place of cold economic calculation, a place where the Evil Empire of copyright was replaced by the Garden of Information.

Meanwhile, the copyleft (a favorite term of Stallman's) was being fueled by artists, musicians, and bloggers.

Copyleftism became fashionable in the plastic arts as part of a language of critique and resistance to commercial and popular culture—ironically, therefore, also as a way of reinforcing the special status of artists. It functioned within a well-established tradition of appropriation in the arts. Copying, of course, was one of the oldest traditions in the plastic arts; for centuries apprentices had learned by copying in artists' workshops. But copying as cultural commentary and critique came into vogue as a reaction to modernism's sleekly smug side. Artists, from cubists like Picasso and Braque to Dadaists like Tristan Tzara and André Breton, stuck messy elements of the world around them, including media clippings and art reproductions, onto their disjointed canvases. Duchamp affronted aesthetes with his "readymades"—utilitarian objects such as carpenters' tools and urinals lodged in galleries, challenging the very notion of art while (somewhat paradoxically) insisting on its connections to the preexisting created environment. Surrealists created shocking juxtapositions such as that found in the still unsettling *Chien Andalou*.

In the 1960s, artists such as Andy Warhol, working within a more pervasive commercial culture, challenged assumptions about art and culture with work seized from front pages and popular magazines. The most successful ran into copyright problems. Warhol in fact fought infringement charges—from fellow artists, however, not from manufacturers such as Campbell's Soup. (He at least once negotiated an agreement to pay royalties to a photographer.) The term "appropriation art" grew to prominence in the 1980s in the New York art world, applied to artists such as Sherrie Levine, Barbara Kruger, Richard Prince, and Jeff Koons. Koons, whose work became highly valued, also became a litigation target, as we have seen. But until digital copying and Internet transmission gave artists expanded tools and created new possibilities, the art world's claims to transgressive appropriation had, more often than not, been taken as a prerogative of a self-defined and largely self-referential cultural enclave. Only when the works themselves became high-priced commodities did artists need to tangle with copyright holders directly.

Emerging artists working in mass-media formats developed an ever broader interface with a wider society, often resonating with surprisingly broad audiences. Young people seized upon new video equipment and editing tools, making nationally recognized art that, for all its connections with earlier collage and remix efforts (John Heartfield, Joseph Cornell, Bruce Conner and Rafael Ortiz), was often received as strikingly original. San Francisco video collage artist Phil Patiris produced a wildly popular mashup video criticizing the 1991 Gulf War, *Iraq Campaign*. Craig Baldwin, a student of legendary experimental video artist Bruce Conner and a devotee of Situationist International theorizing, began in the later 1980s to produce collage-style film works that appropriated the terminology of theft to describe his quotation of commercial culture as stealing (for instance, in *Stolen Movie*, produced by sneaking into theaters and filming snatches of popular films off the screen). Baldwin became a major figure on the highly politicized San Francisco art scene—not only a popular festival hit maker, but also a champion of another transgressive sensation, the group Negativland, which he featured in his 1995 film *Sonic Outlaws*. Music sampling rose in popularity, and participation in the scene became a countercultural badge. Hip-hop music—the wildly popular form of street music that flourished among urban Latinos and African Americans in the 1970s and 1980s—captured and remade sounds from others sometimes well-known and sometimes not. Sampling entered the pop-cultural mainstream with, among other phenomena, the Dust Brothers' contributions to Beastie Boys' 1989 *Paul's Boutique*.

The sampling practices of hip-hop artists eventually were challenged by rights holders. Many took shelter in complex mutual licensing arrangements—arguably to the cost of the music itself. Others chose resistance. Negativland, a collage band with prankster tendencies founded in the late 1970s, had come to national attention in 1991, when it released a parody of a U2 album, prompting U2 to sue for trademark infringement. Negativland steadfastly maintained that their uses fell under fair use, a claim that was, unfortunately for them, irrelevant to a trademark lawsuit, although they also faced threats of a copyright lawsuit. The Canadian musician John Oswald called his style of sampling popular music "plunderphonic." He quickly fell afoul of the music industry, however. In 1989, the Canadian Recording Industry Association persuaded him—interestingly, with a mere cease-and-desist letter—to destroy copies of a CD production that featured extensive musical quotation. His work was widely admired in the United States, and his positioning of himself as outlaw creator became a trope. Unreconstructed, unlicensed sampling practice (though rarer and rarer in reality) could be held up as an example of romantic resistance to the status quo.

Another highly publicized act of resistance came in 2004, when new enabling technology like P2P file-sharing was firmly established. Mixing a capella Jay-Z lyrics with Beatles music, Danger Mouse's *Grey Album* was released (to only a few spots on the Internet). EMI, which coheld Beatles copyrights, ordered Danger Mouse to stop. That did not work; the album moved around cyberspace even more rapidly and attracted enough attention to be listed as the best album of 2004 by *Entertainment Weekly*.

Girl Talk, a solo performer whose work is composed entirely of sampled popular lyrics, rose to national prominence with his third album, *Night Ripper*, in 2006. He openly claimed to be relying on fair use, and so far there have been no copyright challenges to his richly allusive, layering sound art. Nevertheless he was celebrated as a copyright rebel. Girl Talk is a good example of how strong the trope of the endangered, resistant artist defying intellectual property laws (rather than taking advantage of their flexibilities) has become.

In 2003, copyleft activist Carrie McLaren, who published *Stay Free!* magazine, organized the Illegal Art Exhibit, featuring quilts, photographs, videos, and more examples of remixed work incorporating copyrighted material as well as famous trademarks. The exhibit, which traveled to several cities throughout the United States, portrayed the intellectual property situation of the artists as dire: "Borrowing from another artwork—as jazz musicians did in the 1930s and Looney Tunes illustrators did in 1940s—will now land you in court. If the current copyright laws had been in effect back in the day, whole genres such as collage, hip hop, and Pop Art might have never have existed."

The Illegal Art Exhibit, its website proclaimed, "will celebrate what is rapidly becoming the 'degenerate art' of a corporate age: art and ideas on the legal fringes of intellectual property." Ironically, the material showcased was—for the most part—anything but illegal. To the contrary, the exhibit represented a range of work demonstrating energetic and creative use of the balancing features of copyright permitting free expression. But for the organizers, the frisson of the word "illegal" was worth the erroneous impression. Kembrew McLeod cheerfully acknowledged that the term "illegal art" was a misnomer, but described it as a "provocation." During the exhibit, as a prank, he applied for and actually got a (very limited) federal trademark for the term "freedom of expression," and sent a cease-and-desist letter to AT&T for using the term in an advertisement. Although his thin trademark clearly gave him no right to sue (and he did not intend to), the *New York Times* ran a story. As he recounted in *Freedom of Expression*, he was thrilled because "my media prank did succeed in broadcasting to millions a critique of intellectual-property law

False-Alarm Horror Story: Tom Forsythe

The cultural copyleft fed off horror stories, sometimes drawing dubious or even wrong conclusions. For instance, a Utah artist, Tom Forsythe, produced a work of art, *Food Chain Barbie*, featuring a photograph of a Barbie doll in a blender. This was no accidental or incidental use, but a deliberate provocation. It was part of the copyleft moment of protest against corporate culture. Mattel sued him for copyright infringement, and he and his pro bono lawyers argued that he had employed fair use. Judges agreed with Forsythe, and Mattel had to pay him $1.8 million in lawyers' fees. That was not only a victory for fair use, but also a strong signal to any content industry actors about what could happen to them if they sued for infringement. It was a powerful test case that discouraged further lawsuits. However, the Forsythe saga was often retold within the copyleft as a cause for alarm.

that wouldn't normally get national or international attention." Such antics did indeed provide a broad-brush critique, but at the same time they often obscured, for the vast majority of people positioned between the extremes of piracy and hyperprotectionism, the possibilities for practice and change of practice within the law.

That art by appropriation can create complex responses, even within progressive communities, is illustrated by an incident that attracted comment and controversy in 2004. Digital artist Joy Garnett, who creates her own paintings using visual work she samples on the web, used a photograph by political photographer Susan Meiselas of a Nicaraguan revolutionary about to heave a grenade in a collage of images called "Riot." As a matter of principle, Garnett treats all imagery she encounters on the Internet as equally available for her repurposing. She and others regarded this act as transgressive. In this case, without being aware of its significance, she had chosen a richly resonant and even (for some) iconic photograph. It had become one of the most popular images of the revolution in Nicaragua, appearing in murals and leaflets, and was even taken up by the winning revolutionaries the Sandinistas. Meiselas had never attempted to control its use, and as a Sandinista supporter was proud of its diffusion in revolutionary circles. But she was furious at seeing it brutally de- and recontextualized. Incensed, Meiselas sent a cease-and-desist letter to Garnett, for "pirating" her image. Garnett took the image off her site, but Garnett's friends in protest had already begun mirroring it on many other websites.

These acts of rescue were widely seen as a copyleft victory, and Garnett's friends saw themselves as champions of digital freedom valiantly bucking analog-era censorship. The controversy was often discussed in the art world as a copyleft versus copyright conflict. Meiselas's supporters were just as adamant in their defense of the principle of artistic integrity. In fact, both groups took absolutist positions that in different ways reflected a Romantic-genius view of authorship. They saw themselves as defending the right of artists to control their work—the only difference being which artist they had in mind. Recent litigation, and especially the most recent *Koons* case, demonstrated that there is no need to choose, because fair use works effectively to mediate controversies about the quoting of copyrighted material in art. It is enlightening, and encouraging, to know that Meiselas and Garnett eventually dodged the larger issue entirely and solved their problem by talking to each other.

The copyleft flourished in the blogosphere. Blogging picked up speed after 1998 with the creation of the first social networking software, Open Diary. It burgeoned with the creation of templates, and bloggers both promoted copyleft agendas and aggressively used their blogs to copy and paste copyrighted material. Bloggers, exemplified by blogosphere celebrity Cory Doctorow, both exemplified and advocated "free culture." Doctorow, a science-fiction writer and co-curator of the immensely popular blog *Boing Boing*, became a major voice of the copyleft, wittily crafting rhetoric that pointed and sharpened the alternative-reality vision of copyright critique. He became a spokesman for free culture among bloggers, advocating free circulation of digital culture; he wrote his own books under a Creative Commons license (discovering in the process that providing free downloads to readers made for great publicity); and he loudly protested use of digital rights management to protect content. He enthusiastically embraced (and self-applied) the epithet of pirate. He argued, as John Perry Barlow had, that business needed to follow customers and opportunities, not stop them, and that law would inevitably follow. He used scorn, ridicule, and contempt to portray content companies as hindrances to progress. Doctorow actually used fair use effectively and knowledgeably in his work, even while celebrating free-culture rhetoric. Other bloggers were not nearly so clear about the access fair use gives to the generation of new culture. A snarling conversation began between mainstream media (known disparagingly to bloggers as MSM, but ironically essential to many bloggers' work), whose practitioners became convinced that "fair use" was stealing their business model, and bloggers who awaited the arrival of free culture.

Fair Use, Free Use, and Free Culture

"Free culture" discourse developed rapidly in the twenty-first century, following on speeches by Lawrence Lessig and propelled by his book *Free Culture*. Lessig became an increasingly passionate advocate after 2000 of what he termed "free use," by which he meant the consumer practice of reusing and relocating copyrighted material at will. He argued that this time-honored analog practice deserved to be maintained in a digital environment. His goal was to liberate whole sections of the culture—especially amateur, noncommercial expression—from copyright altogether.

In the process, Lessig's denigration of fair use became ever more virulent. At the Comedies of Fair Use conference in New York in 2006, Lessig said in his keynote, "I *hate* fair use. I hate it because it distracts us from free use."

In his 2004 book *Free Culture*, Lessig had explained his hostility more calmly. "The law has the right aim; practice has defeated the aim," he wrote. That is, balancing features are a good idea, but this balancing feature didn't work because of its ambiguity:

> But fair use in America simply means the right to hire a lawyer to defend your right to create. And as lawyers love to forget, our system for defending rights such as fair use is astonishingly bad—in practically every context, but especially here. It costs too much, it delivers too slowly, and what it delivers often has little connection to the justice underlying the claim. . . .
>
> Judges and lawyers can tell themselves that fair use provides adequate 'breathing room' between regulation by the law and the access the law should allow. But it is a measure of how out of touch our legal system has become that anyone actually believes this. The rules that publishers impose upon writers, the rules that film distributors impose upon filmmakers, the rules that newspapers impose upon journalists—these are the real laws governing creativity. And these rules have little relationship to the 'law' with which judges comfort themselves. . . . It takes a studied blindness for people to continue to believe in a culture that is free.

Lessig described well the hurdles that ordinary people, undefended by institutions used to making such calculations, faced in the dark days of an economic interpretation of fair use, and before the assertion of their rights under fair use. He also correctly identified a very real problem: Much creative expression depends on gatekeeper approval, which requires better shared understanding of the practice of fair use than existed at the time. The problem was not so much with the diagnosis as the

Fair Use: You Be the Judge >> Video Games

You are writing a book about massively multiplayer online role-playing games and are creating a related website to showcase what you are talking about. You have both shot footage off the screen and created machinima—action sequences that use video game characters to tell a story that is not within the video game. You will use this material to inform website visitors what the worlds look like, and also to create new sequences that make the argument of your book. For instance, two of the video game's characters may exemplify a standard trope, and then stop to explain what they doing. You expect to use some screenshots as illustrations in the book. You've had no luck getting any video game company to respond to your requests to license this material. Should you proceed under fair use?

Answers at the back, and more at http://centerforsocialmedia.org/fair-use.

prescription. Lessig appeared to abandon hope in fair use, and pinned his hopes on a reformed legal system with wider room for "free culture," providing for a larger "commons" of truly copyright-free material. (Several years later, when he grasped the nature of stakeholder politics, noting that large copyright holders distorted legislative outcomes for copyright reform irrespective of the insights of scholars, he decided to refocus his considerable energies on the project of reforming congressional decision making.) It should be noted that, after documentarians and others began applying fair use successfully to their practices (sometimes, as in the case of Robert Greenwald, with his legal assistance), Lessig moderated his public stance on fair use and even created a Fair Use Project at Stanford Law School to contribute to normalizing fair use. In a 2010 address to the Open Video Alliance, he even praised efforts such as American University's initiative on best practices in fair use for widening the space for creativity and began to refer to "free/fair use." But he continued to believe and to say that fair use was too chancy for most people to use reliably.

In 2003 Students for Free Culture seized upon both the term and the concept of free culture. The organization spread through liberal arts campuses. Downhill Battle, created by college students in 2003, amplified the copyleft voice with "electronic civil disobedience" acts. For instance, it organized a variety of websites to post copies of *The Grey Album* (to protest the music industry antidownloading stance) and loaded digital copies of the public TV series *Eyes on the Prize* on BitTorrent (to call attention to the fact that it was out of circulation because rights clearances had expired).

The free-culture movement was overwhelmingly identified with dissi-
dence, protest, and secession. Its actions and antics were designed to call
attention to a problem, but did not and perhaps could not offer a solution.
(However, young people attracted to this movement often later adopted
more sophisticated approaches, sometimes becoming fair-use advocates.) The common themes were that culture was endangered because
of copyright itself; that mass-media corporations were the dead hand of
history; that a participatory, noncommercial circulation of digitally produced and reproduced work was not only the future of culture but also
the morally correct position. Its discourse thus developed, ironically, in a
precisely complementary way to the imperial position of the mass-media
corporations. Both argued that morality was on their side; both accepted
the terms of piracy and theft; both employed fear to push their agendas;
both conflated business model problems and copyright issues. One used
these positions to argue for copyright as enforcement of economic values.
The other denounced copyright for its enforcement of economic values.

The 2008 release of the Canadian film *RiP: A Remix Manifesto* is an over-
the-top expression of the unreconstructed free-culture position. Director
Brett Gaylor, a Lessig devotee, created an essay designed to alarm audiences about the crippling effects of copyright on culture. Gaylor informs
the audience in voiceover that he must mute the sound in a section of his
work, because he had not cleared the rights. For a US audience, at least,
this is a powerful piece of miseducation. (Gaylor does not even bother
to explain the different balancing features offered by Canadian and US
copyright law.) A star exhibit in the film is the US remix artist Girl Talk,
once again described as someone indulging in highly risky cultural acts.
Gaylor positions himself heroically as a cultural resister, encouraging
noncommercial mashups of his work, of which he posts outtakes online.
However, this is anything but an act of resistance to the clearance culture.
He and his funder, the National Film Board of Canada, which maintains
copyright in the film, are exercising copyright authority to license use.
Their gesture tells us nothing about anyone's right to quote from copyrighted material without permission. As several commentators noted,
RiP: A Remix Manifesto floats giddily on top of a resistance rhetoric of the
copyleft. It makes no contribution to meaningful reform, however, because it is not anchored in the reality of copyright law or practice. Nonetheless, *RiP* was the darling of film festivals, shown on campuses across
the country and bought by many university libraries. Loaded with misinformation as it is, it was even used by private foundation executives as a
primer for understanding copyright problems.

The copyleft rhetoric is now well entrenched in many professional, ar-

tistic, and intellectual circles. It has become part of liberal cultural bag-
gage to cultivate a cynicism around copyright. Unfortunately, this cynicism is profoundly disempowering.

Politics of the Victim

Pranksterism, protest, and resistance all have powerful precedents in
social movements that have used them to great effect. They can, however,
also participate in a politics of the victim—typified by public acts designed solely to call attention to one's plight and strategies designed to
get recognition for a class of victims. The danger of victim politics is in
essentializing of victimhood, developing a moralist language of politics
in which the victims are good and the perps are bad. This gambit does not
work in situations where morality does not line up nicely with the con-
tours of the problem. It has the effect of validating powerlessness; as soon
as victims gain any agency, they start to look more like the enemy. This
way of thinking works particularly poorly in copyright, where a range of
rights and interests are in play. Exaggerating or misrepresenting the acts
of fair users, and their consequences, can unnecessarily deprive people of
the agency to accomplish routine acts of cultural expression.

Commenting on Internet pioneer and EFF board member Brad Temple-
ton's alarmist discussion of fan fiction as copyright infringement in 1998,
Henry Jenkins wrote, "With friends like these, who needs enemies?" Indeed. This disparaging of fair use from the copyleft was in the nature of
friendly fire. Fair use has predictable enemies in large content companies.
In 2009, the Associated Press announced that it would attempt to stanch
the flow of profits from its member journalistic organizations by limiting the fair-use quotations bloggers were making of its members' work.
Soon after, News Corp chairman Rupert Murdoch, in discussion of how
his company would limit reuse of its material online, famously and erroneously suggested that fair use was a dubious part of US law that could be
categorically challenged in court. There has been no sign of such a lawsuit
yet, but these public announcements, in which the content industry's
various business model crises are blamed on copyright exemptions, are
in sharp contrast to the routine way in which media corporations themselves take advantage of fair use. Indeed, shortly after Murdoch's indis-
creet and inaccurate pronouncement, Fox News had to publicly rely on
fair use to fend off a lawsuit claiming that it should have licensed Murdoch's material when using it on air in news coverage of Michael Jackson's
death.

But it is a shame, and largely an inadvertent consequence of well-intentioned efforts to alert the public to the implications of long and strong copyright, that passionately devoted copyleftists have contributed to sidelining fair use, or even labeling it part of the problem. Supporters of fundamental revision of copyright law—policy wonks of all kinds—have no good reason to disparage a part of the law that actually addresses the problems they so eloquently describe.

It is also a shame that some copyleftists have represented themselves as fringe cultural actors. The problems that vidders, samplers, bloggers, and remix artists face are problems that affect us all, at every level of production. The outrage of long and strong copyright is not that it excludes the offbeat and the marginal. It is that it threatens to censor the future for everyone.

Finally, it is a sad irony that so many of the tropes found in copyright industry "educational" materials can also be found among free-culture enthusiasts. Both industry and copyleftists use the language of piracy. In this way, copyleftists capitulate to content industry assumptions about the hegemony of copyright ownership in the current system, rather than emphasizing the importance of balanced rights. Both sides portray their positions as morally superior ("Thou shalt not steal" versus "It is more blessed to give than to receive"). This unhelpfully sets up a black hat–white hat paradigm, rather than allowing people to see that balance within copyright is key, that copyright is about promoting culture and not about property rights as an end in themselves, and that context is critical.

Fair users are only now beginning to develop an assertive language around their acts and around its importance for freedom of expression. Its most vocal participants to date are people working in mainstream America as teachers, lawyers, media makers, and librarians, who reject the white hat–black hat paradigm and who regard a balanced collection of rights as a good goal. Fair use needs to be part of daily life, and people need to say that loudly.

5 Fair Use Resurgent

Fight for your fair use!
Heard at the Free Culture X conference, January 2010

In January 2010, the Washington, DC, think tank Public Knowledge held the first World's Fair Use Day, organized by some of the organization's youngest staffers. Held at the high-tech Newseum, which celebrates the media's devotion to free speech, it attracted a crowd of inside-the-Beltway, wonkish attendees, with hundreds more watching online. A congressman (Mike Doyle of Pennsylvania) spoke in defense of fair use, and artists, lawyers, and advocates heralded the need to employ, defend, and celebrate the importance of fair use in copyright law.

It was a marking moment, a pivot point in a process of reviving fair use's reputation, characterized not only by trends in legal decisions, but also by movements in other areas of society. Among them were legal scholarly research; the creation of codes of best practices in fair use; the rapid spread of online video and the need to employ fair use to share and showcase work; and institutional adoption of fair use. This change had nothing to do with legislation. It had much to do with people asserting their fair-use rights and discovering that doing so expanded those rights.

The shift in legal scholarship on fair use was part of a general turn toward writing that focuses on the history, context, and consequences of legal doctrine. Copyright scholars have begun to investigate the social cost of long and strong copyright, and to explore the implications of the legal trend toward a transformativeness-based interpretation of fair use. These scholars looked closely at culture as well as law, opening up new possibilities.

In the emerging, participatory digital culture, Yochai Benkler's sophisticated and integrated argument for policies to support and nurture that culture, *The Wealth of Networks*, distilled longstanding arguments. Rebecca Tushnet, a veteran and supporter of fan subcultures, asserted

---

Fair Use: You Be the Judge >> YouTube Takedown

You created a hilarious (at least to you) commentary on common clichés of standup comics, and it received a lot of traffic when you posted it on YouTube. But suddenly your video disappeared. You are confident your unlicensed uses were entirely fair. Now what?

Answers at the back, and more at http://centerforsocialmedia.org/fair-use.

---

that "remix is the human condition," and harshly criticized author-heavy copyright policy. Jack Balkin vigorously reinforced the case for the importance of sharing and quoting in the emerging networked society and culture.

Scholars focused upon fair use as a key mechanism for facilitating expression, and found reassurances about its utility. Michael Madison reanalyzed many legal cases in which judges typically invoked the four factors and seemed to come to very different conclusions. Their actual decisions showed, he argued, that something else was going on as well. They were, implicitly or explicitly, asking about habit, custom, and social context of the use, using what Madison termed a "pattern-oriented" approach to fair-use reasoning. If the use was normal in a community, and you could understand how it was different from the original market use, then judges typically decided for the user. James Gibson noted the obverse: Where users and creators did not employ their fair-use rights, a vicious circle of fair-use denial could ensue, in what he called "doctrinal feedback." More attention was brought to the question of how fair use really works by the work of Barton Beebe, who surveyed dozens of fair-use cases statistically to see how they were decided. Although he had to grapple with the problem that many cases almost frivolously invoked fair use as a fillip to other defenses, he also found that transformativeness—whether or not designated as such—was the factor that most explained a pro-fair-use outcome, even when other factors were not found favorable. Pamela Samuelson qualitatively mapped the same material that Beebe had looked at quantitatively, and also found clear patterns—including the increasing importance of the concept of transformativeness. Samuelson's work clearly refutes the notion that the decisional law about fair use is too chaotic or unpredictable to be relied upon. Wendy Gordon, who in the 1980s had argued that fair use was evidence of market failure, made clear in her later work that her position was far more nuanced than, as it had been interpreted, a crude economic argument.

Meanwhile, cultural studies scholars were both writing about the dangers of long and strong copyright and developing projects that vigorously and publicly employed fair use. Lewis Hyde's work *The Gift: Imagination and the Erotic Life of Property*, which thought of and treated artistic endeavor as a spiritual gift to be shared rather than property, was rediscovered, and in 2010 he published a book specifically focused on copyright and its cultural consequences: *Common as Air: Revolution, Art, and Ownership*. Hyde, in his capacity as a fellow at Harvard's Berkman Center for Internet and Society, began researching how to employ fair use in the academic environment. Henry Jenkins at MIT launched the New Media Literacies (NML) project, which explores how to teach in a participatory culture; for Jenkins, fair use is a critical enabling tool for all his projects. (He took the NML to the University of Southern California when he moved there in 2009.) The University of Southern California cultivated cross-unit research interest in do-it-yourself culture, showcased at the 2008 event 24/7: *A DIY Video Summit*, organized among others by Mizuko (Mimi) Ito and Steve Anderson. Anderson then launched the Critical Commons website, which employs fair use to quote and comment upon popular culture. Jenkins and Ito became part of the team that created a code of best practices in fair use for online video. Media Education Foundation, established by cultural studies professor Sut Jhally, became a poster child for fair use.

The coalescence of a changed view on copyright was signaled in *Creative License*, a 2011 book by Kembrew McLeod, with Peter DiCola, following on McLeod and Benjamin Franzen's 2009 film *Copyright Criminals*. In discussing the tribulations of music sampling, among other things, they strongly described copyright policy as grounded in cultural, not economic, logic; praised the concept of balance in copyright; and called for change in behavior in the field—rather than legislation—as a top priority. They singled out the creation of a code of best practices in fair use as a rich potential strategy for musical artists.

In a number of real-life cases close to the heart of academia, fair use proved effective. In 2003, a couple of Swarthmore undergraduates reposted corporate e-mails from Diebold Election Systems, showing that the company was aware of security weaknesses in its widely used voting machines. The students pushed back when the company sent a cease-and-desist letter to Swarthmore, and Diebold backed off. Then the students, with the help of the Electronic Frontier Foundation and the Stanford Cyberlaw Clinic, sued for costs and damages, and won. The judge found that their reposting of the e-mails was a clear fair use.

At the Stanford Fair Use Project (FUP), Anthony Falzone began defending those who face challenges to their fair uses, looking for ways to establish case law by challenging copyright bullies with litigation. FUP successfully vindicated scholar Carol Schloss's right to make fair use of a trove of (James) Joyce family letters. Later, Falzone litigated the 2008 *Expelled* case, in which Yoko Ono unsuccessfully tried to stop the use of John Lennon's "Imagine" in a documentary.

New businesses have flourished employing fair use, and their trade associations have supported them. For any business depending upon search, fair use guarantees the ability to feature small "thumbnails" (tiny pictures) or "snippets" (small excerpts) of the material referenced. Court decisions have assured this right to businesses that depend upon search. Google is the largest example of a company for which fair use is essential. Another category of business that depends upon fair use today is equipment manufacturers and vendors. The people who help us download our music, our TV programs, and our podcasts want us to be able to do as much as possible with our gear. In 2007, the Consumer Electronics Association formed a Digital Freedom Campaign to rally consumers around this message.

Many people in core businesses producing learning materials need fair use to do their work. Some of them are individual or mom-and-pop operations; some are employed by nonprofit educational businesses (such as K–12 education and higher education); and others work for commercial companies (market research, for-profit businesses executing research on a contract basis, and for-profit K–12 and higher education). They all use fair use every day in their work.

How big is the economic sector that depends upon fair use? In 2007, the Computer & Communications Industry Association released the first of a series of reports called *Fair Use in the U.S. Economy*. They showed that industries based on the fair-use doctrine (such as search engines, electronic shopping, audio and video equipment manufacture, market research, and Internet publishing and broadcasting) grew far more rapidly than the gross domestic product overall. Furthermore, these businesses contributed 17 percent of the total United States GDP. (This number came close to that touted by International Intellectual Property Alliance, a lobbying group for copyright owners, which estimates that their members' businesses contributed about 23 percent of the GDP.) An update on this research in 2010 showed that in 2007 alone, fair-use-dependent industries increased revenues by 5 percent, employed 100,000 more workers, and expanded their exports by 12 percent.

Think tanks, legal advocates, and law clinics have taken positions on and developed tools and services for fair-use work. The Electronic Frontier Foundation created standards for responsible copyright holders to use with online media content. It advised, for instance, that copyright holders use people, not machines, to make takedown decisions on YouTube and other such sites, and also that they set up "dolphin hotlines" for the accidentally caught fair-use "dolphins" in their piratical "tuna" trawling. Duke University's Center for the Study of the Public Domain put a spotlight on fair use with its witty comic *Bound by Law*. Intellectual property clinics at law schools around the country help clients with fair-use questions. The Organization for Transformative Works was founded in 2007, to help fan fiction creators and vidders understand how to use copyright. And public interest organizations, including EFF and FUP, have begun offering pro bono legal services to fair users. American Civil Liberties Union lawyers also targeted fair-use protection as a free-speech issue, worth litigating on a pro bono basis, and law school–based clinics around the country are interested in the issue as well. Anyone who wanted to mount a fair-use challenge was then in a very good position to find a pro bono lawyer. Many highly competent (and reasonably priced) lawyers in private practice became interested in finding fair-use work.

Meanwhile, creators and users were quietly putting fair use to work without any legal drama. Documentary filmmakers, pioneers of the model of building codes of best practices in fair use, paved the way, followed by media literacy teachers—English teachers, communications teachers, after-school workshop teachers, social studies and even health teachers—who needed fair use to be able to teach about popular culture in their middle-school and high-school classrooms. They empowered their students to understand their fair-use rights too, as the students completed assignments that would get uploaded to YouTube. Film and communications professors, fed up with ambiguity about whether they could use film clips in class and online, and whether they could incorporate copyrighted material into multimedia research projects, created codes of best practices. Poets, befuddled about how much of a poem can be quoted and when existing work can be made part of a new one, developed a code. Archivists and librarians worked to develop codes of best practices to help them help their users and make the best use of their materials. People who designed open curricula—web-based course materials—in higher education created their own code to help them decide when they could include copyrighted material into the teaching modules they made available to the world. These codes went immediately to

Fair Use: You Be the Judge >> Music in Curricula

You are a teacher preparing an online curriculum for a middle-school class on musical careers. You want to insert into it some video material from a rehearsal of an orchestra playing classical music. You have permission from the performers to record them for this purpose, but what about the music itself? Will you run into licensing problems, or could this be fair use?

Answers at the back, and more at http://centerforsocialmedia.org/fair-use.

work in their communities, and they changed how people could get their work done.

These codes of best practices bore out the scholarly insight that practice matters in making fair use useable. They also showed, in their success, that fair use is not unreliable within communities of practice, when the capacities of the law are matched with cultural missions that range from making new work to education to facilitating research.

Organizations that responded to these communities of practice also began to be nodes of information about the utility of fair use. Dozens of organizations associated themselves with the various codes of best practices, each of them further boosting the reputation of fair use. For instance, the University Film and Video Association—many of whose members are documentary filmmakers and who teach video- and filmmaking—now encourages all its members to insert a fair-use clause into their syllabi. Many online video contests tell participants to use the *Code of Best Practices in Fair Use for Online Video.* Lawyers now offer and take continuing education courses in how to make fair use available to their clients.

Fair users who had organized themselves as communities to shape codes of best practices then became vocal in their demand to assert their rights. With organized and representative groups invested in their ability to employ fair use, it became possible to address, in small but significant ways, the damage done to fair use by the DMCA, which prohibits circumventing the coding of encrypted copyrighted material (say, the book on your Kindle, or the DVD in your video player, or the song on your music player). If you want to get at that material in order to employ fair use, the law explicitly says that that is not a good enough reason.

Thanks to civil society stakeholders' efforts in the run-up to the DMCA, anyone who finds the prohibition against encryption to be a real problem in creating legitimate work using fair use can come before the Copyright Office in hearings held once every three years and ask for an exemption. The first few exemptions were extremely narrow or specialized—for instance, one for breaking encryption to access digital files in obsolete formats. The first person to win a broader fair-use-based exemption was Peter Decherney. On behalf of film scholars nationally, he asked the Copyright Office for an exemption so that film scholars could access DVDs of films (generally protected by the Content Scrambling System, an anticopying technology) and create clips of particular scenes to teach more effectively. He argued persuasively that other options were far inferior. Cueing up the section on the DVD itself took too long; using a VHS version to make the clips meant vastly inferior image quality; shooting a home-video version off a screen running the DVD version typically produced a distinctly homemade looking product subject to light distortion. The Copyright Office granted film scholars this exemption; they could now use decrypted sections from films from their own institutions' libraries in classrooms.

It was a remarkable precedent. The next time the chance to ask for exemptions rolled around, Decherney was back, on behalf of the Society for Cinema and Media Studies, this time to ask for this exemption to be extended to students and independent teachers, and to professors in nonclassroom situations. The libraries, supported by Jonathan Band, advocated extending it to college and university teachers in all disciplines. Documentary filmmakers argued that they needed exemptions in order to do their work. The International Documentary Association, supported by law professor Jack Lerner and the students at the University of Southern California Intellectual Property Law Clinic, along with Los Angeles copyright specialist Michael Donaldson, made the submission. Its spokesmen were filmmaker Gordon Quinn and engineer Jim Morrissette, both of Kartemquin Films. Morrissette methodically showed the tribunal the costly, complicated process of making legal copies of images to use under fair use in documentary film, and also showed the tribunal the degraded quality of the copies. Renee Hobbs, who had shepherded the media literacy community as they created the *Code of Best Practices in Fair Use for Media Literacy Education*, showed up to argue that media literacy educators needed the ability to rip and burn in order to teach students basic skills for a digital age. The American University intellectual property clinic advised her. Finally, several vidders—people who alter and recut popular television shows with the goal of critiquing the ideology of the original—including creator and scholar Francesca Coppa and supported by copyright professor Rebecca Tushnet, argued that they needed to step out of the Internet shadows and claim their right to edit and reimagine popular culture. They pointed out that they could never, even if they could afford it, license their raw material; the owners of *Star Trek* might decide that they do not want to see an episode in which Captain Kirk and Spock have a love affair.

Industry lawyers sat stolidly through the proceedings, with very little to add. They argued that recognizing the interests of broad communities such as documentary filmmakers and media literacy teachers through exemptions would fundamentally undermine the purpose of the DMCA anticircumvention provisions, repeating the copyright holders' arguments that they need seamless DMCA protection to put the lid on piracy. They demonstrated that it is possible—with the right (long) room, right light conditions (pitch dark), and right camera equipment (high-end prosumer)—to copy a film by shooting it off a screen. Peter Decherney argued that these conditions were not duplicable in most universities; Renee Hobbs later pronounced the conditions nonexistent in K–12 settings.

More than a year later in July 2010 the Librarian of Congress issued a new rule based on the Copyright Office's recommendations, granting broader exemptions than anyone had anticipated. The librarian authorized the breaking of encryption on motion pictures on DVD by documentarians, college teachers of all kinds, film and media studies students, and noncommercial video creators. The rule was solidly within the current judicial logic on fair use. The librarian required that the excerpts be used in the service of new work (as transformative fair uses typically are). He also stipulated that the excerpt must be "relatively short," but wisely chose not to define the term, thus making the user able to decide how much use is really necessary. He stipulated that the uses must limited to criticism and commentary, but the restriction was lessened by the fact that much fair use can be interpreted within those two categories. (The rule applies only to "motion pictures" on DVDs, but under the law this term is extremely ample—anything audiovisual and sequential is covered.) Media literacy teachers lost out because—unlike the other beneficiaries of the exemption—they were found not to have shown convincingly why an inferior quality, like a screen shot or VHS dupe, was not good enough for their purposes. They did benefit indirectly, since they and their students often produce noncommercial work, which is under the exemption.

This was a remarkable demonstration of the power of communities of practice acting as political constituencies to access benefits that the law offers. The effort put into designing, making, and using codes of best practices had also been an educational process and a process of gaining political agency.

DIY makers and "free culture" enthusiasts, once so strongly marked by oppositionality, acts of civil disobedience, and resentment against copyright, began to embrace and aggressively use fair use once codes of best practices demonstrated its utility. Cory Doctorow was an early supporter of the codes of best practices in fair use, celebrating each one on his influential *Boing Boing* blog. Carrie McLaren, erstwhile copyleftist, became an enthusiastic supporter of fair use. The 2010 conference of Students for Free Culture featured a dedicated session on fair use as a "floating public domain," and students and faculty at the conference began brainstorming how to bring fair-use issues to campus. Remixers spread the word among each other that fair use was the name for their practice of quoting copyrighted materials in their work. Influential remixers such as Jonathan McIntosh and Elisa Kreisinger boldly linked to the fair-use doctrine and to the *Code of Best Practices in Fair Use for Online Video* in each of their videos, labeling their excerpts as employing fair use and challenging takedowns. Other remixers followed their example.

As communities of practice have empowered themselves to employ fair use with codes of best practices, entities that serve them have incorporated fair use into their business practices. For instance, law practices around the country now specialize in fair use for the entertainment industry. The Copyright Society of the USA, a national organization for legal specialists, highlighted fair use at its 2006 annual conference because of the attention brought by the *Documentary Filmmakers' Statement of Best Practices in Fair Use*, and hosted regional events to showcase how the field was changing. Continuing legal education courses sprang up to provide training in fair-use practice. Media literacy workshops, provided as continuing education for teachers, now provide fair-use training for the classroom, because of the *Code of Best Practices in Fair Use for Media Literacy Education*.

Internationally, as news of reinvigorated fair use has spread, fair use and similar exemptions have been the focus of copyright critique and reform, both in practice and in law. Most countries do not have fair-use provisions, as such, but South African and Norwegian filmmakers have pioneered interpretation of their own copyright law's exemptions. Both have interpreted their "right of quotation" exemptions productively. A broad range of Canadian creators and users has built interest around expanding the flexibility of the Canadian exemption of "fair dealing." In a 2010 report, *Driving UK Research—Is Copyright a Help or a Hindrance?*, the British

Library called for an extension of fair dealing to match more closely with American fair use in order to enhance research capacity. Israel has incorporated US fair-use doctrine word for word into its legislation. (See our note at the end of this book for more on international issues.)

The resurgence of fair use has been grounded in individual and collective choices to define its interpretation and to employ it publicly. This trend validates the argument that fair use, like copyright in general, is rooted in cultural as well as economic practice. It reminds us, incidentally, that fair use is an excellent platform for economic growth, which supports new enterprises without materially harming the owners of existing copyrights. This trend also follows, with a significant lag time, the move that judges themselves have made toward a friendlier interpretation of fair use.

6 Fair Use in the Courtroom

The goal of copyright, to promote science and the arts, is generally furthered by the creation of transformative works. Such works lie at the heart of the fair use doctrine's guarantee of breathing space within the confines of copyright.

JUDGE PIERRE LEVAL

Long before copyleft advocates rediscovered the advantages of fair use, and even before the creation of codes of best practices in fair use, federal judges embraced fair use with both arms. They have done so fully aware that, in this long and strong copyright era, fair use is a crucial safety valve in the copyright system—or, if you prefer, an escape hatch from the prison of copyright holders' private censorship. Judges also have had good reason to know that in many well-siloed environments, not least those of the mass-media companies themselves, fair use never really went away. These days, the judicial assessment of fair use typically relies on an inquiry into whether material has been "transformed" (or in nonlegal parlance, repurposed) rather than simply reproduced for the same audience. It also takes into consideration the community of practice's customs and habits.

How judges approach the interpretation of fair use is important to understand, because the law is deliberately written to require decision making on a case-by-case basis. Users make those decisions before the fact, and judges (very occasionally) do so afterward—but the criteria are the same. Judicial interpretation is a critically important piece of understanding where "normal" is in using fair use. Individual judicial decisions, of course, are made within the accepted climate of legal opinion. That climate of opinion changes, whether judges are interpreting common law or statutes like the Copyright Act. Understanding today's climate of judicial opinion allows creators of all kinds to understand what will be possible and, within that, the safest approach.

Today's Fair Use

The 2006 *Bill Graham Archives v. Dorling Kindersley Ltd.* decision indicates the current trend, which has been dominant now for almost two decades.

Grateful Dead: The Illustrated Trip, a project done in coordination with Grateful Dead Productions, was a huge coffee table book—four authors, 480 splashy and graphic-heavy pages, 2000 images, and more information than anyone but a Deadhead would want to know about the Dead, all organized scrupulously by date. Bill Graham Archives, which owned the copyrights to posters and other graphic materials associated with the musical group's historic appearances at the Fillmore Auditorium and other Bay area venues, had rejected two offers to license this material. The publisher, Dorling Kindersley (DK), went ahead and used seven of them anyway, and the archives sued.

The judge ruled against the archives, and so did the appeals court. The appeals court's analysis may be the most extensive analysis of transformativeness that we have to date. Looking at fair use's first "factor," that of the nature of the use, judges agreed with the trial court that the "use of images placed in chronological order on a timeline is transformatively different from the mere expressive use of images on concert posters or tickets." This was because "the works are displayed to commemorate historic events, arranged in a creative fashion, and displayed in significantly reduced form." In other words, the work was transformative because the material had been recontextualized and re-presented for a new purpose, and to a new audience.

The Court also reemphasized another important point: If the user's purpose was transformative, the mere fact that it was also commercial does not rule out fair use, or even weigh strongly against it. In fact, the Court noted, most fair uses are conducted for profit. The unfortunate dictum of the *Betamax* decision, which seemed to disfavor commercial fair use, no longer held sway. The Court, like others before it, recognized that there needs to be a space—in fact, a big space—for commercial fair use.

The second factor, nature of the work used—here, judges often favor copyright plaintiffs—was judged here to be inconclusive because of the importance of transformativeness: "The purpose of DK's use was to emphasize the images' historical rather than creative value." Thus, while the posters were creative works, this use focused on their value as historical artifacts.

The third factor, the amount and "substantiality" used, also was deemed a toss-up, since to accomplish its transformative purpose, "DK displayed reduced versions of the original images and intermingled these visuals with text and original graphic art. As a consequence, even though the copyrighted images are copied in their entirety, the visual impact of their artistic expression is significantly limited because of their reduced size."

Finally, the fourth factor, the effect on the market, tilted conclusively for the defendant. That was, the judges argued, because original copyright holders cannot control new markets opened up for transformative (as opposed to derivative) uses of their material: "DK's use of BGA's [Bill Graham Archive's] images is transformatively different from their original expressive purpose [and] [i]n a case such as this, a copyright holder cannot prevent others from entering fair-use markets merely by developing or licensing a market for parody, news reporting, educational or other transformative uses of its own creative work." They concluded, "[C]opyright owners may not pre-empt exploitation of transformative markets." The economics-and-law perspective that had so dominated fair-use thinking in the 1980s and early 1990s no longer ruled. It was a long way from the time Jeff Koons was found to be an infringer, rather than a fair user, because photographer-plaintiff might hypothetically have been able to license his work to other sculptors.

Furthermore, in *Bill Graham Archives*, it did not matter that the publisher actually had first tried to license the work. The Court continued by noting that "a publisher's willingness to pay license fees for reproduction of images does not establish that the publisher may not, in the alternative, make fair use of those images."

The *Bill Graham* case was a dramatic, synthetic statement of how courts today interpret fair use.

The Rise of Transformativeness

We have seen that from the 1960s to the 1990s fair use had fallen into a decline, too often treated in the courts and by legal scholars as an exemption you could use only if your activities did not invade the copyright holder's market in any way. Since fair use inevitably involves not paying a license fee, there was an obvious problem of circularity. This dilemma made it very hard to use without some guidance. Some users, of course, could hire expert lawyers to provide advice. Others were lucky enough to get support and guidance from their organizations or industries; broadcast and newspaper journalists, print publishers, some producers for network and cable TV, and librarians at some large institutions quietly employed fair use. The rest of us had been told by content companies—not to mention alarmist academics—that fair use was way too risky.

The judicial response began, unusually, in the pages of a law review. By the early 1990s, a distinguished federal trial judge in New York, Pierre N. Leval (who was promoted to the court of appeals in 1993), had grown dis-

> **Fair Use: You Be the Judge >> Checklists**
>
> Your university has asked you to create some guidelines for faculty on using copyrighted material on their Blackboard sites for their classes. You've seen a number of "four factors" checklists, and think this might be a solution, especially since faculty want clear, bright-line advice. You can even design a simple step-through process to take them through the four factors online. Will that be a helpful approach?
>
> *Answers at the back, and more at http://centerforsocialmedia.org/fair-use.*

satisfied with the state of fair-use law. Married to a distinguished curator and historian of contemporary art, Judge Leval may have had some personal insights into the straitjacket that strong copyright and weak fair use had placed on creators. He set out to correct matters by creating a standard to make the doctrine more useable.

He chose to forgo the typical (and glacial) method of influencing the law by deciding individual cases and hoping those decisions would become precedents. In 1990, Judge Leval chose to try leveraging his authority through scholarly publishing. He wrote a long, heavily footnoted article, "Toward a Fair Use Standard," in the highly influential *Harvard Law Review*, where he had once been a student editor. Leval asserted that the purpose of copyright law was "to stimulate creativity for public illumination," and that fair use was critical to that goal. He thus returned to the cultural understanding of copyright's function that visionaries like Benjamin Kaplan and L. Ray Patterson had espoused—one that had been largely overwhelmed by more economically oriented theories of the field. Specifically, Leval argued that the "transformativeness" of a work is the most critical element of the fair-use analysis. This explanation also helped explain why it was sometimes fair to use copyrighted material, even if there was a potential for the copyright owner "losing" potential licensing revenue as a result. It was a good way to account for the actual way that people create, and to make copyright law fit practice a little better. As is sometimes the case with strongly reasoned articles in prestigious law journals, this one had a profound and relatively rapid effect on the field.

One of the very first decisions to rely on the article's reformulation of the doctrine was a 1992 fair-use lawsuit that Judge Leval decided himself, usually referred to as the *Texaco* case. In that case, executives at Texaco had made photocopies of articles from scientific journals available to its employees. The scientific journals wanted Texaco to buy the copies. Leval found against Texaco, precisely because he judged that this was not a transformative use, and because it was within a purely commercial context. The company appealed, but the appeals court strongly endorsed Judge Leval's analysis, which greatly reinforced the stature of his influential legal article. The decision was not, of course, a victory for fair use as such, but it did serve to validate the approach that subsequently would produce a series of such victories.

The most important of these was the Supreme Court's decision in the *2 Live Crew* case, which showcased transformativeness as a key value for fair use. The case involved parody, one of many ways in which transformativeness can be achieved, and a long-time locus of fair-use jurisprudence. In 1989, the rap music group 2 Live Crew composed a song called "Pretty Woman," a darkly comic, misogynist reinterpretation of Roy Orbison's rock ballad, "Oh, Pretty Woman." Acuff-Rose Music, the song's publisher, refused a request to license the song. 2 Live Crew went ahead to produce and market the new version.

Almost a year later, after nearly a quarter of a million copies of the album including the song had been sold, Acuff-Rose sued for copyright infringement. The trial judge found that the 2 Live Crew song was a fair use because it was parody, but the court of appeals reversed that decision. The court of appeals chose the pre-Leval interpretation of fair use, and ruled against 2 Live Crew because of the highly commercial nature of the use. The appeals court took the fourth factor—effect on the market (here, for licensing the original song)—as the most important one.

2 Live Crew took their case to the Supreme Court. In *Campbell v. Acuff-Rose Music, Inc.* 510 US 569 (1994), the Supreme Court sent the case back to the lower court, directing that it reconsider its opinion, and incidentally giving the parties the chance to work it out. The lawsuit did not continue; instead, 2 Live Crew and Acuff-Rose Music made a licensing deal. But the language the Supreme Court justices used to explain fair use, before sending the case back, described a clearer, more useable standard and convincingly explained why even a highly commercial use like the one in 2 Live Crew's song could be considered fair.

Justice David Souter's majority opinion quietly dismissed the notion that the fourth factor—the effect on the market for the quoted work—should be given greatest weight. He wrote, "All [the factors] are to be explored, and the results weighed together, in light of the purposes of copyright." The majority opinion criticized the court of appeals for having applied "a presumption about the effect of commercial use" on the analysis. Instead, it came down squarely in favor of the approach that Judge Leval had advocated in his 1990 article:

> The central purpose of this investigation is to see, in Justice Story's words, whether the new work merely "supersede[s] the objects" of the original creation . . . or instead adds something new, with a further purpose or different character, altering the first with new expression, meaning, or message; it asks, in other words, whether and to what extent the new work is "transformative." Although such transformative use is not absolutely necessary for a finding of fair use, the goal of copyright, to promote science and the arts, is generally furthered by the creation of transformative works. Such works thus lie at the heart of the fair use doctrine's guarantee of breathing space within the confines of copyright.

Transformativeness Moves to the Center

After 1994, with the Supreme Court's blessing of Judge Leval's arguments, "transformativeness" reasoning gradually rose to become the most important principle in interpreting fair use among judges. It therefore became a central principle by which ordinary people could interpret fair use.

You can see the change by comparing one of the last fair-use decisions to ignore transformativeness, *Monster Communications v. Turner Broadcasting System*, with later decisions that also involved movies and TV shows. The decisions are similar, but the process by which they are reached shows the big shift in judicial thinking around fair use.

In *Monster Communications*, the judge found that fair use was acceptable mostly because it had not caused economic damage (financial loss to the owner). In 1995, the Turner cable programming service TNT produced a low-budget documentary, "Mohammad Ali: The Whole Story," about the famous boxer. In it, some two minutes of clips from an Academy Award–winning film, *When We Were Kings*, were used without permission or payment. The earlier film had the only footage available of a boxing match between Mohammad Ali and George Foreman in Zaire (Congo). The producers of *When We Were Kings* sued the Turner Broadcasting System.

Judge Lewis Kaplan marched through the four factors, finding that the Turner documentary's status as a biography of a public figure favored fair use; that the material taken was a recording of historical fact, making the fair use easier to accept than if the user had taken a "fanciful work or a work presented in a medium that offers a greater variety of forms of expression"; that the amount taken was small, both quantitatively and (in light of the different topical emphases of the two films) qualitatively; and that neither the commercial reception of *When We Were Kings* itself, nor the prospects for spinoffs (such as music videos) from the film, were likely to be affected by the existence of the TV program. That was the end of the era in the courts for the by-the-numbers approach to analyzing fair use in audiovisual works.

Just five years later, in 2001, in *Hofheinz v. A&E Television Networks, Inc.*, the fair-use judgment was squarely made on transformative arguments—a trend that would continue. The cable programming company A&E produced a *Biography* program about the career of actor Peter Graves, who had a long career working in most of the movie genres—westerns, science fiction, comedy, action pictures. Among the film clips that were used under fair use to illustrate his career was one from the 1956 Roger Corman B movie, *It Conquered the World*. The widow of one of the principals of American International Pictures, Susan Hofheinz, sued A&E for copyright infringement.

She lost. Judge Robert Sweet ruled that the producers of the segment were entitled to fair use, because the clips in question were "not shown to recreate the creative expression reposing in plaintiff's [copyrighted] film, [but] for the transformative purpose of enabling the viewer to understand the actor's modest beginnings in the film business." Once this was established, the other factors weighed, overall, in the defendants' favor. Where the fourth factor (economic harm) was concerned, the Court held that "[t]he proper question is whether the Graves biography was, in effect, a substitute for Hofheinz's film clips"—not whether the widow stood to lose licensing revenue if the fair-use defense was upheld. The fact that the filmmakers might have licensed the clip rather than appropriating it was not, in itself, enough.

Since then, transformativeness has been a core value in judicial decisions on fair use. (The arguable exception is a clutch of music sampling cases, which we discuss later.) Therefore, transformativeness also should be a touchstone for anyone making an individual decision on whether a use they are considering is or is not fair.

Consider the 2003 *Elvis* case (*Elvis Presley Enterprises., Inc. v. Passport Video*), in which the fair-use defendant lost. Passport Video—a company that specializes in DVD sets like *The Jungle Girls Gone Wild Collection* and the *Bob Hope Comedy Pack*—had produced a massive documentary about the life of Elvis Presley, *The Definitive Elvis*. The makers had interviewed more than 200 people, including old girlfriends and ex-managers. The documentary segmented the life of Elvis into sixteen hour-long segments. It absolutely depended on material copyrighted by Elvis's estate, including Elvis's TV appearances, film performances, photographs of him and others, and interviews with him. It featured the entire performance of "Hound Dog" on *The Steve Allen Show*. Elvis's songs play in the background while people talk about him, and TV shows featuring him play while the narrator talks. In fact, the cover of the boxed set boasted that this biography would give you the best parts of the Elvis films you might otherwise have to wade through.

"The King is dead," Judge Richard Tallman noted. "His legacy, and those who wish to profit from it, remain very much alive." He then applied transformativeness analysis to the video biography. He found the filmmakers' uses mostly nontransformative, both because they used the material for the same purpose as the original and because so much of it was taken. "In the aggregate," the judge wrote, "the excerpts comprise a substantial portion of Elvis' total appearances on many of these shows. . . . Thirty-five percent of his appearances on *The Ed Sullivan Show* is replayed, as well as three minutes from *The 1968 Comeback Special*." Often, "clips are played without much interruption, if any." He found that "[t]he purpose of showing these clips likely goes beyond merely making a reference for a biography, but instead serves the same intrinsic entertainment value that is protected by Plaintiffs' copyrights."

Judge Tallman was not objecting to the fact that the video reused entertaining material. His objection was that the original purpose of this copyrighted material was the same kind of entertainment, so the material wasn't "transformed," or repurposed. Without transformativeness, the statutory fair-use factors began to pile up against the defendants. Many of the works quoted were creative in nature (rather than merely factual), and too many of the defendant's uses involved unnecessarily long quotations, repetitions of shorter ones, or quotations that represented the "heart" of Passport's use of television clips of Elvis, "in many cases singing the most familiar passages of his most popular songs."

Finally and fatally for the defendant, the appeals court majority argued that the television appearances excerpted in the film (unlike the music and still photographs) were "in some instances, not transformative, and therefore these uses are likely to affect the market because they serve the same purpose as Plaintiffs' original works." Once the defendant had lost the battle over "transformativeness," the rest of the factors lined up neatly in the plaintiffs' favor.

The same copyright lawyer who lost the 2001 Hofheinz cases, having apparently not noticed the shift in judicial thinking, brought another lawsuit featuring monsters. In a *Good Morning America* segment on Americans' fascination with space aliens, the movie critic Joel Siegel argued that "big or small, cute or icky, alien life as portrayed in pop culture inevitably shares some human-like traits." He used clips from *Robot Monster*, *The Brain from Planet Arous*, and *Plan 9 from Outer Space* to make his point.

In the 2005 *Wade Williams Distributors, Inc. v. ABC*, the Court found that because the use was transformative, it should be considered fair. Indeed, the Court specifically rejected the argument that uses cannot be both transformative and entertaining. Along with other weighty authorities, it quoted the judge in the final Hofheinz case, saying that fair use "does not explicitly distinguish between entertaining and serious, plausible and implausible, or weighty or frivolous commentaries, and I do not propose to engage in such subjective line-drawing."

It was becoming safe to employ fair use for vulgar parodies, in commercial work, and to entertain—so long as your use was genuinely transformative.

Transformativeness has also been key to judicial decisions in other media. In 2003, the Ninth Circuit applied the concept in a case, *Kelly v. Arriba Soft Corp.*, which involved Internet search engines. The defendant had created a visual search engine that retrieved information about photographs available online and displayed its results in the form of low-resolution "thumbnails": by clicking on one of these images a user could follow a link back to the web page where the photo originally appeared. This wasn't good enough for photographer Les Kelly, who wanted to be sure that visitors to his website entered by the front door, where he offered various items for sale to the public. He lost because the appellate court agreed with the defendant that the reference use of copyrighted images was "transformative": "The thumbnails do not stifle artistic creativity because they are not used for illustrative or artistic purposes and therefore do not supplant the need for the originals. In addition, they benefit the public by enhancing information gathering techniques on the Internet."

Transformativeness was important as well in a 2009 ruling about art in a movie magazine. The story began back in the late 1950s, when James Warren began publishing magazines with names like *Famous Monsters of Filmland*, *Creepy*, and *Erie*, celebrating movie monsters. One of his favorite cover artists was Basil Gogos. Decades later, in 2004, J. David Spurlock decided to do a book on the art of Basil Gogos—called, unsurprisingly, *Famous Movie Monster Art of Basil Gogos*. He included in the book 24 images (out of 160) of movie magazine cover art. Some were smaller than the original, some almost the same size. Warren sued him.

District Judge Michael Baylson in Pennsylvania decided that it was clearly a case of fair use. After all, whatever you think of movie monster comic book covers, Spurlock was focusing on a person's art and had created a work that allowed aficionados and scholars alike to study it. Baylson considered each of the four factors, but devoted extra time to the notion of "transformativeness." He cited Judge Leval's by-then famous article:

> The use must be productive and must employ the quoted matter in a different manner or for a different purpose from the original. A quotation of copyrighted material that merely repackages or republishes the original is unlikely to pass the test; in Justice Story's words, it would merely "supersede the objects" of the original. If, on the other hand, the secondary use adds value to the original—if the quoted matter is used as raw material, transformed in the creation of new information, new aesthetics, new insights and understandings—this is the very type of activity that the use doctrine intends to protect for the enrichment of society.

Transformativeness was also the touchstone of an important visual arts case. In the 2006 case of *Blanch v. Koons*, the Second Circuit Court of Appeals considered a mural by conceptual artist Jeff Koons. The mural had incorporated elements of a fashion photograph by Andrea Blanch into a large (and expensive) painting. Unlike in Koons's earlier fair-use lawsuit, the Court decided that it was not a copyright infringement, partly because Koons had had a different objective in mind from the photographer. The judge wrote, "The sharply different objectives that Koons had in using, and Blanch had in creating, 'Silk Sandals' confirms the transformative nature of the use." The fact that Koons made a lot of money as an artist was no longer important to the Court, given his transformative purpose.

Transformativeness has also surfaced in print, with Harry Potter. In the 2008 *Warner Bros. Entertainment Inc. v. RDR Books*, the district court judge, Robert Patterson, found that, for the most part, the quotations and paraphrases from J. K. Rowling's novels that had been incorporated into a new reference book, *The Harry Potter Lexicon*, were transformative uses:

> Presumably, Rowling created the Harry Potter series for the expressive purpose of telling an entertaining and thought provoking story centered on the character Harry Potter and set in a magical world. The Lexicon, on the other hand, uses material from the series for the practical purpose of making information about the intricate world of Harry Potter readily accessible to readers in a reference guide. To fulfill this function, the Lexicon identifies more than 2,400 elements from the Harry Potter world, extracts and

synthesizes fictional facts related to each element from all seven novels, and presents that information in a format that allows readers to access it quickly as they make their way through the series. Because it serves these reference purposes, rather than the entertainment or aesthetic purposes of the original works, the Lexicon's use is transformative and does not supplant the objects of the Harry Potter works.

The defense failed only because Judge Patterson thought that in some instances the creators of the lexicon had lost sight of their transformative purpose or taken more material than was appropriate to that purpose. After all, the lexicon took not merely names and facts from the novels, but swatches of as much as 211 words at a time. Though the defense failed, the principle of transformative use was—once again—vindicated, as expert copyright lawyer Jonathan Band has argued.

The big exception to the expansion of the transformative logic of fair use was in the area of music sampling, which is tainted by the unhealthy interaction of three legal decisions. Even worse, most musicians—many of them at the fringes of the large music businesses where quiet deals are often struck and fair use quietly invoked when necessary—decided from

---

True Stories of Fair Use: Drew Morton Goldsmith

Drew Morton Goldsmith was a twelve-year-old disability activist and award-winning filmmaker when he created a short video about the sordid history of disability charities using pity-based fundraising pitches, a practice that declined with the rise of the disability rights movement—except for autism groups. He called the film *No Pity*. He used more than 150 clips, mostly from copyrighted material, to make the compilation video. His college-professor parents immediately worried about copyright problems. One of the charities Drew focused on had sent a cease-and-desist letter to another teenage self-advocate when she posted a parody website. "Of course, she was in the right, but she was buffaloed by their legal intimidation, which was their goal," recalled his mother. Drew assured his parents that he had abided by the Documentary Filmmakers' Statement of Best Practices in Fair Use. Extra-cautious, they asked the Stanford Fair Use Project to analyze it. Stanford sent the work to pro bono lawyers at Wilson, Sonsini, Goodrich, & Rosati, who gave it a thumbs-up (and a rave review). Drew's film headed out to a busy life at film festivals, with a clip-loaded trailer on the online video platform Vimeo.

the start not to assert their rights, and instead acceded to the questionable logic of those decisions. As James Boyle has detailed in *The Public Domain*, following analyses by Siva Vaidhyanathan and Kembrew McLeod, this combination of bad law and bad practice has been toxic for musicians, and it has made it difficult for them even to imagine applying fair use to their practices.

Sampling is an ancient practice in music, possibly a core and even inevitable feature. Bach did it, Beethoven did it, every blues musician has done it, and jazz depends upon it. Musicians actively or accidentally incorporate bits and pieces of previous music into their own. There is precedent in case law, in fact, allowing for a small sample to be taken. That is not an exercise of fair use, but an interpretation of how much is "de minimis," or so small as to be insignificant for the purposes of the law.

Sampling is also, however, a new practice among musicians. With electronic music, musicians, led by hip-hop artists, have begun to appropriate not only tropes but the actual recordings, and to build them into their works. As hip-hop became commercially successful, the artists fell afoul not only of copyrights in musical compositions, but also of a new category of copyright, created in 1972 under pressure from the recording industry, specific to those sound recordings themselves. In this environment, samplers had only three choices: to ignore the law, to license, or to employ fair use.

For the first decade of its existence, modern music sampling operated, in effect, on the assumption that its quotation practices were fair—in part because so many musicians were participating actively in the new trend. But the legal case for modern music sampling got off to a bad start in 1991, when hip-hop artist Biz Markie was sued by the publisher of pop crooner Gilbert O'Sullivan for using the three-word phrase "Alone again (naturally)" with its accompanying musical phrase in Markie's song "Alone Again." The sample was a bold feature of the work, and it was repeated throughout large parts of it. O'Sullivan's publisher asked for and received a preliminary injunction to stop distribution until a trial could take place. In rendering the decision in the case, known as *Grand Upright*, Judge Kevin Duffy argued simply that Markie's behavior "violates not only the Seventh Commandment [thou shalt not steal] but also the copyright laws"—without ever addressing the issue of fair use. Nevertheless, this emphatic phrasing not only discouraged the defendants from pursuing their case—it never did go to trial—but cast a pall over the legal status of sampling in general. The samples were certainly too extensive to be considered *de minimis* (trivial in extent). Whether fair use might have applied, had it been raised, remains an unanswered question. The effect of the decision within the music industry was to drive risk-averse artists and record labels toward licensing of samples—a booming new rights market.

Music publishers, recording companies, and agents for hip-hop artists seized upon the decision, not only to protect themselves or their clients by adapting practice to this latest decision, but also in order to collect revenues from downstream creators, as Benjamin Franzen and Kembrew McLeod described in their film *Copyright Criminals*. But licensing was always expensive and sometimes time-consuming. Gradually, rich, layered sound collages were replaced by simpler, thinner varieties of sample-based hip-hop.

The *Bridgeport Music* (*Bridgeport I*) decision seemed to make things worse for musical innovators. In this case, the rapper group NWA used less than two seconds—three notes—of a George Clinton song, looped and distorted it, and did not clear it. Bridgeport Music sued, and the Court (which refused to draw upon *Grand Upright*) decided that there was no *de minimis* defense for sound recording sampling, as there was for musical composition sampling. Astonishingly, the defendants seem never to have claimed fair use for their quotation—and eventually the decision was rewritten to make clear that fair use had never been part of the case. By then, however, self-designated experts in music copyright had put out the (erroneous) word that fair use simply did not apply to sampling practice. That misunderstanding gave further impetus to the cross-licensing between record labels to clear samples. The Court sent the case back to the lower courts, with the message that they could consider fair use. As so often happens, the case then settled.

In 2009, another Bridgeport lawsuit came up for appeal. In this case, in its "D.O.G. in Me" the rap group UMG had quoted elements from George Clinton's iconic "Atomic Dog." One of the issues in the appeal was whether the jury behaved reasonably. Although Judge Martha Craig Daughtrey found that the use was clearly transformative, she found it hard to ignore the commercial facts. She found that the jury could reasonably have been swayed by the evidence that there was a substantial market in licensing rights and that "Bridgeport could lose substantial licensing revenues if it were deprived of its right to license [such] content." She also noted that the defendants had failed to introduce any evidence to explain their artistic choice of these elements—that is, to further bolster their claim of "transformativeness"—and had failed to acknowledge Clinton in their credits (never a good practice). Ordinarily, the existence of a licensing market should not trump a finding of transformative use, but this case was different because artists and producers had widely accepted the sample-licensing system in the wake of *Grand Upright*. It was exactly the twist in the tale of consensus-based fair use norm-formation that legal scholar James Gibson had predicted.

These three outlier cases make up a disturbing, vicious circle. Judges made economically based judgments; musicians and their agents and distributors embraced a licensing model; then fair use was undermined by the pervasiveness of that model.

The cases point as well to the tangled relationship between law and practice. As legal scholar Michael Madison has elegantly noted, while transformativeness has become the key to open the fair-use door, transformativeness in itself can also be broadly interpreted. Looking carefully at a wide range of cases in which transformativeness was key, some of which conflict with each other, Madison found that when judges use the transformativeness standard, they also consult the pattern of use in the surrounding community of practice. Judges ritualistically pay honor to the four factors, but when courts, including the Supreme Court, interpret those four factors, they turn to questions of what people are actually doing with the material and how that use fits into larger practice. To the extent that communities of practice can articulate how they understand their fair-use rights, and describe them within the terms of their practice (rather than having people individually measure their practice against the highly abstract four factors), they can strengthen not only their own understanding but also the ability of lawyers and judges to make reasonable decisions.

7 Documentary Filmmakers

PIONEERING BEST PRACTICES

Don't skulk around. Do it out in the open, with pride.   KATY CHEVIGNY

Best practices projects—the creation of codes of best practice in fair use that provide consensus interpretation targeted to particular communities of practice—have played an important role in excavating a place for fair use in the copyright reform conversation. They have been created in an era generally friendly to fair use, and have been welcomed in their fields of practice. These codes have set standards, created interest in fair use, and inspired others to set their own standards. They are focused not on legal change, but on change in practice and behavior, as a result of changed understanding of what the law permits.

The story of how filmmakers got their code of best practices shows both the challenges and opportunities of this approach. By 2004, documentary filmmakers had already become poster children for copyright scholars critical of imbalanced copyright policy. Scholars such as Lessig and Boyle had featured the problems of documentary filmmakers who had faced absurd situations. For instance, Jon Else, a revered veteran filmmaker who had begun an illustrious career working on the landmark TV series on civil rights *Eyes on the Prize*, had been forced to remove images from Major League Baseball playing on a TV in the background during a scene in his film *Sing Faster*.

But for all their poster-child status to copyright critics, in 2004 most documentary filmmakers did not perceive that lack of access to fair use was a major problem for them. They were far more concerned with the threat of digital piracy through downloading, and afraid of doing anything that would jeopardize their ability to collect on their work over the long run. They typically regarded the draconian limits they imposed on their own use of copyrighted material as the price to be paid for copyright security as owners. They were prisoners of their own romantic conceptions about creativity and their own narrow expectations of copyright.

That is what we learned when American University researchers conducted long-form, open-ended interviews with nationally distributed, independent documentary filmmakers across the United States, with the help of funding from the Rockefeller Foundation.

Filmmakers also told us their frustrations with copyright, which were legion. Even when documentary filmmakers wanted to license copyrighted material, they often couldn't find anyone to pay. Large copyright holders such as Disney or Viacom either didn't answer an e-mail (probably because the transaction costs would be too high for such a small licensing fee), or set a grossly inappropriate licensing fee, or weren't certain who owned the copyright. Every time they licensed a piece of film or a snatch of music or an image, that single piece of film might include a host of rights to be cleared—and one hour of film could involve dozens of such licenses. Music writers and performers, celebrities, and actors all might have signed contracts with the company from which the filmmakers licensed the material. And once signing the license, filmmakers were obligated to honor all those contractual arrangements as well.

But perhaps the most galling of the copyright problems doc filmmakers faced in using other people's materials was that of including copyrighted material accidentally or incidentally in a documentary scene. Perhaps someone sang "Happy Birthday," or was listening to the radio in the car, or was sitting in a dorm room with posters on the walls, or chatted in a café with a TV in the background. Or maybe a stagehand was watching baseball on the television while waiting for the next scene change in a Wagner opera (Major League Baseball, like many commercial sports associations, both guards its copyrighted material and charges high prices for it).

When researchers asked filmmakers about those problems, filmmakers stopped sounding like hard-bitten small business people and started sounding like outraged First Amendment activists. They were angry because they felt it just wasn't fair. And they really hated doing what they had to do to get around this problem. Before they went into a scene, they asked people to take stuff off walls, turn off radios and televisions, even change their clothes. Some filmmakers even went on location with prelicensed music, for easy substitution. They took out images and sound in postproduction and substituted something they could license. They cut out scenes. The people in charge of documenting reality were systematically changing it to film it.

The report we issued, through the Center for Social Media and the Washington College of Law at American University, about filmmakers' licensing problems, *Untold Stories*, was released in November 2004, and made a splash at the 2005 Sundance Film Festival—the annual gathering and de facto marketplace for independent filmmakers. The biggest news wasn't the licensing snarl. The biggest news was that documentary filmmakers were actually avoiding entire areas of production out of self-censorship. Because they understood as professionals the problems they would face, they regularly avoided topics that would involve popular music, popular films, politics and elections, and historical archival material. They also avoided genres such as parody and criticism. Even when Robert Greenwald, the gutsy left-wing filmmaker, took on Fox News with his bold critique *Outfoxed*, he proceeded only once he had secured Lawrence Lessig as a copyright consultant to ensure that every quote he took from Fox News was within fair use. Most people didn't have that kind of access to top lawyers. They decided it wasn't worth doing. Too risky. Too time-consuming. Too many headaches.

So the people in charge of documenting reality were not just changing reality, but avoiding it altogether. They were in fact avoiding realities that were among the most popular and pervasive elements of their culture.

That news was enough to make five national organizations for working filmmakers each agree to participate in shaping a code of best practices in fair use for documentary film. (The Rockefeller and MacArthur Foundations funded this phase of the work.) Over the next year, filmmakers in the major cities for documentary production—New York, Los Angeles, San Francisco, Washington, D.C., and Chicago—met in thirteen small-group meetings of veteran makers. Each meeting was hosted by a film organization. We opened each meeting with the highlights from the report, and asked filmmakers to talk about the situations in their own work where they would like—if they could—to employ fair use.

Each group came up with very similar lists within an hour or so. Filmmakers typically thought they should be able to use copyrighted material without licensing it in four common situations: when they were critiquing a piece of media (*Outfoxed*); when they were using media as illustration of an argument or point ("Hip-hop music of the mid-1990s was characterized by the density of its textures and the range of its social references"); when copyrighted work appeared accidentally or incidentally ("God Bless America" at a political rally); or when they were making a historical reference that wasn't the primary subject of the film ("During the Roosevelt Administration, jobless men and women often could be seen lined up at free soup kitchens"). The group would often become vociferous in their defense of using copyrighted material for free. Then we asked the group to consider how they would feel if another filmmaker used their own material for one of those purposes. Suddenly they began to rethink. That conversation took longer.

By the end of three hours, filmmakers had usually come to pretty much the same place: *I need fair use to be able to make work with integrity, and therefore I also need to acknowledge others' right to use it. But people shouldn't use my work just to save themselves money or time; if they want to do that, they should pay me. And by the way, I would like other people to give me credit, even if they use it for free. Even if they have the right to use my work for free, they shouldn't give anyone the impression that they did work that they took from someone else.*

Filmmakers had come, on their own, to a place that looked basically like judges' current interpretation of fair use, more specific to their own practices.

This knowledge did not console them, however. They did not believe that even if they could come to a consensus about the interpretation of fair use, it would make any difference. "We're not the people who get to make the decision," one said. Distributors typically expect that the filmmaker will give them a completed product that is insured against any errors and omissions in licensing. Without errors and omissions (known as E&O) insurance, no broadcaster, cablecaster, or distributor with an asset to their name was going to risk taking the film. The fact that lawsuits are so rare in this area just made the risk calculation scarier—because even though people "never" sued, every once in a while somebody did. And then even if you won, you were out a lot of money.

It had been perhaps two decades since E&O insurers had routinely insured against fair-use claims. Sure, some films did receive such insurance after elaborate negotiations, some famous filmmakers were treated with special care, and many films received insurance that excluded fair-use claims. But neither the insurers nor the filmmakers wanted to discuss having fair-use claims recognized, for fear of calling attention to themselves. Indeed, some filmmakers and their lawyers became angry when we asked them. E&O insurers, without any way to understand what "normal" interpretations of fair use were in filmmaking, were not about to take uncharted risks.

With plenty of experience with insurers and broadcasters, a filmmaker would say to us, "Why are *we* doing this? Why not the broadcasters, or the lawyers or the insurers? It won't change anything if we develop consensus around fair-use interpretation." Peter would explain, "Your gatekeepers don't really care if you make a pretty good film or a great one. You do. Until you have a code of best practices created by the field, nothing will change. Maybe nothing will change even if you do, but until you do, there's no way to change the conversation, because only then will the risk calculation change. And you may be giving them a tool they can use."

Peter could say this with some confidence, because he had helped the Society for Cinema and Media Studies create a code of best practices in using film stills and frame grabs in scholarly literature. Film scholars, formerly frustrated by publishers' demands to license illustrations used solely for scholarly discussion, now found themselves routinely able to include such illustrations without licensing them. Often the publishers themselves did not know the extent of fair use, and needed to see the scholars' statement of best practices to educate themselves.

Documentarians typically came to the meetings with a very strong investment in their status as creators and their need to protect their own work. They were afraid that fair use would undermine an already precarious artistic existence (filmmakers often depend on long-term revenues from sales and from footage licensing). Their investment in their creativity, however, was also a valuable motivator to employ fair use. Fair use was often the only way to achieve the highest quality in the production. As artists, they were the only ones who cared whether the film was truly excellent or merely pretty good—good enough, broadcasters and cablecasters would say, for television. So they had to hold out for quality, and that meant giving their gatekeepers a tool to lower their risk and accept fair use.

Another reason why filmmakers were so skeptical, even as they were grateful that academics and lawyers were worried about their problems, was that they thought fair use was a question for lawyers to settle. "Why talk to us?" said one filmmaker. "Why not talk to the lawyers? They're the ones who are always telling us we can't afford the risk of using fair use. And who knows better than them?" Filmmakers had located fair use as a legal issue, rather than a right to their own freedom of expression.

The answer went back to the question of mission. Lawyers are, of course, professionals hired to protect their clients' interests. Frequently, clients want to be as safe and secure as possible. When using copyrighted material in a documentary film, absolute safety is in licensing. That is a contract—a binding agreement. The owners cannot sue; they agreed to the terms. A right is different. Like any right—the right to free speech, the right to self-defense—it could always be contested. So just as you choose to run that risk when you exercise other rights, you will do the same with fair use.

That is why knowing what is normal makes a huge difference. People routinely decide what is reasonable and normal when exercising free-speech rights. They could be liable for charges of defamation, when public speaking, or libel, in writing. They have a general sense of what is appropriate, however, and are guided by that understanding when they speak and write. The same is true for fair use, if the community of practice has expressed what it regards as normal.

If filmmakers want to use their right of fair use, they have to let their lawyers know that they want to incur that small risk. Otherwise, lawyers will do their level best to protect their client—even if it means spending huge amounts, changing reality, or shelving a project. Besides, lawyers have no crystal ball on how a community interprets fair use; they need a code of best practices to inform them. If the lawyer is representing not the filmmaker but the television company or the insurer, then the programmers have to let the lawyers know that the company needs this small level of risk in order to do business. And these gatekeepers will not act without something that minimizes risk—such as a code of best practices defining the community's norms.

Then a filmmaker would say, "But wouldn't it be better if we could have a test case that would really establish what fair use is?"

The "test case" argument was common not only among filmmakers but among copyleftists. Everybody has the dream that they won't have to work out for themselves how to interpret the law, but that a definitive case by a wise judge somewhere will lay down clear rules. That, however, is simply wishful thinking. First, it is hard to get a test case on fair use, because big companies have good lawyers who see the disadvantages in launching any lawsuit on fair use. Even if they won, they would expose the utility of fair use. So they tend to avoid litigation altogether. Of course, they still *threaten* to sue. Indeed, many companies send out scary cease-and-desist letters regularly, as documented on the website http://www.chillingeffects.org, pointing out that charges from a successful lawsuit could run into the hundreds of thousands of dollars in statutory damages. But the threats are rarely followed up by action, and the dollar figures are almost guaranteed to be vastly inflated. Second, if a company actually engages in litigation, it may be because there is a good chance of actually winning—something that could destroy the entire logic of a test case. Third, one case is never the end of the story—it's only another chapter in it. It could be an outlier, a pathfinder, or a middle-of-the road case. And since fair use decision making is case by case, there is no guarantee that knowing how one controversy has turned out will help in predicting the future. Fourth, as we saw in chapter 6, there is no guarantee that a judge will actually understand copyright law—or the cultural contexts in which quarrels about copyright come up. Any test case would be far stronger if the judge charged with deciding it could turn to a public document saying what community standards and expectations were.

Filmmakers' response to our answers to the Why me? question was generally: "Hmph." That meant, We'll see.

They had to wait for several months. During that time, Peter and Pat distilled the common conclusions of the filmmakers in the different group discussions into a code of best practices in fair use. Then the code underwent close scrutiny and fine-points discussion by a legal advisory board. The board was made up of three lawyers, some of whose clients come from the entertainment industry, and two legal scholars. All were familiar with recent judicial decisions on fair use, and all were acutely conscious of the need for clarity and legality. By the time they had thoroughly worked over the code, it was sturdy and reliable. And it still said what the filmmakers had said. The five filmmaker organizations that had helped to identify participating filmmakers and to convene the meetings now became cosignatories to the final document.

On November 18, 2005, the *Documentary Filmmakers' Statement of Best Practices in Fair Use* (available at the end of the book) was released at a launch event at American University's Washington College of Law. It was a family party of sorts. Gordon Quinn, the Kartemquin Films founder, talked about owning his rights. Byron Hurt, an independent filmmaker, talked about being empowered to make films without fear. Michael Donaldson talked about being able to reassure clients. Tamara Gould of the Independent Television Service, part of public broadcasting, celebrated the ability to work with PBS more smoothly to get programs to air. And eighty-nine-year-old George Stoney, who began making documentary films in the 1930s, thumped on the podium and asked, "Who owns our history?"

Then the changes started rolling in. Within eight weeks, three films used the statement to do copyright clearance for films to be shown at the 2006 Sundance Film Festival. All three of them were works that could not have been made without fair use. *This Film Is Not Yet Rated*, Kirby Dick's exposé of the Motion Picture Association of America's flawed ratings system, used more than a hundred clips from Hollywood and independent films—all under fair use. He never had an alternative. The licensing contracts for Hollywood films included clauses saying that he would not criticize either the film or the film industry with them. *The Trials of Darryl Hunt*, by Ricki Stern and Annie Sundberg, used video from two decades of local television to document the history of a prisoner falsely charged with murder. Upon the overturning of his conviction, the local TV station had suddenly decided that it would under no circumstances license any of the material; the TV station apparently was considering making a film of its own. That film's use of all the TV footage rested firmly on fair use. Finally, Byron Hurt's *Hip-Hop: Beyond Beats and Rhymes* critiqued misogyny in hip-hop by quoting and commenting on hip-hop lyrics, music, and videos. Hurt never even considered asking hip-hop stars for permission to use their material to criticize them.

What happened next was more surprising: All the films were picked up by television programmers, in spite of the fact that they all contained huge amounts of unlicensed, copyrighted material. Cablecaster IFC took *This Film Is Not Yet Rated.* HBO took *The Trials of Darryl Hunt.* Public television, via ITVS, took *Hip-Hop.* Each distribution outlet now faced the challenge of dealing with a film that was in E&O limbo.

Seeing broadcasters and cablecasters take on films that were fair-use heavy was gratifying, but the field couldn't depend on courageous actions by a few. Those actions needed to be the early signs of a wider acceptance. So on the heels of Sundance and the positive reception there, we organized a lunch meeting, hosted by the Rockefeller Foundation, for cable programming and public broadcasting executives. Some twenty-five executives attended, every one skeptical of the notion that fair use would be good for their businesses but afraid to miss an opportunity their competitors and colleagues might spot. They left politely clutching their copies of the statement, but often without making eye contact.

In the ensuing months, though, several of those executives quietly found a reason to employ the statement to justify decisions to acquire or start new projects. Jessica Wolfson, then at IFC, brought the statement back to IFC president Evan Shapiro, who had a problem. He had commissioned a documentary to be called *Wanderlust* about road films. The producer had budgeted $200,000 for film clips, but the final, take-it-or-leave-it best offers of the eighteen studios involved came to over $450,000.

At the 2006 Sundance Film Festival, Shapiro had met with lawyer Michael Donaldson and, in the process, had come to see how empowering fair use could be. They worked out a strategy to preserve IFC's important relationships with the various studios while lowering costs. IFC offered the studios a reduced fee for all the film clips that could be justified as fair use—$1,000 per title. Meanwhile, Donaldson, guided by the statement, worked with the filmmakers to bring the film clips that could be reshaped within the purview of the fair-use doctrine.

Of the eighteen owners, thirteen—including Sony Pictures Entertain-

True Tales of Fair Use: Sundance Compared

How much have things changed for documentary filmmakers? Michael Donaldson did the numbers: In the 2005 Sundance Film Festival, eleven months before the Documentary Filmmakers' Statement of Best Practices in Fair Use was issued, none of the documentaries he worked on exercised their fair-use rights. "Zero. Nada. Nothing." In 2010, five Sundance documentaries that his office worked on extensively employed fair use, as seen in this chart:

Table 1. Number of clips used pursuant to fair use

Film	Film clips	Music clips	Photos, etc.
Bhutto	424	0	26
Countdown to Zero	11	1	6
Gasland	16	1	21
Lucky	9	4	13
Waiting for Superman	140	0	4

In spite of the fact that music is as eligible for fair use as other copyrighted material, filmmakers continue to be skittish. But licensors know the truth. Before the statement, said Donaldson, "Evan Greenspan, a leading music clearance house in New York City, would include a button in all the materials he sent to prospective clients. It said, 'USE A NOTE, GO TO JAIL.' He doesn't use that button anymore."

ment, MGM, Universal Studios, Miramax Films, and Warner Brothers Entertainment—agreed to license the clips at $1,000 a title. The other owners did "not want to set a precedent," so the filmmakers obliged by using clips from their films for free without a license, under fair use. The total cost came to under $50,000; a *New York Times* story on the negotiation gave valuable publicity to the new approach to fair use.

The insurers for errors and omissions were still a problem. These insurers had always considered fair-use claims, but on a case-by-case basis, and without a word in public. (None of the filmmakers we talked to were any of these lucky people, of course, nor did they know any.) Simon Kilmurry, codirector of public TV series *POV*—a haven for documentary filmmakers—helped coordinate a meeting of representatives from the only four companies that handled such insurance for documentaries in the United States. Insurers sat at the table poker-faced during the presentation. They thumbed gingerly through the statement. One said, "I wouldn't even show this to my account executives; I don't want them distracted."

Veteran broker Debra Kozee, a friend of Kilmurry's, watched the reaction with great interest. Kozee's next job was hunting for the best insurance deal for *Hip-Hop*. Usually this would be a big problem; the film was laced with fair-use clips from a part of the music business plagued with litigation, and insurers usually did not insure for fair use. She decided to test the waters. She sent out a letter to all of the insurers, inviting them to bid on *Hip-Hop*. She called it a "test case" of insurance companies' willingness to insure fair-use claims, given the new era created by the statement. She often passed the representative from AIG on her way to work. "How about that fair-use film?" she would ask.

She did get more than one bid. Not only that, the representative of AIG, one of the four insurers, was willing quietly to insure fair-use claims routinely, now that there was a statement to lower the risk. The Center for Social Media offered to put out a press release announcing the breakthrough. AIG was not ready to make that public a commitment. But others were.

In California, Donaldson had had a similar experience. Like Kozee, he had quietly obtained insurance coverage for a fair use—for the song "Fuck the Police" in the documentary *The History of the F Word* (released simply as "F*#&!!!"). Media Professionals (MediaPro) Insurance company agreed that fourteen seconds of that song fell within fair use. Donaldson suggested to the senior claims counsel of Media Professionals, Russell Hickey, that documentary filmmakers would benefit enormously if they knew that such coverage was available. He agreed. Within days, Hickey had approval and they set to work drafting a rider.

Meanwhile, Stanford University's Fair Use Project director Anthony Falzone had met with the chairman of MediaPro, Leib Dodell, who agreed to move forward with a special policy. The insurance company would issue a policy covering fair-used material, and Stanford would agree to provide free legal defense if there were a lawsuit.

This coverage of fair use by MediaPro was announced to a sellout audience attending an evening celebrating the documentaries that were nominated for the Oscar. There was a spontaneous, standing ovation. The MediaPro executives were on stage and in shock. They never expected such a reception. Errors and omissions insurance is a highly competitive business; the few companies were all competing with each other for those contracts. Chubb announced its new policy within a week, and AIG went public as well. Within a month the last remaining US-based E&O insurer, OneBeacon, simply added fair-use coverage to its announcement of offerings as if it had always been there.

True Tales of Fair Use: Katy Chevigny

Katy Chevigny, a distinguished documentary filmmaker and cofounder of the media production house Arts Engine, became, as she described it, a "born-again" fair user, and began conducting workshops with the emerging filmmakers featured in Arts Engine's Media That Matters film festival and at Independent Feature Project workshops. She used her own experience as an example: "When I made *Deadline* [a film on the death penalty], I was not yet educated in fair use and I was at the mercy of what lawyers told me—both broadcast and archive lawyers. An enormous part of our budget went to archival, even though ten percent or less was archival. We spent about $75,000 on clearances on a low budget film, in which the filmmakers only made $30,000.

"In addition to paying inordinate sums and not negotiating, we lost a precious moment that is no longer in the film. We were comparing the situation today with a decision on death penalty made in 1972. To transition back to 1972 we cut to Walter Cronkite—the iconic voice of news at the time—intoning that the death penalty is now illegal in the US. The clip situates the viewer back in that era, and it tells the story crisply and authoritatively. We told the archival clearance person, we'll pay for it. She said, 'No, Walter Cronkite has a rule that he doesn't let his image be used.' [If you license material, you inherit the contractual agreements that the copyright holder has with, for instance, the talent, such as Walter Cronkite. If you fair-use the material, these contracts don't travel with the material.] Later we found that he's a nice guy, but his handlers stop everything from getting to him. So now we think we can't even license this footage from CBS, because Cronkite is involved. We replaced him with an image of an NBC guy who nobody knows, who rambles and doesn't have the definitive sound bite. It's much less effective, and we had to pay a lot of money for it. If I could do it again, I would fairly use it, and we would have had a rock solid case for fair use in case he came after us, which I don't think he would have. [Cronkite would have had to complain to CBS, which would then have had to sue Arts Engine, in order to trigger his contractual rights, unless he relied on publicity rights, which also would likely not apply in the circumstances.] That clip is still not in the film, and I still mind it.

"So that's what happens if you don't know what you can do. You do something that's less effective, more expensive, and you feel like crap about it.

"Then when we were editing *Election Day* [a 2007 film about the 2004 presidential election] I was armed with the Documentary Filmmakers' Statement, and knew my rights. In that film, we have a scene in a bar-

(continued)

bershop in Harlem, and on the TV they're showing people with Puff Daddy [PD], wearing the Vote or Die T shirt. It was a historic image. Tons of people have asked me, 'How did you clear the image of PD?' Well, I didn't clear it, and I didn't need to. Our characters were watching it. At the end of the film, we created a montage of all the characters we had been following watching the TV. They were all watching different channels—some of them ABC, some Fox, some Jon Stewart. That diversity alone was a statement about the media in our time. If I had had to clear it, I would only have been able to pay for one. The only way we could do it was by fair using it. If I hadn't had my fair use conversion experience, what would I have done in *Election Day?* We would have lost some of the texture of what was happening, which will be important to people 30 years from now.

"So it went to the public TV series *POV* and nobody sued me.

"I try to let people know that employing fair use like this is not some semi-illegal thing, where you hope you can 'get away' with it. We need it to do our work; it's not a favor, it's a right. And the more we use it, the more we can use it. So don't skulk around. You need to do it out in the open, with pride."

Every single insurer of errors and omissions in the United States began to offer fair-use coverage routinely and often without even a small incremental fee—because the statement had lowered the risk so dramatically. The landscape had shifted fundamentally. For documentary filmmakers, fair use was no longer a gray area, an area of indecision and anxiety, an area that put your distribution in jeopardy. It was part of normal business practice.

There were even "test cases"—or attempts at them, anyway. In 2007 a Chicago filmmaker, Floyd Webb, posted to YouTube clips and a trailer of a film he was making about Count Dante, a martial arts expert who founded Chicago's Black Dragon Fighting Society. A leader in the martial arts group sued Webb for using the count's image. Webb defended himself using the principles and limitations of the statement, with the help of Anthony Falzone and Stanford's Fair Use Project, which provided legal services for free. The case was summarily decided for Webb. That was great news for Webb, but the downside of this particular decision was that there was no written text to use as precedent.

The makers of the 2008 *Expelled*, a pro-creationist documentary, quoted a John Lennon song, "Imagine." Their lawyer, Michael Donaldson, applied the Documentary Filmmakers' Statement as he worked with them to make the segment easily defensible under fair use. (He expected Yoko Ono to sue.) The filmmakers massaged the segment to emphasize the connection of the music to the point the filmmakers were making, and they got MediaPro insurance. Yoko Ono indeed sued, and once again the Fair Use Project defended without cost to the filmmakers. In this case as well, the case never went to trial. The judge dismissed it because he believed the lawsuit would not have merit. Yoko Ono never pursued the case, although she is notoriously and stubbornly litigious.

Documentary filmmakers had pioneered a new approach to changing copyright policy. They educated themselves about the law, claimed their own right to interpret fair use as citizens and creators, worked together to clarify their common understandings, and used those understandings in their work. They also changed their understanding of who they were. They were not only creators, but also users, of culture. They learned to value the selection and repurposing of culture as a creative act, and they learned to accept that other people would sometimes be able to use their work without paying or getting permission because those people too would be creating something new.

This changed vision did not happen overnight, or universally. At the University Film and Video Association annual meetings, the notion of teaching fair use to budding filmmakers made some teachers nervous. "I'm not a copyright expert—what if they ask a question I can't answer?" was a common question. Center for Social Media primers, videos, and lesson plans addressed some of those concerns. More common still was this attitude: "I don't want my students using copyrighted material; I want them to be original and creative."

That last answer showed that the Romantic notion of individual creative genius was alive and well, and living in academia. But teachers were also willing to consider the notion that compilation might involve creativity. Once again fair-use advocates argued that creativity could be demonstrated effectively by the well-applied reuse of existing materials. Indeed, that was the heart and soul of documentary, which reorganized reality. Gradually, film professors began teaching what documentary filmmakers were already practicing. Fair use was becoming part of the ordinary lexicon of media makers, although at every film festival there were filmmakers who hadn't yet gotten the word.

In one highly visible arena, makers of new culture had changed the practice of copyright policy. The actions of the seemingly powerless documentary filmmakers—who had seen themselves as hostage to their broadcasters, cablecasters, and insurers—had changed the way a media business did business. But was that just a fluke? Did a small group of documentary filmmakers really amount to a hill of beans in this crazy world?

8 Codes of Best Practices Catch On

We need one of those for media literacy teachers.

PROFESSOR RENEE HOBBS, Temple University

Documentary filmmakers had changed their world, and they had done it themselves. They had created a small, eight-page educational brochure that, because of its power to represent community norms, changed the minds and the work of broadcasters, cablecasters, lawyers, and insurers. There were even test cases rolling out—the Holy Grail of fair-use advocates.

But compared with the problem of public ignorance of fair use, this seemed insignificant to many copyright critics. "How many documentary filmmakers are there?" said one scholar skeptically at a convening of intellectual property experts held by the MacArthur Foundation in Washington, D.C., the following year. "A few thousand? Tens of thousands?"

A few thousand, maybe.

Not enough to change the way copyright squashes creativity today, was the opinion that ran around that room. We need something that's a game changer. Something that will put lawyers everywhere on notice, shake up the copyright holders, and empower creators at every level of production—especially those grassroots folks making new digital media. Codes of best practices were nice, but laborious to produce, and they focused on small, defined communities. What about high-profile legal cases, or new legislation, or maybe even an international treaty on copyright limitations?

These were techniques for achieving change that involved experts and professionals pulling levers of power to influence governments on behalf of creators. They did not have to involve the actual communities of users, many of whom were hopelessly confused about their copyright rights and thus disempowered. These techniques fit the model of most think tanks and inside-the-Beltway public-interest groups focused on direct policy intervention. The nonprofit lawyers could take the good ideas of the legal scholars into policymaker briefings and, with luck, into courtrooms or diplomatic conferences. The users and creators would be the beneficiaries, not the agents of change.

Meanwhile, the code of best practices model pioneered by filmmakers had impressed another group: teachers of media literacy. They define media literacy as the capacity to access, analyze, evaluate, and communicate messages in a wide variety of forms. Like literacy in general, media literacy is about both making and consuming, and media literacy teachers typically focus on commercial popular culture—advertisements, movies, TV shows and characters, popular music performers. Teachers teach media literacy in courses ranging from English to history to public health and journalism. They teach in classrooms and after-school programs. They teach critical thinking and the importance of interactivity, especially feedback, for learning.

One leader in the field, Temple University communications professor Renee Hobbs, had just completed a media literacy website designed for tween girls, MyPopStudio. It was loaded with popular culture material. She had depended on the *Documentary Filmmakers' Statement of Best Practices in Fair Use* when she stocked her website. At a conference in June 2006, she ran into us and shared that news. "We need one of those for media literacy teachers," she said.

She explained that many teachers of media literacy were hamstrung when trying to teach critical thinking or develop interactive or participatory projects using popular culture. Mary Jane Sasser in Howard County Public Schools, in Maryland, was charged with creating a do-it-yourself film festival with high-achieving students. But no one was sure if the work could be released on DVD or even shown on the school's cable system without getting the school system in trouble. Shay Taylor at Blair High School near Washington, D.C., kept hearing from administrators that she couldn't bring her own videos into the classroom for any purpose. A lot of teachers were used to getting conservative advice in workshops and orientation sessions and then blithely ignoring it once the classroom door was shut. But many were discovering that the students just as quickly opened a new door, when they uploaded their class work to YouTube.

The pressure on teachers had intensified in recent years, we discovered, when thanks to grants from the MacArthur Foundation and Ford Foundation, we interviewed more than sixty media literacy educators for a report called *The Cost of Copyright Confusion for Media Literacy.* "Up until the late 1990s," said one teacher, "there was no concern. We used copyrighted materials in whatever way we wanted to. I never thought much about it. We used popular music, clips from videos, films, whatever. Sometime in the late 1990s, we got the message: This will cease 100 percent." Many teachers faced this kind of problem from their gatekeepers—the vice-principal, the board of education, sometimes even their own school librarian. Teachers were not really sure they understood what fair use was; indeed, some hoped never to find out, because they were afraid they might learn that what they were doing was wrong.

They had a lot of reasons for confusion. First, US copyright law contains several explicit exemptions just for educators, the most important of which (section 110[1]) permits them to use copyrighted materials in face-to-face classroom discussion. It has now been extended, with some strict new limitations, to some kinds of distance learning as well, through the so-called TEACH Act (section 110[2]). Teachers often confused fair use, an ample and flexible doctrine, with their own narrow and specific exemptions.

Second, many school systems depended on unhelpful guidelines about fair use, guidelines distorted by powerful industry interests. One set of guidelines was created during the 1976 revision of the Copyright Act, when congressman Robert Kastenmeier brought together representatives of publishers and educators to negotiate the *Agreement on Guidelines for Classroom Photocopying in Not-for-Profit Educational Institutions*. Although Kastenmeier's intentions were of the best, the result was not a balanced document. What emerged (and is now on educational websites everywhere) was drafted primarily by the publishers. It was included in the legislative history—*despite* letters of protest from representatives of the American Association of University Professors and of the Association of American Law Schools.

These guidelines are sadly outdated, as well as highly restrictive. They are not part of the Copyright Act, and thus have no binding legal force. But because they are part of the record of congressional deliberation, they continue to carry some weight among educators, as does a sister document, *Guidelines for the Educational Use of Music*. They were followed by a third, *Guidelines for Off-Air Recording of Broadcast Programming for Educational Purposes* in 1981, also after negotiations called by Kastenmeier. (This third document was not even part of the legislative package.)

As you might expect from negotiated settlements where one side is much more powerful and invested in weakening fair use, the guidelines were harshly limited. The photocopying guidelines, for example, spoke of

···

Fair Use: You Be the Judge >> Curriculum

You are a biology teacher making a slide show on photosynthesis for Thursday's class. Much of the material comes from resources that the school district has licensed. You would also, however, like to provide some introductory material to different sections, quoting scientists from different eras. Your goal is to show students the process of scientific discovery as an individual, human process. Some of these quotations come from books, and others from quotation websites. Your slide show will go up on the school district's resources pages, which are open, as well as on the students' passworded homework platform. Is your unlicensed use of those quotes fair use?

Answers at the back, and more at http://centerforsocialmedia.org/fair-use.

···

making copies for class that included "not more than 1,000 words or 10% of the work, whichever is less." There is, of course, no grounding whatever in the Copyright Act for such a numerical limitation. Indeed, it goes against the very logic of fair use, which is case-by-case and depends on the nature of the use and the nature of the copyrighted material to decide how much is appropriate.

Still, these narrow, often arbitrary, and fear-inducing guidelines created a tiny but entirely undisputed center of more-or-less guaranteed safety—a kind of fair-use fortress—in a much larger field of possibility that the doctrine provides. And, in fact, the text of the guidelines documents makes it clear that that was all they were intended to do.

They were not used that way, however. Publishers pushed hard to promote a false interpretation of the guidelines as defining the outer limits of educational practice. And too often, as legal scholar Kenneth Crews has shown, they were treated that way within school systems across the country by administrators (and sometimes librarians) who had been charged with providing teachers clear instructions based on these documents. This was the path of least resistance, and one that led to certainty about fair use—even if it was a false certainty. The guidelines had become counterproductive. They actually kept teachers from their work and from understanding the law.

To make matters worse, from 1994 to 1998 another round of negotiations between educators and vendors had taken place, in an attempt to use the same failed strategy to address digital innovations that had occurred since the original guidelines had been issued. The US Patent and Trademark Office had facilitated a series of meetings known as the Conference on Fair Use (CONFU). This time, the negotiations simply fell apart. Stakeholders failed to agree about "safe harbors" for various kinds of educational and library uses involving new digital technologies.

One of the participants, the Consortium of College and University Media Centers (CCUMC), on its own, produced a highly restrictive set of guidelines for educational multimedia production. These guidelines were quickly endorsed by the publishing, movie, and record industries. They were just as squarely rejected by library and educational organizations, including the major national library associations, the National Association of State University and Land Grant Colleges, and a K–12 coalition led by the National School Boards Association. Although educational stakeholders in general had rejected them, Copyright and Patent Office officials went ahead and endorsed the guidelines as a success of the CONFU process. This gave the CCUMC guidelines no special legal status, but it certainly provided them with a great deal of publicity.

These days, CCUMC's *Proposal for Fair Use Guidelines for Educational Multimedia*—a document endorsed only by the large content holders that discourage others' fair use—is found on educational websites everywhere, and is used by well-meaning librarians to tell teachers what they cannot do. This is in spite of the fact that CCUMC has now begun to consider rescinding its support for its own multimedia guidelines. No wonder the teachers were confused. What they did in their confusion impaired their teaching and weakened the field of education. As we learned in research summarized in *The Cost of Copyright Confusion for Media Literacy*, teachers had three responses: "See no evil" (refuse to learn the law for fear there might be bad news in it); "Close the door" (do whatever you want within the classroom); or "Hypercomply" (follow every rule). The combination of these responses meant that teachers could not bring needed materials into the classroom; that they could not share their materials or strategies with colleagues; and when they or their students did produce materials, they often could not share those materials because either they did not comply with legal standards or somebody else thought they did not.

The report inspired the teachers to develop a code of best practices in fair use, with support from the MacArthur Foundation. We identified key media literacy organizations and put together a set of meetings to come to consensus around a code of best practices in fair use. Unlike filmmakers, teachers were good at forming committees and undertaking a collective project to assert norms. They did things like that all the time. And they immediately saw the need for more flexibility and freedom to teach well. But they brought new questions and problems to the task.

True Tales of Fair Use: Kristin Hokanson

Renee Hobbs tells this story: Kristin Hokanson, a technology integration specialist at Upper Merion High School, was one of those "hypercompliant" teachers before she learned about fair use. She had maintained a rule that students could use only 30 seconds of video in their media presentations, when a student came to her to tell her that she would be using 37 seconds of video, even though she knew this would lower her grade. "I need 37 seconds to get the message across," the student explained.

Now that she's learned about fair use, Kristin Hokanson allows her students to use all kinds of visual, audio and image-based media in constructing their projects. All she asks is for them to document their fair-use reasoning in writing using a simple form based on the Code of Best Practices in Fair Use for Media Literacy Education. "The quality of student work has improved remarkably," she says.

Teachers were used to skirting complex and restrictive rules and stifling bureaucracies to do their face-to-face work with children. They often were short on equipment, and maybe even textbooks; they would buy "their" kids art supplies with their own lunch money and copy TV programs at home to bring in to class. They were trying to teach skills to survive a high-octane consumer economy, and they were doing it mostly in spite of their own administrations. They had developed powerfully persuasive explanations for why it was OK for them to break the rules: We have to, if we want to get our work done. The kids come first, they would say. We put up with it all because we have a vocation. We are teachers.

So they often brought to their deliberations the attitude that they should not have to honor copyright ownership, if teaching the kids was at stake. For people on a mission, for *under-resourced* people on a mission, honoring copyright ownership was nearly an insult. It almost seemed as if commercial copyright holders had a moral obligation to let them use materials as they saw fit.

The media literacy teachers had the opposite problem from filmmakers. Filmmakers came into the room deeply attached to their control over their material. Media literacy teachers came in passionately committed to using copyrighted material when good teaching demanded it. But it was more complicated than that. Teachers were not only users of copyrighted material. As they learned in discussion, they were also modeling appropriate and legal use of copyrighted materials. They were teaching their students about copyright by example. They might be willing to skirt the law to perform their mission, but were they willing to teach their students to disregard it? They were not.

Furthermore, teachers also came to understand that they themselves were creators of teaching tools, which meant both that they needed access to copyrighted material and that they were acquiring ownership rights of their own. Media literacy teachers often design their own curriculum materials, in which they quote magazine covers and ads and lyrics. It was one of their aspirations—thwarted, they believed, by copyright restrictions—to be able to share their curriculum materials with others and to publish and sell them for use in classrooms around the country. To make things still more complicated, when teachers assigned students to create work as part of a media literacy project, the student creators often would turn around and upload their creations to YouTube.

For many teachers, the meetings were the first time they saw themselves—and their students—as producers of potentially valuable, and certainly distributable, copyrighted media, invested in the ownership side of the copyright balancing act.

This was sometimes hard to grasp. The teachers' world was a nonprofit environment, where making money was not just unfamiliar, but somehow a little suspect. They thought of themselves as good people partly because they had a nonprofit mission, helping kids, and many distrusted those with a profit motive. When they thought about copyright reform, they confused fair use with other mechanisms to expand access to knowledge, such as Creative Commons licenses and open-source software. They, like others in the copyright conversation, had turned the discussion into a good guy/bad guy conflict. To think in terms of balancing rights meant conceding that some ownership rights were legitimate. Indeed, sometimes those rights belonged to themselves and their students.

The commitment of the teachers to their mission was impressive, even inspirational. At the same time, they needed to understand that however good a nonprofit mission might be, for-profit circulation of work was not inherently evil. Indeed, sometimes both the teachers and the students might want to sell their own work, even if it was simply to raise money for the media department of the school. For too long, both teachers and students had been told that their own work should not circulate.

Some of them also noticed that the boundaries between their nonprofit classrooms and the for-profit world outside it were fairly porous anyway. Their best source of material was in the commercial realm of popular culture that their students responded to, an arena where Creative Commons licenses and open-source material are scanty. When they distributed their work online, even if it was posted with a Creative Commons license, it was typically on a site with advertising—that is, an arguably commercial venue.

The teachers had some of the same questions as documentary filmmakers had, as well. They were just teachers, the frontline workers. Why did they have to do this work of interpreting fair use? What about their media specialists, their principals, their school system rules? That's who was stopping them from using copyrighted material creatively. Why didn't we work with the gatekeepers instead? And if the teachers did create a code, how could they expect principals and school system administrators to listen to them?

The answers for media literacy teachers were similar to those for filmmakers. It was teachers, not their administrators, who knew what students really needed to learn and what materials they needed to do it. No one could promise them that their librarians, principals, and school system lawyers would listen. But surely no one would listen without information that could change the status quo. They were up against the fact that well-meaning educators were circulating misinformation. A consensus document from teachers would, like the one from documentary filmmakers, make it easier for gatekeepers to understand the real level of risk, the real capacities of the fair-use doctrine, and what was at stake. It could begin a conversation that had languished for too long.

On November 11, 2008, at the National Constitution Center in Philadelphia—a stone's throw from Independence Hall—teachers and students gathered in the auditorium to unveil the *Code of Best Practices in Fair Use for Media Literacy Education*. The code spelled out the principles and limitations on fair use for teachers when they used copyrighted material in teaching, in making their own curriculum materials, and in sharing them, for instance, on a website. It also explained the same thing for students when they made and distributed work.

On the panel was Joyce Valenza, a library information specialist in a Pennsylvania high school, who had initially been deeply suspicious of the idea that a code of best practices in fair use was useful to teachers. Now, she said, this was an auspicious beginning of new possibilities for teachers. "Tell someone," she said. "We need you to teach your peers."

Almost immediately, teachers began taking advantage of the new tool. Hundreds of copies of the code flew out the doors as teachers seized upon them at in-service trainings and conferences. Individual teachers began making use of the code. Teachers in Ohio, New York, and Pennsylvania began incorporating assignments that involved producing media as part of high-school English classes. Some of their students' work was posted online. Frank Baker, a media literacy teacher, developed curriculum materials using copyrighted material and posted them online.

Within a year, organizations began incorporating the code into their work. Dozens of universities, including Johns Hopkins, Penn State, and the University of Arizona, used the code to teach teachers. School systems in Wisconsin, Virginia, and Maryland incorporated it into their guidelines. The National Writing Project trained all its members on the *Code of Best Practices* in the context of multimedia composition projects, so that K–12 writing teachers across the United States could be more confident in having their students use copyrighted materials in their own creative work. National student video competitions used the code to guide student submissions. Public television station KQED and national associations such as Educause, Library Leadership Network, and the American Council of Learned Societies all put the code on their websites. The first curriculum guides laced with copyrighted material went online and into print. Renee Hobbs wrote a book, *Conquering Copyright Confusion*, to guide educators in their fair-use decision making.

Teachers could finally stop whispering and slipping each other bootleg DVDs. Their work had been recognized and put to use, not only by them but by their gatekeepers. And there hadn't been a ripple of complaint. Within a year of its release, the code had affected the working lives of hundreds of thousands of teachers, and they were all eager to blog about it on their websites. Their administrators were making presentations about the changes at their conferences.

Word was spreading fast.

But now they faced new challenges. Teachers needed to move from the position of consumers to that of consumer-producers, in conjunction with their students. They needed to see themselves and their students both as copyright owners and copyright users. They needed to redefine their work space not as a zoned and protected area but as a workplace open to connect to the world (as indeed it was).

While teachers were preparing their code of best practices, Stephanie Lenz was watching her toddler Holden learn how to walk, and posted the fateful video of Holden jiggling to the sound of a Prince song, "Let's Go Crazy," in the background. Stephanie Lenz's problem was symptomatic of a much bigger one: lack of clarity around use of copyrighted material in online video. Before the dawn of YouTube in 2005, this was almost not a problem.

True, there were geeks and techies and, increasingly, film students

Fair Use: You Be the Judge >> School Projects

You are a high-school media literacy teacher. Your students all find popular music to be a key part of their culture, and they want to use entire songs from popular artists in their video and slide show presentations. If it's just for class projects that will not be distributed outside the classroom, is that fair use?

Answers at the back, and more at http://centerforsocialmedia.org/fair-use.

who made videos and schlepped them around the web. Sometimes they did so on private and passworded sites, like many vidders (the people who imaginatively re-edit popular culture such as *Star Trek*, *Lost*, and *Buffy the Vampire Slayer* to remake the narrative). No one outside a privileged group would ever know about them. Sometimes they moved their creations around via FTP, to designated addresses. It was clumsy and only semiprivate. Privacy protected the makers, but it also isolated them.

With YouTube's simplification of the process of uploading and sharing, online video had become far more popular. Soon video downloads were accounting for a significant minority of all bandwidth use in the United States. And more and more people—mostly young people—were making them.

At first, YouTube's founders imagined the platform as a service for home movies. But almost instantly it became a place where people uploaded material they thought lots of people could like—material like the latest *South Park* or *The Daily Show with Jon Stewart* or *Project Runway* episode. That began to sound like piracy to large media companies. By the DMCA's rules, they could notify the platform of copyright infringement. They started using detection software to identify copyrighted material on the site. But this process could leave the video around for up to three days. When Google bought YouTube in 2006, and brought assets into the game, Viacom sued Google for copyright infringement—a case that in 2010 continued on appeal even though Google won the first round. Viacom was the industry's advance guard in attempting to coerce a settlement that could cut copyright holders in on any profits from a popular online service that still had no revenue model of its own.

Suddenly, the prospect loomed of a settlement between two large industry players that could pre-empt new users' creative choices. What if Google agreed to remove videos that used copyrighted material? The future of a new form of expression could be crippled at birth by a settlement that could keep users from quoting copyrighted material. Once again, the prospect of hobbled imagination—Blake's "mind-forged manacles"—loomed. Once again, that prospect was largely invisible, even to many practitioners. The old problem surfaced: how do you demonstrate a loss from something that doesn't happen? What is the social cost of *not* letting people develop a cultural trend?

Creators of remixes, vids, and fan fiction were also worried. The Organization for Transformative Works was founded in 2007 by legal and cultural studies scholars. Its website proclaimed,

> One of the most exciting and helpful developments in copyright of late has been the development of "best practices," principles and procedures establishing what constitutes fair use in the judgment of a community of creative users. Best practices can successfully defend fair use rights even without litigation—see the statement of best practices in fair use. It is our position that, at a minimum, noncommercial, transformative fanworks are fair use, and the OTW will defend that position, just as the documentary filmmakers are using their best practices to make films and do business without litigation.

But there still was no standards document to work from, nor was there understanding of practices and attitudes outside the copyleft. The first step was research. With funding from the Ford Foundation, we went in search of people who, at that early stage in the history of online video, were making videos and uploading them to YouTube. We hunted in one of the likeliest places: colleges that have film programs. We interviewed several dozen young people about their habits and choices. In our report, *The Good, the Bad and the Confusing: User-Generated Video Creators on Copyright*, we found something surprising. Although these budding professionals often used and uploaded unauthorized copyrighted material, they usually believed that they were flouting the law and demonstrated great anxiety and concern. They were far from stereotypical copyright rebels. Some avoided uploading their work altogether, to avoid possible trouble. Others trusted that as noncommercial works they would be ignored by copyright holders, and they believed they would not be able to do such work in a commercial environment. Their knowledge of their rights as users—and these were college-age young adults, mostly in college—was abysmal. Our small survey had netted a small bit of knowledge: emerging online video practice among people who did not see themselves as rebels was tentative, and easily discouraged or at least distorted.

We then embarked on a study to map existing practices in using copyrighted material for online video. American University's graduate film students and law students fanned out over the Internet to log practices and understand what people were using copyrighted material for. In the report, *Recut, Reframe, Recycle: Quoting Copyrighted Material in User-Generated Video*, we summarized our findings. There was a wide range of reasons why people would repurpose copyrighted material: satire and parody, commentary both negative and positive, as a trigger to discussion, as illustration or example, incidental use, diaries, preservation, and pastiche/collage—or as many now called it, remix. Within a few months of YouTube's launch, people had already figured out more than a handful of different transformative uses that turned old copyrighted material into part of a new cultural expression.

That new cultural expression was not necessarily in good taste. Some of it was ludicrous, humiliating, or pointless. One foundation's program officer, looking at our findings, sniffed and said, "You'll have to find something more worthy, if you want to impress on our board of directors that this is culture worth saving." But "Numa Numa" (a nerd sings along with a popular song in his cubicle) and "Dramatic Chipmunk" (five seconds of a hamster looking bemused accompanied by a three notes of a horror soundtrack) were part of the process of developing an emerging culture. The survey of creative work during the first two minutes of an emergent cultural practice showed a wide range of strategies for reusing copyrighted material. The report demonstrated that a vigorous, exploratory, creative new cultural practice was at risk from summary rejection of all copyrighted material without owner permission.

We shared the data in a closed session with executives from a variety of Internet businesses, lawyers, and legal scholars, who strongly recommended the creation of a code of best practices. They pointed to the existence of an industry code of best practices, *Principles for User Generated Content Services*, endorsed by CBS, Fox, Viacom, Microsoft, and other content holders, which strongly inveighed against copying but offered empty pieties regarding fair use. These companies were in the habit of demanding that platforms like YouTube take down videos making unlicensed uses of even small amounts of copyrighted content. The platforms generally went along, to maintain a shield against liability under the DMCA. However much the commercial actors here claimed to respect fair use, the result was that legitimate examples of it were being caught in the nets extended to catch infringers. The Electronic Frontier Foundation had developed a set of guidelines for industry to follow to make online video "dolphin-safe" for the fair user, *Fair Use Principles for User Generated*

Video Content. But no one had yet made clear to an ordinary user what fair use looked like in the context of online video.

We took on the challenge of building the *Code of Best Practices in Fair Use for Online Video.*

Deciding on the body to shape the code was a challenge. Codes of best practices function well because they represent a common understanding in a community of practice (rather than, say, the opinion of a group of "expert" lawyers or a negotiated treaty of sorts with organizations invested in copyright ownership). But online video practice was only emerging, and no business models yet existed to establish how and who would be rewarded commercially. Therefore early adopters often disregarded or even disdained the entire question of copyright ownership, often choosing to believe that their nonprofit practice was outside the purview of copyright. No stable, broad-based associations of practitioners had yet grown up, probably for the same reason that there were yet no business models among producers.

Eventually, and as a result of consultation with professionals who had been involved in the study and in earlier projects, we decided to form a high-level, interdisciplinary committee of experts in two areas: popular culture and copyright law. The scholars of popular culture understood firsthand both the kind of work being created in this participatory environment and the motivations behind it, and they often sympathized passionately with new media makers. The legal experts understood the recent history of fair-use practice and litigation, and the historical arguments justifying fair use in an analog, professional media environment. Some were clueless about participatory media practice, and came to it with sympathy and curiosity but reserve. We thought these two groups would be able to educate each other, and would mutually be invested in creating a document that would encourage new makers to use their rights without encouraging them to take unnecessary risks. We also believed that the group's credibility was enhanced by the fact that no one in it had a direct market investment in the outcome.

The group brainstormed over four months. At first, some of the lawyers struggled to fully grasp the new media environment involved. Sometimes the group was able to find analogies with more traditional media, or to describe online video practice in terms that allowed consideration of how it could be transformative. Some of the cultural studies experts resisted the idea that the law might frown on activities they knew were common, such as sharing of entire texts of copyrighted works in order to be able to work from them. The group eventually agreed that such practices might fall beyond a code of best practices, but not necessarily beyond the doctrine of fair use.

The *Code of Best Practices in Fair Use for Online Video* described fair-use reasoning, stressed the importance of demonstrating good faith (for instance by attribution), and organized the presentation according to situations in which fair-use questions typically emerge in current practice. These included such common situations as critique, reposting for commentary, and remixing. As in earlier codes of best practices, each category was described and provided with a general fair-use principle with appropriate limitations.

The code was downloaded tens of thousands of times within the first two months, and was referenced on a variety of websites, including those of *Revver*, *Boing Boing*, *Rocketboom*, and leading remix practitioners such as Jonathan McIntosh.

There were no industry criticisms of the code, other than one nonlawyer's disparagement of it on the website of the Copyright Alliance (funded by large copyright holders and chartered to promote their interests in Washington, D.C.). Alliance executive Patrick Ross wrote,

> This is a dangerous effort. We at the Copyright Alliance support education on fair use and have information on our site. But our information is intentionally broad; we do not want to be in the position of giving legal advice to specific end-users of copyrighted works. . . . But that is precisely what the best practices guide writers run the risk of doing. . . . What is implied suggests a significant expansion of the current established thinking of fair use, going far beyond legal precedent.

William Patry, a fair-use expert who had become senior copyright counsel at Google, responded sharply on his personal blog:

> Let's see what this means: a guy who isn't a lawyer, much less a copyright lawyer, thinks it is a dangerous effort for copyright lawyers, educators, and those who deal with real world fair use problems on a daily basis to address some of the common problems presented, not as legal advice, but as "best practices." The safe sex approach, according to Mr. Ross, is the type of education that Mr. Patrick's group—a front for large corporate copyright owners—gives, namely always ask permission. . . . I can say, based on my over 25 years of experience with fair use, over 25 years more than Mr. Ross has, that the site doesn't "imply" "a significant expansion of the current established thinking of fair use, going far beyond legal precedent," as he states. Mr. Ross's purpose is not to engage in a constructive debate about specific

examples and whether those examples are appropriately a fair use, something reasonable minds might disagree on. Rather, his purpose is to silence those who try to provide responsible, thoughtful guidance to those on the ground, and ultimately to silence those who dare to suggest there can be fair use at all.

Patrick Ross did not respond. But Google did. Google funded the Center for Social Media's creation of a short film, which was showcased on YouTube, about the code: *Remix Culture: Fair Use Is Your Friend.*

The notion of creating codes of best practices was now spreading well beyond the activities based at American University. In 2007, Dance Heritage Coalition members were inspired by the news of documentarians' work on fair use, as they faced enormous frustrations in their own. Many dance organization administrators are either former dancers or lifetime members of the dance community. For them, dance is both an art form with a particular beauty because of its evanescent, momentary quality and also a fragile and poorly preserved tradition. As administrators, they maintain the tradition and attempt to cultivate a new generation of lovers, students, and teachers of the form. They are not only archivists, but champions of their art form. They won a grant from the Andrew Wood Mellon Foundation to create a code of best practices, and their then-executive director Barbara Drazin contacted us to learn the best practices model.

With our help, the DHC staff, led by Libby Smigel, the organization's director, collected stories from their networks. They found for example that many administrators of collections of dance materials—photographs, videos, notated choreography—were so concerned about copyright that they wouldn't even copy items from their holdings for preservation, let alone make them available to the public through exhibits, websites, and the like. Administrators were also loath to supply material to dance scholars for inclusion in course materials or publications. Their fear and anxiety was keeping them from their basic mission.

DHC staff organized eight small-group meetings around the country. The rich mix of professionals—not only archivists and librarians but also scholar-teachers and choreographers—discussed passionately their problems, needs, and interpretations of the law. Each meeting ended with the effervescent feeling that their mission could be served better with fair use. Out of these discussions came *The Statement of Best Practices in Fair Use of Dance-Related Materials.*

Dance archivists targeted five areas in which they needed fair use to provide support: preservation, exhibition, teaching, scholarship, and the use of materials on collections' websites. As was true with other codes, this one carefully balanced rights. For instance, archivists found that they should be able to employ fair use to quote dance materials in websites where the curators were doing something very different from an original dance—for instance, explaining a kind of choreographic style. At the same time they suggested that such use would wisely involve contextualizing clearly, crediting the copyrighted material, building an explanation for why they chose the amount they did, and where possible making it hard to copy.

The sense of optimism among these administrators is hard to capture. They believe that their statement can transform the field by making illustrations of dance history available even to people who live far from the centers of dance programming and documentation. They believe it can be instrumental in the vitality of dance as an art form. They were promptly joined by some of the major organizations in their field, who endorsed it.

Meanwhile, at the Society for Cinema and Media Studies (SCMS), Peter Decherney had been watching the process of creating codes of the best practices closely. In his research on early cinema, he had become interested in the development of copyright in film, and had come to see how practice shaped law as much as law shaped practice. He presented a series of papers, elements in his forthcoming *Hollywood's Copyright Wars*. He knew how frustrating it was to try to teach about film when boxed in by copyright restrictions. Indeed, he had organized a successful effort to win an exemption from the DMCA penalties for breaking encryption, for film professors who make clips of films for classroom teaching. (The effort was supported by the Glushko-Samuelson Intellectual Property Law Clinic at American University's Washington College of Law.)

Decherney worked with members of the SCMS policy committee to design a survey of problems in the field and, ultimately, a code of best practices for film professors in classroom teaching, *SCMS Statement of Best Practices for Fair Use in Teaching for Film and Media Educators*. Again with help from the AU clinic, the policy committee identified appropriate fairuse practices in typical situations: classroom teaching, archiving and use of broadcast materials, presentations both by students and professors.

Film professors embraced the code, but they wanted more. They were frustrated by their publishers and other gatekeepers in their scholarship. They wanted to quote frame grabs and stills, and use clips on websites and in media packaged with scholarship. But gatekeepers frequently told them they needed to license all such material. Back in 1993, as we have noted, film scholars through SCMS had addressed this with a code of best practices. Digital innovations had further challenged scholars, and an SCMS policy committee, again led by Decherney, decided to rewrite the scholarly advice, which resulted in the organization's second guide, *SCMS Statement of Fair Use Best Practices for Media Studies Publishing*.

The creators of OpenCourseWare also wanted to make the most of their fair-use options. They chafed at the kinds of courses they had to put up online when professors used a lot of copyrighted materials. They called them "skeletons"—courses so bare that they were unhelpful teaching tools—and "swiss cheese"—full of holes where crucial copyrighted material had been removed. Indeed, cultural studies scholar Henry Jenkins had refused to let his courses go online, because they would be so deformed by the choice not to include third-party material.

Led by Lindsey Weeramuni of MIT, with funding from the Hewlett Foundation, the group first surveyed their own small field to get a good sense of shared problems, and circulated their report, called "Skeletons and Swiss Cheese," within it. Then, with help from the Center for Social Media, they shaped a *Code of Best Practices in Fair Use for OpenCourseWare*, which enabled them to fill out the skeleton-and-swiss-cheese courses and meet their mission. In the process, they faced a challenge in crossing the line between the alternative-public-domain environment of Creative Commons and copyrighted environments. The OpenCourseWare efforts, part of a general trend toward open educational resources, depended in part on Creative Commons licenses of different kinds that promised users worldwide that these materials could be used and reused at will for noncommercial purposes, regardless of the details of local copyright law. Inserting third-party copyrighted material into course materials in reliance on fair use threatened to compromise the portability and integrity of those materials. It meant that the entire package of material might no longer be available under the one blanket license, since that license would not cover others' copyrighted materials. The group's allegiance to the alternative-public-domain concept was central to its mission.

But so was the belief that OCW should be of as high a quality, and as complete, as possible. The group finally decided that the benefits of employing fair use to flesh out courses outweighed the inconveniences. As their code made clear, it was extremely important to them to label all third-party material clearly, so that its special status would be clear to users. Those users could then decide how they wanted to use it beyond simple consumption, and they would bear all the responsibility for doing so.

There was another problem. This group was made up of creators of OpenCourseWare, and they were typically somewhere in the middle of the administrative hierarchy of large organizations. They were not independent actors like many independent filmmakers, although they were creative workers with a lot of autonomy. The group began its efforts hopeful of attracting support from their university administrators, who often shared with them their frustrations on this issue. But such decisions move within a glacial timeframe. Nor could they get the imprimatur of their own international association, the OpenCourseWare Consortium, which also answered to many of these same administrators. The group took advantage of its main strength—the collegial relationships among the creators across the different universities. The signatories, who typically were the people who headed the OpenCourseWare initiatives at their institutions, signed on to the code as individual creators—not as representatives of their institutions.

Nonetheless, by spring 2010, OpenCourseWare designers were launching courses in fields as diverse as engineering, ethics, music, nuclear technology, and robotics with fleshed-out curricula. They were having success in persuading university lawyers to give fair use in OCW a chance. They were interweaving third-party copyrighted material in the form of text, images, and video clips. "Now we're sitting around waiting for the sky to *not* fall!" said Weeramuni.

Meanwhile, communities interested in codes of best practices were popping up in unexpected places. Communications scholars, through the International Communication Association, in 2010 issued its *Code of Best Practices in Fair Use for Scholarly Research in Communication*. Poets decided to clarify their fair-use interpretation, with help from the Poetry Foundation.

Then, in 2010, librarians began to organize. With the help of a grant from the Andrew Wood Mellon Foundation, the Association of Research Libraries began, with us, to explore the problems that research librarians face in meeting their mission, given their confusions and concerns with copyright and fair use. Prudence Adler, ARL's associate executive director and head of government relations, was well aware of the success of earlier codes of best practices and agreed to shepherd the process of diagnosing the problems correctly and shaping a consensus document. The standards that the research librarians established would be highly influential for the entire library community. Of all the communities of practice that had picked up the best practices model, none to date was so pervasive throughout society as the librarians. The librarians' code promised to answer definitively the good question that the scholarly skeptic had been asked, in that meeting of MacArthur grantees, about the scope of best practices initiatives.

The growth of fair-use codes of best practices, and ensuing activism around the DMCA, has not gone unnoticed in the content industries. But even there the reaction has been largely favorable. Unofficially, we have heard from many people in TV networks, cable programming companies, and archives that having codes of best practices in fair use makes their lives easier. They get fewer calls and e-mails that they have to ignore. They are also able to show people what the limits of fair use are, which speeds licensing negotiations. Finally, in recessionary times, large content companies have increasingly turned to fair use themselves to lower budgets, and they have turned sometimes to codes of best practices in fair use to assist them in decision making.

When fair use becomes easier to use, friction in marketplace transactions is reduced. Copyright holders don't lose significant money. In most cases, no licensing went on previously, because the amounts of money were too small for the transaction costs. Copyright holders may gain in other ways, for instance with publicity for their work. But mostly the big benefit is that more culture is created with less fuss.

This has been achieved in part because fair-use advocates have avoided moralizing about the value of exemptions and fair use in particular. They do not need to demonize one side in the copyright balance; they can value both. Fair use is highly valued, if often secretly, by large content companies, and quite openly by other large businesses such as Google. It is a liberator of culture at the smallest and most informal scale, such as amateur online videos and elementary schoolchildren's homework. People who use and need fair use often are the same people who use and need copyright ownership rights as well.

9 How to Fair Use

Practice makes practice. DAVID VAN TAYLOR, filmmaker

Changing the balance of copyright involves building up fair-use practice. Fortunately, it is easy and legal to expand your opportunities to employ fair use, and to help others to do the same. Three immediate options are to develop a code of best practices in a creative or user community; apply the best learning from others' codes; and encourage such action as a gatekeeper, teacher, and enabler of good choices.

Smart fair users are also informed citizens with regard to copyright policy, as we have seen from the savvy interventions some user groups have made at the Copyright Office over the DMCA exemptions. Smart fair users may be interested in joining policy activists working on targeted copyright problems that can expand the pool of copyrighted material available for everyone to use without permission or payment.

Make Your Own

Many creators—musicians, software developers, corporate trainers, bloggers, journalists, and others—do not yet have a code of best practices in fair use to refer to. They may have to deal with lawyers, supervisors, insurers, publishers, or some other authority who will not take their word for it that fair use is available. Lawyers, insurers, television executives, and publishers have changed their minds when they see codes of best practices.

How does a group of people design a code of best practices in fair use? This is a process that involves many individuals, but it depends on a few of them coordinating the activity. (This is why foundation support for efforts to date has been so important, to guarantee the attention of a few coordinators.) Those people need to keep good records, in part to make

Making a Code of Best Practices in Fair Use

Find networks and organizations in the community of practice (not the gatekeepers, but the creators/users).

Document the kinds of problems the community has with using copyrighted material; get good stories!

Circulate the results of this documentation to the community; tell the stories.

Host or cohost small-group conversations on interpreting fair use; use the stories to locate the problem areas and discuss how to apply fair use to those problem areas.

Draft a code of best practices, using templates to the extent they are helpful.

Have an advisory board of supportive lawyers review and revise the draft, to ensure that the code of best practices conforms to the law.

Get endorsements from community organizations for the code.

Circulate news through community networks and organizations.

Document your successes.

Publicize your successes.

sure that all the people who have become involved with the process can become part of a fair users' network as it grows.

The first step of those organizers is to find one's friends. Professional associations are ideal sites for activity; they have regular meetings, membership lists, and e-mail forums, and they want to serve their members. Some have a standards body—for instance, an accrediting association. The industry executives or brokers who license the copyrighted material a community uses are never good friends for this purpose (no matter how lovely or helpful they are in other ways), since they are not interested in making your fair-use rights easier to use. If they were, they already would have. Social networking is a great way to spread the word once a group has something in hand, but it is not a good way to start out, since the work involved depends on the credibility of organizations.

The next step is to find out what problems the community of practice has with using copyrighted material. The problems of teachers, filmmakers, courseware developers, and dance archivists were similar in some ways, but also particular to their areas. Each community has its own stories and problems. Representative organizations are the ideal agents to conduct research, perhaps with a survey, or through long-form interviews, or both. Nothing else provides the rich detail of long-form interviews, even if they take time to plan, carry out, transcribe, and analyze. They are especially valuable because people explain not only what their problems are, but how they experience and even imagine them. If the interview process is not possible, open-ended survey questions can provide an opportunity for richer detail.

The data you collect have to be analyzed to explain how people in the field actually experience their problems with fair use. The research needs to be limited, then, to fair use, not the full range of copyright complaints. For instance, licensing, where it is necessary, is frustrating; fair use does not make the actual process of licensing any easier, although it may obviate it. If people need access to materials that are held by only one source, or conveniently available from only one source, fair use will not help with that either. Research can focus on when people need to reuse copyrighted material in their own work; why they use that material rather than, say, creating similar work; what they do when they cannot get it; what gatekeepers stop them from using it, and how; and what they would make or do if they did not have these concerns.

The research results will show not just a list of miscellaneous complaints, but a set of obstacles to creative practice. They will describe in what way creative action is hobbled by incomplete or incorrect understandings of the doctrine of fair use. They will conclude with recommendations for next steps, prime among which could be creating a code of best practices in fair use. These results can be shared with the field of practice, as widely as possible, with an awareness of timeliness. It may be much more appropriate, for instance, to publish in a newsletter than an academic journal, if journal publishing may take years. Understanding the networks of the community helps us understand how to reach the people in it, including by using social networking. With luck, the report of problems starts a conversation in the field, particularly if the associations involved engage with the problem. The conversation should pave the way for an engagement with a code of best practices in fair use, if desired.

The next step, creating a code of best practices, is a process that involves experienced members of the community, possibly identified by representative organizations. They are chosen not for their legal understanding but for their ability to understand the core mission of the creative community. These people will discuss, ideally in a series of small groups of eight to twelve, their most common fair-use problems; what fair-use principles apply in those cases; and limitations on fair-use principles appropriate to the field . (A template is provided at the end of this book.) They do not need a lawyer to deliberate on their appropriate employment of fair use, if they have grasped the logic of earlier fair use codes. Indeed, many lawyers find the prospect of nonlawyers making decisions on their own threatening, even though we all do that every day without incident. If they want guidance, organizers can draw upon the resources of an intellectual property law clinic (see next page), or contact the Center for Social Media.

Organizers certainly need a facilitator who understands the larger objective of developing categories of practice, and who can help the participants effectively to brainstorm descriptions of those categories, how fair-use principles apply, and what limitations are important. That facilitator probably needs a good note-taker. As with all good meeting management, a clear agenda and a good timekeeper are essential. Staying on topic is not always easy with such juicy material. An easy way to derail the conversation is to open the discussion to other aspects of copyright that people find hard to deal with, such as licensing.

Some discussions benefit from prior development of sample scenarios, drawn from the research. Members of the group can then discuss the scenarios, and their discussion can be used to clarify both principles of fair use and associated limitations. The facilitator needs to pose the problem to the group from two angles: What do I truly think is fair unlicensed use in a particular situation (whether or not I am permitted to do it, and whether or not I've been told I shouldn't)? And second, Would I still think such a practice was fair if someone used the material I had copyrighted (or that belongs to someone I especially respect) in that way?

Often, the hardest part of these conversations is convincing people to imagine their practice outside the constraints, fears, and misinformation about use of copyrighted material that they experience in their work. Too often people bring their inner lawyer—or boss, or insurer—into the room with them. Before they get to what they think is fair, they default to "I wouldn't be permitted to do that." The facilitator must be on point to remind the participants of two points. First, it is they, as the creators/users, who know what they really need to fulfill their mission, not the lawyers or the gatekeepers. Second, the creation of a code is not about setting down in writing what is being done or what people think that they can "try for" or "get away with." Instead it is about establishing the best practices that the field in question should adhere to whenever possible, within the fair-use doctrine.

Intellectual Property Clinics in the United States and Canada

Berkman Center for Internet and Society, Harvard University

Center for Intellectual Property Law and Information Technology, DePaul University College of Law

Franklin Pierce Law Center

Glushko-Samuelson Intellectual Property Law Clinic, Washington College of Law, American University

Intellectual Property and the Arts Clinic, Vanderbilt University Law School

Intellectual Property and Nonprofit Organizations Clinic, Washington University Law School

Intellectual Property and Technology Law Clinic, Gould School of Law, University of Southern California

Intellectual Property Law Clinic, University of Maine School of Law

Intellectual Property Law Clinic, William Mitchell College of Law

Samuelson Law, Technology & Public Policy Clinic, School of Law, University of California, Berkeley

Samuelson-Glushko Intellectual Property and Information Law Clinic, Fordham School of Law, Fordham University

Samuelson-Glushko Canadian Internet Policy and Public Interest Clinic, Faculty of Law, University of Ottawa

At many points, people in such meetings say, "What's the point of talking among ourselves? The real problem is the copyright holders (or gatekeepers, or lawyers). We need to get them in the room and negotiate with them, if we're ever going to get anywhere." But in fact, the people in this community of practice wouldn't even be in the room with each other if they could persuade content holders or their gatekeepers or their lawyers to take them seriously individually. They will be able to begin a change-making conversation with their gatekeepers, and act with confidence in front of content holders, only if they first act collectively. That is a lot of work, but it is also effective.

What would be death to such meetings is inviting gatekeepers or content holders to them. The gatekeepers are invested in the security of their own operations, and the content holders cannot be asked to agree to fair use of their own materials. Fair use gives you permission to use their materials whether they want you to or not. Usually they do not want you to. Certainly they cannot be asked preemptively to give you permission.

These conversations need to be synthesized into a rough draft of a code of best practices, structured around the most common situations in which practitioners in the field experience problems. This document should say, essentially: "In our field, these common situations occur, where fair use applies. In each of these situations, here is how fair use applies." For each situation, an example is given ("People in this field usually do *this*, and need *that* to do it"); fair use is asserted ("People in this field can employ fair use in this situation because . . ."); and limitations are itemized ("They have to be careful to . . . and not to . . ."). Usually the principle derives from discussion of the first question ("What is fair unlicensed use in this situation?") and is related to a claim to transform the material. The limitations come from the discussion of the second question ("When would I think it was unfair, whether I liked it or not, if my own material were used this way?"), and they are usually linked to the question of how much borrowing or copying is appropriate.

In drafting any code of best practices, it is crucial to make clear that although the principles and limitations it contains express a strong consensus of the community of practice involved, they by no means exhaust the full range of potential fair use by members of the community. There will always be examples—sometimes many—of situations in which individuals can and do go beyond what their communities can widely agree on. Many of these uses are ones that also would be found fair if they were tested in court. The code makes it easy to understand where the center of gravity or safe harbor is; it should never discourage those who want to explore the wider, less-charted territory of fair use from doing so.

The next step is making sure that the code stays safely within what is known about the law itself. All the codes of best practice developed through American University have benefited from outside legal expertise contributed by lawyers highly conversant with the fair-use doctrine and its balancing role. The selection of lawyers is extremely important. Any lawyer asked to become involved with creating a code of best practices needs to understand the nature of the project, and needs to understand copyright law and the doctrine of fair use. Too many lawyers have bought into the assumption that what people need is better rules, not the ability to reason on their own. To be useful in a project of this kind, lawyers have to accept that codes of best practices are grounded in the expectation that people can reason competently about their own rights, given the right information. In addition, some lawyers are related to communities but not necessarily sympathetic to their aims. For instance, if a group of history teachers is getting together, they may have access to school board lawyers, but the history teachers are not the lawyer's clients—the school board is.

Once the code of best practices has been vetted by lawyers and/or legal scholars, it needs to be sent for review to all potential organizations that can lend credibility, promote, and publicize the information. In each case, the organization's decision is thumbs-up or thumbs-down; the document once vetted is complete, and text cannot be negotiated. It is also a potential asset to every group that endorses it. Once endorsements are in place, the document is ready for formatting and publication.

The release to the community of practice and the world is coordinated with all the signatories and endorsers, the allies and friends. At this point, the extensive database of contacts developed in the course of the project and today's social networking tools become immensely helpful. The release might be coordinated with a major event within that community— an annual conference, a festival, an awards ceremony, a board of directors' meeting.

The launching of the code is the beginning of the community's education. Now that the code exists, it can (but doesn't have to) change practice. Success will depend upon people accepting it as the "new normal" in their field. The work after the launching of the code is just as important as all the work in creating the code. This means spreading the word and prompting discussion, at professional meetings, in e-mail forums, in award competitions, within professional practice. It means documenting successes, and spreading the news about them back to the field, through websites, blogs, and newsletters. When people start putting the code to work, change starts to happen. "I get it!" said documentary filmmaker David Van Taylor after he heard the news about insurers accepting fair-use claims. "Practice makes . . . practice!"

This is a basic lesson of codes of best practices in fair use: Practice makes practice. When people use their rights, their rights are stronger, and more people can use them. Changing practice is not something that happens because a document is created; it happens when enough people use that tool to change their behavior, and tell someone else.

Learn from Others

The kinds of communities that have developed these codes so far have usually been fairly small—or at least highly self-conscious. It's not surprising that small, self-conscious communities create such codes; they are relatively light on bureaucracy and therefore on naysayers, they have a strong sense of mission ("I'm not just a customer, I'm a creator"; "I'm a teacher, I teach the next generation!"; "We're sharing knowledge with the world!"), and they have a clearly identified need.

Less obvious is the role that seemingly small communities play in larger ones. Ideas spread via networks, and little ones intersect with big ones. For instance, the documentary filmmakers' work has inspired change in practice not only in large television networks but in studios producing feature fiction films. Michael Donaldson reports that since the Documentary Filmmakers' Statement came out, he has worked on several fiction features that employed fair use: *The Stoning of Soraya M.* employed fair use for a photo of Soraya at the end of the picture; *Bitch Slap* fairly used six clips of dancing women over the main title credits; and *Dakota* fairly used clips from the *O'Reilly Factor* under fair use, as the lead character struggles with her decisions around an unwanted pregnancy.

Scholars facing publishing problems outside the film area turn to the Society for Cinema and Media Studies' codes of best practices for help with their arguments. Educators in English, history, and even mathematics turn to the media literacy teachers' code for sound practice. Librarians who are frustrated by both clients and vendors turn, at least for now, to the decisions of the dance collections and open courseware communities for guidance on when they can use materials from their own archives for public exhibitions, and how they can incorporate illustrative material for online courses. Online video makers impressed by Jonathan McIntosh's work on the website Rebellious Pixels pick up on his assertion of fair use, perhaps not even knowing that he grounds his assertions in the *Code of Best Practices in Fair Use for Online Video*.

Those not represented within a community that has interpreted fair use still may be able to learn from the conclusions that they have drawn. Right now, someone is making a PowerPoint presentation for work or for a spouse's fortieth birthday party; some teacher is teaching history or science rather than media literacy; someone is organizing the exhibit for your small town's centennial, not running a dance archive; someone is working on a podcast about conducting genealogical research, not making a documentary film. They all may benefit by referring to existing codes of best practices in fair use.

The starting point for freelance decision making on fair use has to be the doctrine itself, which currently is organized around transformative use in appropriate amounts. It can be lonely to make a decision on fair use without such consensus as has been developed in codes of best practices, but it can be done, by using the same reasoning that infused the codes. (By contrast, for the reasons we discussed earlier, trying to use the four factors to conduct a fair-use analysis can be frustrating and inconclusive.) The questions that people making those codes asked themselves to test their fair-use instincts are the same ones we discussed at the outset, representing a distillation of what courts now focus upon:

· Was the use of copyrighted material for a different purpose, rather than just reuse for the original purpose?
· Was the amount of material taken appropriate to the purpose of the use?
· Was it reasonable within the field or discipline it was made in?

Also, people usually asked themselves how they could demonstrate their good-faith understanding that they were employing fair use, by making gestures of acknowledgment such as crediting the original.

Increasingly, we see uses that are both widely popular and yet in a fair-use gray zone or even not yet clearly acceptable under fair use. By and large, they go unchallenged. For instance, it is common for people to use popular commercial songs to accompany their homemade slide shows or video. Increasingly, they also take advantage of new technology to create their personal takes on familiar cultural artifacts. Then they post them on the Internet, for the pleasure of a small circle of family and friends. These works may quickly spread to wider networks and even commercial sites. Consider this case: During a 2010 snowstorm in Washington, D.C., Alison Hanold, suffering from cabin fever, asked her equally bored friends to create video of themselves singing new and topical words to Alanis Morissette's "Ironic." They then sent her video of themselves, and she edited it into a group video that went viral and was showcased on public radio. The video, "Ironic Blizzard," used the entire track of the song, but the transformative use was manifest; the ability to share the song was crucial to the nature of the work. Public radio station WAMU had no problem posting it on its website, and there were no legal repercussions. As people gain confidence in fair use and develop transformative arguments, these practices may move closer to the safe center of fair use.

Those who wish to remain squarely in the safe center of fair use today can apply the reasoning that has guided those developing codes of practices. A fair-use judgment is applied common sense. Anyone, an individual or group, can make common-sense judgments about fair use. In general, those judgments will be reliable because this is a doctrine of reasonableness. (Whether common sense can persuade a publisher, a boss, a lawyer, or some other gatekeeper without a code of best practices is another question.)

As always, context is everything in fair use. But there are situations so recurrent in different codes that they end up echoing each other. Three areas in which several of the codes have identified a role for fair use are critique, illustration, and incidental capture. These are also areas that recur in case law. Even though the situations each code sets forth are specific to that community, one can learn from that analysis in developing common sense judgments on fair use. For instance:

Comment and critique. People who are commenting on, critiquing, satirizing, making a parody, or just plain making fun of some piece of copyrighted work cannot do that without quoting it in some fashion. Imagine, for instance, that a husband is preparing a slide show for his wife's birthday and wants to open with a rewritten version of a song from one of the wife's favorite popular music groups. His version pokes gentle fun at the group while evoking good memories of his wife's fascination with it. He should be as confident as 2 Live Crew was in recasting, however vulgarly, "Pretty Woman." Indeed, the use of copyrighted material for such purposes is so well established in the law as fair use that some people think that it is the only kind of fair use. They are wrong, because these days the guide to fair use is in the concept of transformativeness (allied with its sister concern, appropriate size of use, and the question of community's custom). But commenting, critiquing, and poking fun at copyrighted work is a perfect example of transformative use. Such efforts may be parodic or satiric, but they do not need to be, in order to be fair uses.

Illustration. In many cases, the use of copyrighted material simply to refer to it within another context may also be fair use. For instance, if in that same slide show the husband wants to represent his spouse as the Wonder Woman of the household, or to use photographs of famous events to mark the passage of the years, he can be confident in his use of copyrighted works. How much is too much? That depends on what you need for the repurposed use. Take the case of the filmmakers who made *This Film Is Not Yet Rated.* The film quotes lots of Hollywood films to show the arbitrariness of the MPAA ratings board. One of their interviewees argues that Hollywood sexual prudery is worse now than in the 1970s, when *Coming Home* featured an extended scene in which Jane Fonda's character has an orgasm. The filmmakers cautiously clipped a few seconds of that scene into the interview, to provide a reference point. Their lawyer advised that they put more of the scene into the film, because otherwise they had not actually demonstrated that the scene really was extended. Even though they added a few more seconds, they didn't give viewers a substitute experience for the film. They merely were able to make their point.

Recall as well the book, *Grateful Dead: The Illustrated Trip*, in which entire concert posters from Bill Graham's Fillmore Auditorium were reprinted in illustration of the evolution of the band's career. Showing one corner of the poster would merely have baffled readers. On the other hand, the posters weren't shown at their original size; if you're a poster collector, you won't be able to use the book reproduction to make an image suitable for framing. The judges in this case unequivocally agreed with the book authors; it was fair use. By contrast, look at the uses of Elvis Presley performances in the multivideo biography that resulted in the Presley estate lawsuit. The Presley estate won the case, because the performances were basically used to entertain audiences, just as the originals had. In a more recent case, the *Harry Potter Lexicon* author lost his fair-use argument not because quoting from the *Harry Potter* series was not fair use, but because he had simply used so much of a work of fiction that it exceeded the appropriate amount.

Incidental/accidental. Many creator groups' codes discuss fair use in the context of inadvertently or incidentally capturing some copyrighted material in the process of doing their own work. This too is a specific instance of transformative use. The use being made of the copyrighted material is very different from the market for the work, and the new makers are not using any more of it than is naturally occurring in the course of their getting their jobs done. Perhaps that slide show includes a clip of a home movie where people sing "Happy Birthday" to the spouse, or there is a snapshot of the young couple at a Bon Jovi concert contrasted with later video of the older couple taking their child to a Jonas Brothers concert. Codes created by documentary filmmakers, teachers, open courseware creators, and online video folks all deal with incidental occurrence of copyrighted material. The subjects of a documentary dance at their wedding to a popular song. A teacher's lecture is recorded for podcast in a room that has copyrighted posters on the wall. A child dances to popular music. A cat watches television. In each case, copyrighted material is interwoven in an activity that didn't depend on it, and that the creator never selected.

Choosing deliberately to incorporate copyrighted material, rather than having it present in material captured for other purposes, changes the calculation. Selecting certain music for the background of one's own wedding video is different from capturing that music in the context of

---

Fair Use: You Be the Judge >> Parody and Satire in Slideshows

You are producing a comedy revue sketch satirizing election practices. You would like to create parodic versions of famous people's names, such as Nancy Feroshee and Newt Gangrene. You would like to create a slide show to be projected during the sketch, including photographs of actual election rally signs. You would also like to include some relevant political cartoons that reinforce your message in the slide show. Can you claim fair use for these uses?

Answers at the back, and more at http://centerforsocialmedia.org/fair-use.

---

a video you make about someone else's wedding. The choice to employ copyrighted material in situations where licensing is typical (for instance for soundtrack) could lead to a decision to license the material.

Some creator groups take as their raw material a variety of copyrighted works. They then create something new from that work. They believe that if the original work becomes raw material for something that is not merely a derivative of it (like a novelization of the movie or cover of a song), but something new, then they are employing fair use. In that anniversary slide show, perhaps the end features a remix of a Baby Einstein video with a 1990s music video, the juxtaposition making a comment on life's passages. Remixes, mashups, and political collages have all been identified as fair uses in the *Code of Best Practices in Fair Use for Online Video*, a document that has gone uncontested by content companies. Makers have sometimes seen their work disappear from YouTube because of automatic searches for copyrighted material, but when they have demanded that their work be reinstated, it has been without challenge. (Don't forget that Stephanie Lenz, with help from EFF, sued Universal, not the other way around.) This too is an example of repurposing and limiting uses to the needs of the repurposing.

In making a fair use-decision, inevitably people go through some reasoning process. As you do that, you may find it helpful to make a note of your reasons. If this work is publicly available, it may also be helpful to others to see the rationale behind your decision to employ fair use. This may be something you will want to do anyway, because it is part of the contextualizing of the selected material. Some makers of online video do this. However, no one loses their right to claim fair use because of a failure to leave a record of their rationale. Even users who believe they are infringing may eventually discover that in fact they are fair users.

Worry, Guilt, Etiquette, and Fair Use

Fair use is not only a legal decision but one that reflects relationships and values. Fair use exists because policymakers decided from the beginning of copyright in the United States that it would not be fair for copyright owners to have total control of their copyrights. The decision to employ fair use often calls up a calculation that goes beyond the questions of transformativeness and appropriateness, and makes people reflect on their own values, relationships and social networks.

Some people making fair use of copyrighted materials feel guilty about taking something that belongs to someone else. They are afraid that they may not "get away with it," and don't want to put themselves at risk. No one should be in this position. The law not only permits but encourages limited incursions on copyright owners' monopoly in order to protect the future of culture. No one should be trying to "get away" with anything, and nobody should assume more risk than they are comfortable with, when they can avoid it. Fair use does not usually require courage. It should be something that elementary schoolchildren can do without drama. Codes of best practices dramatically lower risk; understanding the logic and reasoning of fair use in today's judicial climate lowers risk; sharing your deliberations with others who understand the logic and reasoning of fair use also helps you know when you're in the zone of fair use. The more people share their calculations and their employment of fair use, the easier it gets to understand what is acceptable fair use.

Some people also worry about whether someone else will get angry because they fairly used the work. There can be good reasons not to alienate a copyright holder, even if the law permits it. One of the most obvious is that the user may have—or want to have—an ongoing relationship with the rights holder. For instance, some filmmakers deal so routinely with some archives and footage houses, and receive substantial discounts in the process, that they are reluctant to access independently and fairly use a copy of work the archive holds. Others may choose not to alienate museums and archives by independently photographing public domain works that the museums or archives themselves photograph and sell images of, so that they can maintain relationships. They prefer not to make waves. This choice can make good sense for them, but a different maker might make a different choice. Some makers have visited copyright holders to discuss lowering terms for material that they might well take under fair use but can afford not to, if the price is right. They have received substantial discounts in those negotiations.

Often people who employ fair use want to make sure that they give credit for the work they take, so that it is perfectly clear that they are not claiming it as their own, and that they recognize its value. People do this in many ways. They make a reference to the work in passing; they put a label on it; they mention it in credits; they create a footnote. Many creators value recognition more than any other currency.

Users of others' copyrighted material sometimes find themselves in the position of desperately wanting to use some copyrighted material and being afraid that they are stretching the logic of fair use a little far. There is, of course, a large gray area between a solid, comfortable understanding of fair use (this is what the codes of best practices express) and what a court will almost certainly find as infringement. Some people are comfortable taking risks, as previous lawsuits demonstrate, and taking up space in that gray zone. They also sometimes calculate, correctly, that they can always take back their use if they have to. They know that if someone complains, the first act will be a letter asking them to cease and desist, not a lawsuit. People who post something to a blog or a video website are in a good position to "ask forgiveness rather than permission," because it is so easy to take down material that is challenged. People who publish a big initial run of a popular book are not well placed to use this approach.

More risk-averse people consult others in their peer community and discuss their use with friendly nonprofessionals who can help them understand if their desire has overmatched their common sense. These conversations can help fair users put themselves in the position of the copyright holder, to imagine the arguments they might have to confront. How might a copyright holder use the same logic of fair use against the new user? This is a challenging but healthy exercise to test whether you trust your own fair-use reasoning.

Consistently, people find that common politeness is a tremendous aid. It is polite, as well as legally favorable, to provide citations or references to work that is fairly used. It is often polite, although certainly not necessary, to inform copyright holders of the way you found their work valuable. It is much easier to be polite if you understand that you as a new user have solidly grounded rights to reuse when repurposing, recontextualizing, and using the appropriate amount. Then you are not asking permission but saying "thank you" for work you value and have legal access to.

Other Free Uses

Makers of new cultural expression may be able to find free material from other pools:

Public domain works: The public domain is the pool of work that no one can claim ownership of. Work can fall into the public domain when it ages out of its copyright. The original work of Beethoven, Mahler, Caravaggio, Dickens, Machado de Assis, the Upanishads, *The Art of War*, the Lumière Brothers' shorts—they are all in the public domain. If someone issues a new translation, or makes a new performance, or publishes a still-copyrighted edition, though, that will be copyrighted. Photographs of public domain museum art may be copyrighted, although the art itself is not. If you can get at the public domain item independently (say, you take your own photo of the museum sculpture; your cousin performs Chopin; you excerpt some shorts by the Lumière Brothers off the DVD), you don't have to worry about licenses. US federal government works of all kinds—manuals, jingles, movies, books—are all in the public domain, so long as they were made by full-time employees, whether they are the words of federal government employees or camera footage taken in civilian or military service. So are laws and judicial decisions. The purposes for which you use the material, and the source from which you obtain it, are irrelevant from a copyright perspective. One caution on federal government public domain work: Sometimes federal government works are made by contractors whose work is copyrighted, or they may include third-party work that is copyrighted. Also, some kinds of state and local government work can be copyrighted.

Creative Commons: You can use any work that has a Creative Commons license under the terms that the license specifies. The owner has, with that license, given you blanket permission for some uses, and has also usually imposed some limitations. At a minimum, CC licenses all carry the requirement that the work not be distributed with digital rights management. This requirement keeps CC-licensed work from circulating on professionally distributed DVDs.

Exemptions: You might benefit from some exemptions that were written into copyright law to accommodate special situations. For instance, there has been copyright in architectural works in the United States since 1990, but the Copyright Act includes an exemption for "any pictorial representation." Buildings that can be seen from public areas can be filmed for any purpose without permission. It doesn't matter whether the building is the subject of the film or an incidental background. And as we have noted, teachers, librarians, and public broadcasters all have special exemptions.

Finally, work produced in an entirely noncommercial way is especially favored for fair-use consideration. But noncommerciality is probably not enough of a reason in itself. Although the law favors noncommercial uses, as we have noted earlier, it does not provide a free pass.

Giving Away Your Fair-Use Rights

The law permits people to surrender their rights, which people often do by entering into contracts. This happens regularly, for instance, when people surrender their free-speech rights by signing nondisclosure agreements, or by going to work at a place that may require them not to display any regalia endorsing a political candidate.

Many media products come with contracts or licenses attached to them in ways that may be invisible to the user. On websites and in software, these agreements are usually buried in the "Terms of Service" (TOS) or "End-User License Agreements" (EULAs). Frequently, these provisions, on which we must click "I agree" if we want the item, include language that restricts what we can do with it. Much material on electronic databases in libraries is licensed to them on terms that explicitly prohibit or restrict fair use. CDs of images and sounds usually come with fine print limiting your use of them. Film and photo archives typically require users who ask for preview materials to sign an agreement ruling out fair use of the material.

Sometimes it is impossible to avoid this surrender of fair-use rights. Sometimes you can gain independent access to material and employ fair use. But if you are bound by a license, contract, or terms of service already, it will not matter that you have independent access. You are still bound by the terms of that agreement.

Outside Copyright

Some of the most common stumbling blocks people encounter with regard to copyright do not actually belong to copyright at all. Often they are not really stumbling blocks, either. Consider:

Trademarks: The scientist being interviewed in the jungle on the cable documentary is wearing a T-shirt that is weirdly pixeled out—not because it's obscene, but because it is advertising a rock band. Do you have to do that? No, and neither do the cable producers. Incidental uses of trademarks never need to be licensed, unless (perhaps) they incorporate a mark into the title of a film in a way that misleads people about the content, or if such uses lead people to believe that some corporate endorsement is implied. Federal and state trademark laws exist to protect the specially designed ways that a company signals its identity (logos, design, a particular set of colors, even the shape of a bottle). It protects trademarks from competitors (Pepsi versus Coke) and from efforts to confuse customers about the product—or from widespread commercial uses that could "dilute" the value of those marks. The trademark "antidilution" statute has a broad exception for expressive uses. Of course, trademarks can contain copyrighted images or graphics, in which case fair use may apply. When Morgan Spurlock made *Super Size Me*, a stunt film in which he ate only McDonald's food for thirty days and tracked his health (which declined precipitously), McDonald's logos dotted the film. But he wasn't a rival hamburger manufacturer, and he didn't misrepresent the nature of the business. He was not confusing people about what McDonald's trademark stands for or promotes; he was not "diluting" the quality of the trademark. (Although McDonald's representatives did say that most of their customers don't eat there three times a day, the corporation did not take any legal action.)

Patent law: Patents (available under federal law only) are intended to encourage invention of something tangible, useful, and "nonobvious." In general, since patents are about technological innovation, patent law doesn't usually overlap with copyright concerns. That is less true in computer software, however, where both copyright and patent apply. Before adapting a software program without authorization, a user would need to consider both regimes. But for people producing books, movies, songs, plays, photographs and so on, patent law is an irrelevant concern.

Trade secret: This body of state law protects the rights of companies to keep the ingredients or nature of their product a secret, if there is a commercial advantage. It does not usually apply to people making new cultural expressions—though it may matter to employees who are considering using material they have accessed at work for a new, personal purpose. In order to maintain trade secret protection, many firms have standard employee agreements that limit such uses, whether or not they would be permissible under copyright.

Right of publicity: What happens if you refer to a Michael Jackson CD cover? Will the Jackson estate invoke "right of publicity" and say that you are unfairly capitalizing on his image? If simply exploiting his image is the whole point of your endeavor (you are selling Michael Jackson mugs or T-shirts, for example, where the mug or T-shirt in itself has no particular value without the Jackson image), then they might have a case. But is it? "Right of publicity" is state law, and exists only in some states. It confers on individuals an affirmative right to control the commercial exploitation of personal information, especially their names, images, and associated traits. In many places, the right lives on after a person dies, and can be invoked by his or her survivors. However, right-of-publicity laws have been crafted and interpreted to create plenty of space for freedom of expression—in much the same way that copyright law has been limited by the fair-use doctrine. Judicial decisions and sometimes the laws themselves make it clear that the right of publicity bars only the direct commercial exploitation of a celebrity's "persona," and First Amendment–protected expressive uses are specifically exempted. So we can't all go into business selling posters and knickknacks representing Michael Jackson, but any of us could write an "unauthorized biography" of him, and illustrate it appropriately, even if we hope to get rich in the process.

Personal releases: It is a good idea to get a personal release form from someone you single out for special attention in your work. But people who are not the main focus of a production, who are in parks, streets, or other public places where they have no expectation of privacy, cannot complain if they are captured in audio or on film, even for a commercial production.

Advocacy

Some sore spots in the reuse of copyrighted material cannot be addressed with self-help. While global copyright reform is not likely to happen soon, targeted issues that greatly affect the utility of fair use are amenable to reform in the short run. They deserve attention from people who want to form or join advocacy groups in taking political action. Orphan works and the DMCA are two such areas. If these two areas of copyright policy were tweaked in order to permit greater access, both citizen media and professional media works would benefit dramatically.

Orphan works are copyrighted works whose owners are missing. If earnest efforts fail to locate anyone who knows who owns the copyright for a work, then that is an orphan work. This is not much of a problem, if you are employing fair use. But it is a huge problem if you want to license the material. This is a rare copyright policy issue where copyright owners and copyright users can cheerfully be on the same side. The only reason legislation has yet to go forward is the gridlock on larger copyright policy decision making, and the general aversion of rights holders to any legislation that might "weaken" copyright, no matter how well justified. If it can pass, then more copyrighted work can be used with less wasted time and money, and more culture can be made.

Eventually, the DMCA will have to be re-examined for the backward-looking, creatively stifling legislation that it is. By that time, probably new business models will create a different stakeholder configuration. In the meantime, it is important for anyone who has a DMCA-related problem accessing material they have a right to use under fair use to bring that problem to the Copyright Office. Every three years, the Copyright Office hears complaints from users who are stopped by the DMCA from exercising their free-speech rights. The more people appear before the Copyright Office to explain their problems, the better organized they are in showing that entire communities of practice are affected, and the better they can show the Copyright Office that they lack adequate alternatives, the more holes are driven into the DMCA and the more its legitimacy is challenged.

We also see on the horizon an opportunity to make a real difference in the actual terms of copyright law. We expect to see a new campaign to secure copyright term extension for works that would otherwise enter the public domain when the extra twenty years of protection won in 1998 comes closer to running out. Copyright term extension has become a high-profile issue in the copyleft. The issue needs to be shared much more broadly; it is not a partisan issue, and it is one that affects us all. Large companies that benefit from public domain and fair use, such as Google, Yahoo, Microsoft, and equipment manufacturers, could play some counterweight role in the inevitable stakeholder jockeying.

Another urgent issue for activists, as many organizations—including Electronic Frontier Foundation and Public Knowledge—have noted, is statutory damages. These stiff and utterly out-of-proportion penalties, even if rarely invoked at their highest level, powerfully inhibit people from using their rights in the United States. Only well-organized coalitions of broad constituencies will be able to engage in the inevitable stakeholder politics. We believe that as communities of practice exercise their fair-use rights, they will also understand the need for reform of statutory damages.

We think some legislative approaches to improve balance in copyright are not worth pursuing at this time. Some activists have suggested legislative proposals to add noncommercial, personal expression to the list of activities in the preamble to the section of copyright law that describes fair use, section 107. This change certainly would be worthwhile, if it could be achieved. But vastly more likely is that the attempt would open up section 107 to reconsideration, inviting a strong lobbying pushback from content owners against the last decades' developments in case law and practice. Going farther, for instance, to categorically exempt personal noncommercial uses from copyright regulation, would be more problematic. Creating a copyright-free noncommercial zone could create a copyright playpen or, worse, a virtual prison for such information. People who make something valuable enough to share frequently want to share it within commercial venues. Sometimes they have to—for instance, on Flickr, an ad-fed site. There are also suggestions to include lists of other exempted activities in the body of the statute, creating bright-line zones of crystal-clear fair use. We believe that such a measure would entail more problems than solutions. Lists of exempted activities—the strategy used in copyright regimes that employ the continental European approach to exemptions—adapt poorly to new technologies and customs. They also tend, because of the inevitable food fights among stakeholders, to be harshly constrained. Finally, we know from bitter experience that codifying legal safe harbors for fair use is most likely to limit fair use to those safe harbors. Today, fair use does have de facto safe harbors, particularly in the areas where communities have defined their practice. But it also has large gray areas where those using emergent practices or willing to assume more risk may also go, within their rights. Those gray areas are where emerging practices can flourish and gradually move toward the center.

Copyright will continue to be intertwined with important choices we make about the future of culture. How long should copyrights be? How do we balance security, property protection, and access to culture? How should collectively produced work be honored, protected, and shared? How should we treat the products of folk and indigenous cultures? Both as users and as citizens, we should be part of the discussion about such issues, and we can be, if we understand the implications.

Conclusion

This era's version of copyright law is regrettably unbalanced in favor of current copyright holders, and against emergent culture of all kinds. New creators and users need to unlock their mind-forged manacles, assert the rights they have, and understand the vital importance of limiting copyright holders' rights. These limits are not a gift, but a requirement for the creation of tomorrow's culture. Everyone who uses those rights can see the need.

Every person who understands this is also, potentially, another member of a constituency for healthy and sound copyright policies and practices as they change (and they will; they always do). The copyright regime that took shape in the 1976 act and then tipped the copyright balance steadily through to the 1990s developed without significant citizen input. People simply did not realize what was at stake; the world of participatory media creation was still too new. In the name of expanding international trade and economic security, and buffaloed by moralistic talk about copying and stealing, they permitted a harshly limiting version of copyright policy to settle into place.

Fair use is not only the law of the land, but part of the package of free-speech rights we hold dear and an investment in our cultural future. People who use and respect fair use can better defend it, and also defend other policies that permit greater unfettered access to culture.

10 A Note on the International Environment

Do not fear copyright.   P. BERNT HUGENHOLTZ

Fair use is a US doctrine, and while most other nations' copyright laws also contain significant exemptions, few have a close equivalent to the flexible and adaptable doctrine of fair use. This can pose a challenge for people in the United States producing for an international audience, and it has created frustration among creative communities internationally that lack access to fair use. Some scholars have disparaged the value of fair use because it is only a national policy in an Internet world that crosses boundaries. Even so, when US creators have employed fair use, it has typically not been an impediment to international distribution. Some creators who work exclusively in an international environment, such as OpenCourseWare creators, have found that they can successfully rely on fair use to distribute materials globally. And the resurgence of fair use in the United States has creatively affected copyright policy discussion elsewhere.

Large companies may sometimes tailor their licensing practices to account for differences among national rules about copyright limitations and exceptions. In practical terms, however, US-based creators who work across international boundaries have rarely been deterred when they have invoked fair use to complete their work. This has to do more with the practical questions of risk than the technical legalities. Copyright litigation is far less common in other countries than it is in the United States. Moreover, most other countries do not have the statutory damages that make a wrong call so potentially punitive in the United States. Finally, the exceptions and limitations provisions of other nations' copyright policies might very well overlap with domestic fair-use claims.

Perhaps the most significant news in the international environment is not the practical fact that penalties for infringement are low and the risk of litigation even lower. The important news is that there is increasing interest in expanding the utility of limitations and exceptions in other nations. Copyright policy internationally, just as in the United States, is grounded in the public interest, as P. Bernt Hugenholtz and Ruth L. Okediji have argued. Monopolies given to creators are necessarily tempered with other measures—limitations and exceptions—that limit that monopoly. But how should the balance be struck? Each national copyright policy is grounded in that country's values and historical experience, and there is great variety in both the law and its interpretation. Most efforts at harmonization (as it is called in international treaty negotiations) of national limitations and exceptions have been directed more at constraining than enabling them. This has been part of the agenda of copyright industries in trade-based intellectual property negotiations.

There are three general approaches to limitations and exceptions. US-style fair use is a rarity, available elsewhere only in Israel (as of 2008) and the Philippines. Even copyright laws that include fair use have special exemptions—for instance, for libraries, education, the disabled. The fair-use provision backstops the specific exceptions, as well as covering unforeseen situations. So, for example, in the United States libraries may claim fair use for interlibrary loan practices that are not specifically permitted by their special exemptions.

A second approach is common throughout the British Commonwealth nations and in other former British colonies, combining specific exceptions with a provision allowing for so-called fair dealing—based on a weighing of factors similar to those at work in US fair-use analysis. Unlike fair use, fair dealing covers only some kinds of uses, typically those related to education or scholarship. Many uses undertaken by artists, remixers, video makers, even documentary filmmakers typically are not covered. Still, in the areas it covers fair dealing can be potent.

National copyright laws such as those of continental Europe take a third approach, by relying exclusively on creating specific exceptions and limitations. They may single out for special treatment, for example, not only certain library or educational uses, but also critical commentary, parody, pastiche, illustration, or even "fair quotation." Specific exemptions tend to be both limited and static, and often fail to reach some socially desirable uses of works. They may, for instance, exempt the use of print but not the use of images in some situations. They may specify that certain materials may be used in certain ways by certified teachers, but not by independent learners. On the other hand, this approach can be relatively secure; you will know better (if not perfectly) what you can and

Working across Borders: Three Questions

If I am making a work in the United States, can I apply fair use to material I take from other countries—say a clip from a Bollywood film, or a quote from a French text? You always operate under the law of the nation where you are. So if you are using material from another nation under fair use within the United States, you do not need to worry about the laws of that other nation.

   How about a coproduction or a US work distributed internationally? Do I have to make sure my work complies with every country's exemptions policy? In business practice, once a US standard has been met, rarely are copyright licensing issues raised again. This has more to do with the actual risk than with the law of copyright exceptions. Very few other countries have statutory damages. In most cases, a mistaken licensing decision results simply in agreeing to a copyright holder's demand for a standard fee. Furthermore, in most other countries, copyright lawsuits are extremely rare. Therefore, even large media companies do not expend much time or energy on questions of how to manage unlicensed use internationally.

   What if I want to incorporate third-party material under fair use, but my work is circulated internationally under a Creative Commons license? In that case, you simply have to make sure that users understand what in the work is covered by the CC license (that is, the material for which you own the copyright), and what you are fairly using (and therefore is not covered). Consumers have no issue at all; they may use the entire package at will. New international producers who excerpt or repurpose your CC'd work, honoring the conditions you stipulated, must make a decision to reuse the fairly used material under the laws of their own countries.

cannot do. In their narrow grooves, specific exemptions can cut deep. In turn, however, their visibility makes them a potential target of restrictive harmonization efforts, such as the one carried out in the 2001 European Union Information Society Directive.

   While content industry stakeholders have pushed hard to minimize and narrow exceptions, particularly in the European Union, at the same time there have been counterforces pushing to expand them. Wherever copyright reform is under discussion, expanding exemptions, including the policy of fair use, is one of the important issues being debated. The law now exempts parody and satire, and allows some noncommercial use by public-sector institutions such as universities, schools, and museums. In the United Kingdom, the 2006 Gowers Review, in its overall assessment of UK copyright law, suggested the adoption of transformative use as a standard for exceptions. In 2010, the British prime minister initiated a review of copyright policy, suggesting that adopting a fair-use standard could expand business opportunities and improve the British economy. At the international level, an initiative to develop some general norms for limitations and exceptions to benefit the print-disabled seem likely to succeed, as discussions among the many national delegations to WIPO suggest.

The biggest shadow cast over the expansion of limitations and exceptions is the so-called three-step test, stipulating that national legislatures and courts "shall confine limitations or exceptions to exclusive rights to *certain special cases* which *do not conflict with a normal exploitation of the work* and *do not unreasonably prejudice the legitimate interests of the right holder*" (italics added). Some version of this formulation has been a part of international copyright since 1971. In 1994, as part of the World Trade Organization Agreement, the three-part test was made generally applicable as a limit on all limitations and exceptions. Regrettably, more and more countries are also adopting the three-step test as part of their domestic copyright law. This is a purpose for which the standard was never intended. Because the language of the test is so general and open-ended, it is open to a range of interpretations. Copyright owners would like it to mean that whenever a copyright exception interferes with their realization of an actual or reasonably likely stream of revenue, that exception is invalid. On at least one occasion, the World Trade Organization seems to have adopted this approach. But it is far from inevitable, as Hugenholtz and Okediji argue. Alternative ways of reading the three-step test, which give weight to cultural as well as economic concerns, also are possible.

Articulate constituencies need to be developed for limitations and exceptions—not because these serve special interests but because the public interest is at stake here. The United States has emerged as a world leader in promoting long and strong copyright, but policymakers in other countries need to know that what has made US copyright (and copyright industries) successful is the fact that it balances strong protection and meaningful exceptions—thus clearing a space for artistic as well as technological innovation. So-called free-trade agreements negotiated by the United States generally are silent on the issue of fair use, while they mandate higher levels of copyright protection and enforcement. In the end, the choice is up to each government and each citizenry. Both international awareness of the importance of exemptions and limitations, and vigorous and public use of those that exist, are important.

Certainly international creator communities sparked into awareness by US fair-use activity have become political actors in their own countries. The first evidence of this was among documentary filmmakers, probably because documentarians typically produce for an international audience, and often coproduce internationally. The news of the power of fair use spread rapidly and internationally in this community, and prompted a range of reactions and projects.

Canadian filmmakers learned, partly through 2007 events at the documentary film festival Hot Docs, about the American experience of fair use. They were drawn to the way in which filmmakers had been able to help themselves. Through the national membership organization Documentary Organization of Canada, and with the help of Canadian legal scholar David Fewer, they conducted a member survey. Drawing on the *Untold Stories* methodology, they discovered the same pattern that US filmmakers did. They joined with others pressing for the expansion and bending of Canadian fair dealing to make it look and act more like American fair use.

In Europe in 2007, filmmakers enthralled with the US example decided to hold side meetings of producers and programmers at film festivals. This group of enthusiasts met in Rome in 2008, and organized, with our help, a survey of European filmmakers on their copyright problems. They discovered results similar to those of the United States: overlicensing, insecurity, altering of reality, and avoidance of projects based on licensing challenges. They formed what became the group AFACE, to press for the principles of fair use in documentary filmmaking.

Under the leadership of Marijke Rawie, a retired Dutch public television programmer, the group convinced the European Documentary Network and documentary members of the European Broadcasting Union to participate in a European Union docket on limitations and exemptions. The submission made clear the need to create exemptions that would be as useful for commercial producers as for noncommercial producers, and that could be both flexible and adaptable.

Researchers at Norway's University of Bergen emulated the research methods of the *Untold Stories* report, consulting with the Center for Social Media on research design. In 2009, the researchers, with support from a private Norwegian journalism foundation, held a conference in Bergen on the topic of creativity and copyright for filmmakers. European makers, researchers, and lawyers attended the event, which showcased the results of the study. Researchers had found results very similar to the US and pan-

European study, with overlicensing, confusion about rights to use unlicensed material, and avoidance of topics that involved a lot of licensing. Finally, they discovered that the Norwegian "right of quotation" had never been litigated for filmmaking, and that there was no interpretive history. The group decided to develop an interpretation with filmmakers and to involve other Scandinavian nations—each of which had an ample "right of quotation" clause—in developing a region-wide interpretation.

At the event, Dutch legal scholar Bernt Hugenholtz began and ended his presentation with a four-word mantra: "Do not fear copyright." He counseled that filmmakers and creators in general were far too wary of using unlicensed material. In practical terms, he pointed out, the risks and dangers were fairly low, given the lack of statutory damages and low level of litigation. Filmmakers had an unexplored opportunity to discover what national exemptions they did have, to use them, and to coordinate production with filmmakers whose exemptions matched up. Invoking their rights in this way would, at a minimum, help them discover the limits of the current system and provide valuable hard data for EU decision makers. It might create important interpretive precedents, since in Europe, as in the United States, the habits and practices of creative communities cannot help but weigh in any judicial interpretation of exemptions. And filmmakers would be able to use their nation's laws.

While the Norwegians were exploring national action on the right of quotation, South African filmmakers were doing the same. Assisted by Peter Jaszi and Sean Flynn from the Washington College of Law, and with support from the Ford Foundation, filmmakers' associations in South Africa researched their own problems with unlicensed material. Like the Americans and Norwegians, they discovered overlicensing, insecurity, inability to complete projects, and, as always, the most serious problem of avoiding projects that could entail unlicensed material. In a several-day conference, the filmmakers focused on South Africa's right of quotation and set about interpreting it to permit a top priority for the group: telling the most accurate, vivid, and moving stories from the apartheid and immediately postapartheid era in their nation.

In Israel, soon after the Israeli legislature adopted US-style fair use in 2008, professors and administrators in higher education worked together to craft a code of best practices in fair use within higher education. They used the process described in this book as their model.

International interest in limitations and exceptions is in some part due to the effectiveness of grassroots efforts in the United States within creator and user communities. It shows that communities can create viable interpretations of fair use, which then enable those communities to do their work, meet their missions, and accomplish progress in their fields more simply. Even in very different copyright regimes, with different underlying principles, one important and healthy response to long and strong copyright is to understand and exercise the rights that people do have.

Creative projects that span borders will continue to be complex— messier than anyone would like, like so much else in life. But citizens who know what their rights are, or who can show what is lost by not having better rights, can become part of constituencies for copyright that works to nurture, not constrain, the creation of culture.

Codes of Best Practices in Fair Use

Communities of practice are constantly developing codes of best practices in fair use. The Center for Social Media aggregates the codes that it and the Washington College of Law have facilitated and others we are aware of, at http://centerforsocialmedia.org/fair-use.

Codes include:

- *Code of Best Practices in Fair Use for Media Literacy Education*
- *Code of Best Practices in Fair Use for Online Video*
- *Code of Best Practices in Fair Use for OpenCourseWare*
- *Documentary Filmmakers' Statement of Best Practices in Fair Use*
- *Statement of Best Practices in Fair Use of Dance-Related Materials*
- *Society for Cinema and Media Studies' Statement of Best Practices for Fair Use in Teaching for Film and Media Educators*
- *Society for Cinema and Media Studies' Statement of Fair Use Best Practices for Media Studies Publishing*
- *Code of Best Practices in Fair Use for Poetry*

Forthcoming:

- *Code of Best Practices in Fair Use for Research Libraries*

A Template for a Code of Best Practices in Fair Use

Please feel free to use this template freely in your own code design. We would appreciate recognition, with a reference to this book, if you do employ it.

CODE OF BEST PRACTICES IN FAIR USE FOR _____

BY [entities involved in the creation] [Recognition of any funders]
DATE

INTRODUCTION

What This Is

This document is a code of best practices that helps _____ to interpret the copyright doctrine of fair use. Fair use is the right to use copyrighted material without permission or payment under some circumstances—especially when the cultural or social benefits of the use are predominant. It is a general right that applies even in situations where the law provides no specific authorization for the use in question.

This guide identifies _____ situations that represent the _____ community's current consensus about acceptable practices for the fair use of copyrighted materials.

What This Isn't

This code of best practices does not tell you the limits of fair-use rights. Instead, it describes how those rights should apply in certain recurrent situations. _____'s fair-use rights may, of course, extend to other situations as well.

It's not a guide to using material that people give the public permission to use, such as works covered by Creative Commons licenses. Anyone can use those works the way their owners authorize—although other uses also may also be permitted under the fair-use doctrine. Likewise, it is not a guide to the use of material that has been specifically licensed, which may be subject to contractual limitations.

It's not a guide to material that is already free to use without considering copyright (http://copyright.cornell.edu/public_domain/). For instance, all federal government works are in the public domain, as are many older works. For more information on "free use," consult the document "Yes, You Can!" (http://centerforsocialmedia.org/free-use).

It's not a guide to using material that someone wants to license but cannot trace back to an owner—the so-called "orphan works" problem. However, orphan works are also eligible for fair-use consideration, according to the principles detailed below. And it does not address the problems created by the 1998 Digital Millennium Copyright Act, which creates barriers to otherwise lawful fair uses of copyrighted materials that are available only in formats that incorporate technological protections measures (such as encryption).

How This Document Was Created

This code of best practices was created by [explain the process], involving [what kinds of people and how many]. [This statement shows how broadly your document involved the community.] The process was coordinated by _____. The code was reviewed by a committee of legal experts in copyright and fair use.

Characteristics of This Field

[In this section you will make clear why the requirements of the creative process involve use of copyrighted materials.]

Problems Often Encountered

[Here you will make clear the stumbling blocks people encountered when you did your research.]

Fair Use

Law provides copyright protection to creative works in order to foster the creation of culture. Its best known feature is protection of owners' rights. But copying, quoting, and generally reusing existing cultural material can be, under some circumstances, a critically important part of generating new culture. In fact, the cultural value of copying is so well established that it is written into the social bargain at the heart of copyright law. The bargain is this: we as a society give limited property rights to creators to encourage them to produce culture; at the same time, we give other creators the chance to use that same copyrighted material, without permission or payment, in some circumstances. Without the second half of the bargain, we could all lose important new cultural work.

Copyright law has several features that permit quotations from copyrighted works without permission or payment, under certain conditions. Fair use is the most important of these features. It has been an important part of copyright law for more than 170 years. Where it applies, fair use is a user's right. In fact, as the Supreme Court has pointed out, fair use keeps copyright from violating the First Amendment. New creation inevitably incorporates existing material. As copyright protects more works for longer periods than ever before, creators face new challenges: licenses to incorporate copyrighted sources become more expensive and more difficult to obtain—and sometimes are simply unavailable. As a result, fair use is more important today than ever before.

Copyright law does not exactly specify how to apply fair use, and that gives the fair-use doctrine a flexibility that works to the advantage of users. Creative needs and practices differ with the field, with technology, and with time. Rather than following a specific formula, lawyers and judges decide whether an unlicensed use of copyrighted material is "fair" according to a "rule of reason." This means taking all the facts and circumstances into account to decide if an unlicensed use of copyrighted material generates social or cultural benefits that are greater than the costs it imposes on the copyright owner.

Fair use is flexible; it is not unreliable. In fact, for any particular field of critical or creative activity, lawyers and judges consider expectations and practice in assessing what is "fair" within that field. In weighing the balance at the heart of fair-use analysis, judges refer to four types of considerations mentioned in the law: the nature of the use, the nature of the work used, the extent of the use, and its economic effect (the four factors). This still leaves much room for interpretation, especially since the law is clear that these are not the only permissible considerations. So how have judges interpreted fair use? In reviewing the history of fair-use litigation, we find that judges return again and again to two key questions:

- Did the unlicensed use "transform" the material taken from the copyrighted work by using it for a different purpose than that of the original, or did it just repeat the work for the same intent and value as the original?
- Was the material taken appropriate in kind and amount, considering the nature of the copyrighted work and of the use?

If the answers to these two questions are "yes," a court is likely to find a use fair. Because that is true, such a use is unlikely to be challenged in the first place.

Both key questions touch on, among other things, the question of whether the use will cause excessive economic harm to the copyright owner. Courts have told us that copyright owners aren't entitled to an absolute monopoly over transformative uses of their works. By the same token, however, when a use supplants a copyright owner's core market, it is unlikely to be fair. Thus, for example, a textbook author cannot quote large parts of a competitor's book merely to avoid the trouble of writing her own exposition. Another consideration underlies and influences the way in which these questions are analyzed: whether the user acted reasonably and in good faith, in light of general practice in his or her particular field.   's ability to rely on fair use will be enhanced by this code of best practices, which will serve as documentation of commonly held understandings drawn from the experience of _____ themselves and supported by legal analysis. Thus, the code helps to show that the uses of copyrighted materials described here are reasonable and appropriate for the purposes of _____.

Fair use is in wide and vigorous use today in many professional communities. For example, historians regularly quote both other historians' writings and textual sources; filmmakers and visual artists use, reinterpret, and critique copyright material; scholars illustrate cultural commentary with textual, visual, and musical examples. Equally important is the example of commercial news media. Fair use is healthy and vigorous in daily broadcast television news, where references to popular films, classic TV programs, archival images, and popular songs are constant and routinely unlicensed.

In some cases professional communities have set forth their understandings in consensus documents, which may be useful to _____if they are involved with these creative practices. Although professional groups create such codes, no one needs to be a member of a professional group to benefit from their interpretations.

CODE OF BEST PRACTICES IN FAIR USE FOR _____

General Points about Principles

This code of best practices identifies _____ sets of current practices in the use of copyrighted materials in _____, to which the doctrine of fair use clearly applies.

These situations may involve all forms of media. In all cases, a digital copy is the same as a hard copy in terms of fair use.

The situations concern the unlicensed fair use of copyrighted materials for education, not the way those materials were acquired. When a user's copy was obtained illegally or in bad faith, that fact may affect fair-use analysis. Otherwise, of course, where a use is fair, the origin is irrelevant.

The principles are all subject to a "rule of proportionality." _____'s fair-use rights extend to the portions of copyrighted works that they need to accomplish their goals—and sometimes even to small or short works in their entirety. By the same token, the fairness of a use depends, in part, on whether the user took more than was needed to accomplish his or her legitimate purpose. That said, there are no numerical rules of thumb that can be relied upon in making this determination.

Situations

ONE: [you name the situation]
DESCRIPTION: [you describe it]
PRINCIPLE: [you assert that fair use is able to be used to do what needs to be done in this situation]
limitations: [you describe the limits on what should be taken]
TWO: [you repeat]
Etc.

Fair Use Outside These Situations

These [number] situations do not exhaust the scope of fair use for _____. These are merely the most commonly recurring situations at the time that we created this document. In considering other situations, users should be guided by the same basic values of fairness, proportionality, and reasonableness that inform this statement. Where they are confident that a contemplated quotation of copyrighted material falls within fair use, they should claim fair use.

COORDINATORS: [names, titles, associations]
SIGNATORIES: [typically organizations]
LEGAL ADVISORY BOARD: [names, titles, locations]

Feel free to reproduce this work in its entirety. For excerpts and quotations, depend upon fair use.

Documentary Filmmakers' Statement of Best Practices in Fair Use

By the Association of Independent Video and Filmmakers, Independent Feature Project, International Documentary Association, National Alliance for Media Arts and Culture, and Women in Film and Video (Washington, D.C., chapter), in consultation with the Center for Social Media in the School of Communication at American University and the Program on Intellectual Property and the Public Interest in the Washington College of Law at American University, and endorsed by Arts Engine, the Bay Area Video Coalition, the Independent Television Service, P.O.V./American Documentary, and the University Film and Video Association.

This Statement of Best Practices in Fair Use makes clear what documentary filmmakers currently regard as reasonable application of the copyright "fair use" doctrine. Fair use expresses the core value of free expression within copyright law. The statement clarifies this crucial legal doctrine, to help filmmakers use it with confidence. Fair use is shaped, in part, by the practice of the professional communities that employ it. The statement is informed both by experience and ethical principles. It also draws on analogy: documentary filmmakers should have the same kind of access to copyrighted materials that is enjoyed by cultural and historical critics who work in print media and by news broadcasters.

Preamble

This Statement of Best Practices in Fair Use is necessary because documentary filmmakers have found themselves, over the last decade, increasingly constrained by demands to clear rights for copyrighted material. Creators in other disciplines do not face such demands to the same extent, and documentarians in earlier eras experienced them less often and less intensely. Today, however, documentarians believe that their ability to communicate effectively is being restricted by an overly rigid approach to copyright compliance, and that the public suffers as a result. The knowledge and perspectives that documentarians can provide are compromised by their need to select only the material that copyright holders approve and make available at reasonable prices.

At the same time, documentarians are themselves copyright holders, whose businesses depend on the willingness of others to honor their claims as copyright owners. They do not countenance exploitative or abusive applications of fair use, which might impair their own businesses or betray their work.

Therefore, documentarians through their professional organizations, supported by an advisory board of copyright experts, now offer the statement that follows.

Background

"Fair use" is a key part of the social bargain at the heart of copyright law, in which as a society we concede certain limited individual property rights to ensure the benefits of creativity to a living culture. We have chosen to encourage creators by rewarding their efforts with copyright. To promote new cultural production, however, it also is important to give other creators opportunities to use copyrighted material when they are making something new that incorporates or depends on such material. Unless such uses are possible, the whole society may lose important expressions just because one person is arbitrary or greedy. So copyright law has features that permit quotations from copyrighted works to be made without permission, under certain conditions. Fair use is the most important of these features. It has been an important part of copyright law for more than 150 years. Where it applies, fair use is a right, not a mere privilege. In fact, as the Supreme Court has pointed out, fair use helps reconcile copyright law with the First Amendment. As copyright protects more works for longer periods, it impinges more and more directly on creative practice. As a result, fair use is more important today than ever before. Creators benefit from the fact that the copyright law does not exactly specify how to apply fair use. Creative needs and practices differ with the field, with technology, and with time. Instead, lawyers and judges decide whether an unlicensed use of copyrighted material is "fair" according to a "rule of reason." This means taking all the facts and circumstances into account to decide if an unlicensed use of copyright material generates social or cultural benefits that are greater than the costs it imposes on the copyright owner. Fair use is flexible; it is not uncertain or unreliable. In fact, for any particular field of critical or creative activity, such as documentary filmmaking, lawyers and judges consider professional expectations and practice in assessing what is "fair" within the field. In weighing the balance at the heart of fair-use analysis, courts employ a four-part test, set out in the Copyright Act. In doing so, they return again and again to two key questions:

- Did the unlicensed use "transform" the material taken from the copyrighted work by using it for a different purpose than the original, or did it just repeat the work for the same intent and value as the original?
- Was the amount and nature of material taken appropriate in light of the nature of the copyrighted work and of the use?

Among other things, both questions address whether the use will cause excessive economic harm to the copyright owner. If the answers to these two questions are affirmative, a court is likely to find a use fair. Because that is true, such a use is unlikely to be challenged in the first place. Documentary films usually satisfy the "transformativeness" standard easily, because copyrighted material is typically used in a context different from that in which it originally appeared. Likewise, documentarians typically quote only short and isolated portions of copyrighted works. Thus, judges generally have honored documentarians' claims of fair use in the rare instances where they have been challenged in court.

Another consideration underlies and influences the way in which these questions are analyzed: Whether the user acted reasonably and in good faith, in light of general practice in his or her particular field. In the future, filmmakers' ability to rely on fair use will be further enhanced by the Statement of Best Practices in Fair Use that follows. This statement serves as evidence of commonly held understandings in documentary practice and helps to demonstrate the reasonableness of uses that fall within its principles.

Documentarians find other creator groups' reliance on fair use heartening. For instance, historians regularly quote both other historians' writings and textual sources; artists reinterpret and critique existing images (rather than merely appropriating them); scholars illustrate cultural commentary with textual, visual, and musical examples. Equally important is the example of the news media: fair use is healthy and vigorous in daily broadcast television, where references to popular films, classic TV programs, archival images, and popular songs are constant and routinely unlicensed.

The statement that follows describes the actual practice of many documentarians, joined with the views of others about what would be appropriate if they were free to follow their own understanding of good practice. In making films for TV, cable, and theaters, documentarians who assert fair use often meet with resistance. All too frequently they are told (often by nonlawyers) that they must clear "everything" if they want their work to reach the public. Even so, some documentarians have not been intimidated. Unfortunately, until now the documentarians who depend on fair use generally have done so quietly, in order to avoid undesired attention.

In this statement, documentarians are exercising their free-speech rights—and their rights under copyright—in the open. This statement does not address the problems that result from lack of access to archival material that is best quality or the only copy. The statement applies to situations where the filmmaker has ready access to the necessary material in some form.

The statement also does not directly address the problem of "orphan works"—works presumably copyrighted but whose owners cannot be located with reasonable effort.

Generally, it should be possible to make fair use of orphan works on the same basis as clearly sourced ones. Sometimes, however, filmmakers also may wish to use orphan works in ways that exceed fair use. A more comprehensive solution for orphan works may soon be provided through an initiative spearheaded by the US Copyright Office (for more information, see http://www.copyright.gov/orphan).

This statement finally does not concern "free use"—situations when documentarians never need to clear rights. Examples of types of free use are available in documents at http://centerforsocialmedia.org/fair-use.

The Statement

This statement recognizes that documentary filmmakers must choose whether or not to rely on fair use when their projects involve the use of copyrighted material. It is organized around four classes of situations that they confront regularly in practice. (These four classes do not exhaust all the likely situations where fair use might apply; they reflect the most common kinds of situations that documentarians identified at this point.) In each case, a general principle about the applicability of fair use is asserted, followed by qualifications that may affect individual cases. The four classes of situations, with their informing principles and limitations, follow on the next page.

ONE: Employing copyrighted material as the object of social, political, or cultural critique

DESCRIPTION: This class of uses involves situations in which documentarians engage in media critique, whether of text, image, or sound works. In these cases, documentarians hold the specific copyrighted work up for critical analysis.

PRINCIPLE: Such uses are generally permissible as an exercise of documentarians' fair-use rights. This is analogous to the way that (for example) a newspaper might review a new book and quote from it by way of illustration. Indeed, this activity is at the very core of the fair-use doctrine as a safeguard for freedom of expression. So long as the filmmaker analyzes or comments on the work itself, the means may vary. Both direct commentary and parody, for example, function as forms of critique. Where copyrighted material is used for a critical purpose, the fact that the critique itself may do economic damage to the market for the quoted work (as a negative book review could) is irrelevant. In order to qualify as fair use, the use may be as extensive as is necessary to make the point, permitting the viewer to fully grasp the criticism or analysis.

LIMITATIONS: There is one general qualification to the principle just stated. The use should not be so extensive or pervasive that it ceases to function as critique and becomes, instead, a way of satisfying the audience's taste for the thing (or the kind of thing) critiqued. In other words, the critical use should not become a market substitute for the work (or other works like it).

TWO: Quoting copyrighted works of popular culture to illustrate an argument or point

DESCRIPTION: Here the concern is with material (again of whatever kind) that is quoted not because it is, in itself, the object of critique but because it aptly illustrates some argument or point that a filmmaker is developing—as clips from fiction films might be used (for example) to demonstrate changing American attitudes toward race.

PRINCIPLE: Once again, this sort of quotation should generally be considered as fair use. The possibility that the quotes might entertain and engage an audience as well as illustrate a filmmaker's argument takes nothing away from the fair-use claim. Works of popular culture typically have illustrative power, and in analogous situations, writers in print media do not hesitate to use illustrative quotations (both words and images). In documentary filmmaking, such a privileged use will be both subordinate to the larger intellectual or artistic purpose of the documentary and important to its realization. The filmmaker is not presenting the quoted material for its original purpose but harnessing it for a new one. This is an attempt to add significant new value, not a form of "free riding"—the mere exploitation of existing value.

LIMITATIONS: Documentarians will be best positioned to assert fair-use claims if they assure that

- the material is properly attributed, either through an accompanying on-screen identification or a mention in the film's final credits;
- to the extent possible and appropriate, quotations are drawn from a range of different sources;
- each quotation (however many may be employed to create an overall pattern of illustrations) is no longer than is necessary to achieve the intended effect;
- the quoted material is not employed merely in order to avoid the cost or inconvenience of shooting equivalent footage.

THREE: Capturing copyrighted media content in the process of filming something else

DESCRIPTION: Documentarians often record copyrighted sounds and images when they are filming sequences in real-life settings. Common examples are the text of a poster on a wall, music playing on a radio, and television programming heard (perhaps seen) in the background. In the context of the documentary, the incidentally captured material is an integral part of the ordinary reality being documented. Only by altering and thus falsifying the reality they film—such as telling subjects to turn off the radio, take down a poster, or turn off the TV—could documentarians avoid this.

PRINCIPLE: Fair use should protect documentary filmmakers from being forced to falsify reality. Where a sound or image has been captured incidentally and without prevision, as part of an unstaged scene, it should be permissible to use it, to a reasonable extent, as part of the final version of the film. Any other rule would be inconsistent with the documentary practice itself and with the values of the disciplines (such as criticism, historical analysis, and journalism) that inform reality-based filmmaking.

LIMITATIONS: Consistent with the rationale for treating such captured media uses as fair ones, documentarians should take care that

- particular media content played or displayed in a scene being filmed was not requested or directed;
- incidentally captured media content included in the final version of the film is integral to the scene/action;
- the content is properly attributed;
- the scene has not been included primarily to exploit the incidentally captured content in its own right, and the captured content does not constitute the scene's primary focus of interest;
- in the case of music, the content does not function as a substitute for a synch track (as it might, for example, if the sequence containing the captured music were cut on its beat, or if the music were used after the filmmaker has cut away to another sequence).

FOUR: Using copyrighted material in a historical sequence

DESCRIPTION: In many cases the best (or even the only) effective way to tell a particular historical story or make a historical point is to make selective use of words that were spoken during the events in question, music that was associated with the events, or photographs and films that were taken at that time. In many cases, such material is available, on reasonable terms, under license. On occasion, however, the licensing system breaks down.

PRINCIPLE: Given the social and educational importance of the documentary medium, fair use should apply in some instances of this kind. To conclude otherwise would be to deny the potential of filmmaking to represent history to new generations of citizens. Properly conditioned, this variety of fair use is critical to fulfilling the mission of copyright. But unless limited, the principle also can defeat the legitimate interests of copyright owners—including documentary filmmakers themselves.

LIMITATIONS: To support a claim that a use of this kind is fair, the documentarian should be able to show that

- the film project was not specifically designed around the material in question;
- the material serves a critical illustrative function, and no suitable substitute exists (that is, a substitute with the same general characteristics);
- the material cannot be licensed, or the material can be licensed only on terms that are excessive relative to a reasonable budget for the film in question;

- the use is no more extensive than is necessary to make the point for which the material has been selected;
- the film project does not rely predominantly or disproportionately on any single source for illustrative clips;
- the copyright owner of the material used is properly identified.

Fair Use in Other Situations Faced by Documentarians

The four principles just stated do not exhaust the scope of fair use for documentary filmmakers. Inevitably, actual filmmaking practice will give rise to situations that are hybrids of those described above or that simply have not been anticipated. In considering such situations, however, filmmakers should be guided by the same basic values of fairness, proportionality, and reasonableness that inform this statement. Where they are confident that a contemplated quotation of copyrighted material falls within fair use, they should claim fair use.

Some Common Misunderstandings about Fair Use

As already indicated, two goals of the preceding statement are to encourage documentarians to rely on fair use where it is appropriate and to help persuade the people who insure, distribute, and program their work to accept and support documentarians in these choices. Some common errors about fair use and its applicability may stand in the way of accomplishing these goals. Briefly, then, here are some correctives to these misunderstandings:

- Fair use need not be exclusively high-minded or "educational" in nature. Although nonprofit or academic uses often have good claims to be considered "fair," they are not the only ones. A new work can be "commercial"—even highly commercial—in intent and effect and still invoke fair use. Most of the cases in which courts have found unlicensed uses of copyrighted works to be fair have involved projects designed to make money, including some that actually have.
- Fair use doesn't have to be boring. A use is no less likely to qualify as a fair one because the film in which it occurs is effective in attracting and holding an audience. If a use otherwise satisfies the principles and limitations described in the Statement of Best Practices in Fair Use, the fact that it is entertaining or emotionally engaging should be irrelevant to the analysis.

- A documentarian's failed effort to clear rights doesn't inhibit his
  or her ability to claim fair use with respect to the use in question.
  Everyone likes to avoid conflict and reduce uncertainty. Often, there
  will be good reasons to seek permissions in situations where they
  may not literally be required. In general, then, it never hurts to try,
  and it actually can help demonstrate the filmmaker's good faith. And
  sometimes (as in connection with Principle Four) it can be critically
  important.

Legal Advisory Board

Professor Julie E. Cohen
Georgetown University Law Center
Washington, D.C.

Michael C. Donaldson, Esq.
Donaldson & Hart
Los Angeles, California

Professor Michael J. Madison
University of Pittsburgh School of Law
Pittsburgh, Pennsylvania

Gloria C. Phares, Esq.
Patterson Belknap Webb & Tyler
New York, New York

J. Stephen Sheppard, Esq.
DeBaets, Abrahams & Sheppard
New York, New York

Authoring Organizations

Association of Independent Video and Filmmakers (AIVF)

Works to increase creative and professional opportunities for independent video and filmmakers and to enhance the growth of independent media by providing services, advocacy, and information.

Independent Feature Project (IFP)

Fosters a sustainable infrastructure that supports independent filmmaking and ensures that the public has the opportunity to see films that more accurately reflect the full diversity of the American culture.

International Documentary Association (IDA)

Promotes nonfiction film and video around the world by supporting and recognizing the efforts of documentary film and video makers, increasing public appreciation and demand for the documentary, and providing a forum for documentary makers, their supporters, and suppliers.

National Alliance for Media Arts and Culture (NAMAC)

Provides education, advocacy, and networking opportunities for the independent media field.

Women in Film and Video (WIFV), Washington, D.C., Chapter

Works to advance the professional development and achievement for women working in all areas of film, television, video, multimedia, and related disciplines.

Academic Consulting Organizations

Center for Social Media

Showcases and analyzes media for social justice, civil society and democracy, and the public environment that nurtures them, in the School of Communication at American University in Washington, D.C.

Program on Intellectual Property and the Public Interest

Sponsors events and activities designed to promote awareness of the social, economic, and cultural implications of domestic and international intellectual property law, in the Washington College of Law at American University.

Endorsers

Arts Engine
Bay Area Video Coalition
CINE
Doculink
Electronic Arts Intermix
Grantmakers in Film and Electronic Media
Full Frame Documentary Festival
Independent Television Service (ITVS)
P.O.V./American Documentary
University Film and Video Association (UFVA)
Video Association of Dallas
Women Make Movies

Funders

The Rockefeller Foundation
The John D. and Catherine T. MacArthur Foundation
Additional support from: Grantmakers in Film and Electronic Media

For more information, consult http://centerforsocialmedia.org/fair-use.
Please feel free to reproduce this in its entirety. For excerpts, employ fair
use or contact socialmedia@american.edu.

Myths and Realities about Fair Use

MYTH: Fair Use is valid only when it is noncommercial.

REALITY: Fair use is designed to expand the range of cultural production, not just the range of noncommercial cultural production. Almost all the occasional litigation on fair use, which has determined this legal trend of interpretation, has been over commercial uses. (Generally lawsuits aren't begun if there is no money to be gained.) Fair uses can be made of copyrighted material in any commercial context, so long as the four factors of consideration tilt toward the value of new contributions to culture against the cost to current owners. Currently the simplest calculation, the one preferred by the courts, is to find transformation (reuse for a different purpose), and to make sure that only as much of the original has been used as is necessary for the transformation; this is best done with a justification for the habits and practices of a particular creative or user community.

MYTH: Any noncommercial use is fair.

REALITY: The law does privilege such uses in some cases, but you will unfortunately today be in a gray zone if you lean exclusively on the fact that you're not selling your work. That is especially true in online situations, where you may not be making money off your work but somebody else is—usually an advertiser placing ads on a site, or a data miner. Besides, giving work away that contains valuable pieces of other people's work can indeed hurt someone else's pocketbook. If you have a legitimate fair-use claim, that pocketbook problem can be overridden (depending on how severe it is). Simply not making money does not give you a fair-use pass.

MYTH: Fair use is always valid if you're using copyrighted material in an educational context, and especially within a classroom.

REALITY: Being a good guy is not necessarily enough. Educational uses have their own special exemptions, but fair use in any educational context will have to abide by the same logic as in other contexts. However, because fair-use analysis is always done, implicitly or explicitly, within the context of a community of practice, you can refer to the mission and needs of your field. Educational contexts provide some very easy justifications for transformation (such as that students are analyzing the content). Educators need to pay particular attention to their claims to fair use if they are using commercial materials explicitly designed for their educational environment. In that case, an educator's use might not be transformative.

MYTH: Fair use is only about criticism and commentary, such as parody. REALITY: Criticism, commentary, satire, and parody are all great examples of ways in which copyrighted material is reused for a different purpose than for its original market, in the process of creating more culture. (How does satire differ from parody? They are closely related. Parody imitates a particular work, usually for the sake of funny commentary. Satire usually makes ironic fun at anything, including behavior.) But they are not the only kinds of activities that qualify as transformative fair use. Pastiche without a specific point to make—a collage or mashup—can also be a fair use. So might quotation for discussion—and much more.

MYTH: Fair use is just "the right to hire a lawyer." REALITY: In fact, fair use is no vaguer or unclear than other rights of free expression. As with questions of libel, indecency, or obscenity, there are clear areas of comfort and safety, marginal or risky areas, and troublesome areas. Most people most of the time know where they are. Your greatest comfort is in knowing that your peers in a community of practice have already agreed upon standards of interpretation. Many people have taken the comment of legal scholar Lawrence Lessig, made at the beginning of the twenty-first century, that "fair use is only the right to hire a lawyer" at face value and repeated it many times since. But Lessig made that remark before the beginning of the current efforts by communities of practice to exercise their fair-use rights. This has greatly clarified safe interpretations of fair use for many communities. Indeed, he made that statement before he himself founded the Fair Use Project at Stanford, which encourages wider interpretation of fair use.

MYTH: Fair use needs a really good test case in the courts, to set precedent.

REALITY: There are several reasons why we shouldn't wait for litigation to improve our access to fair use. First, fair use is only occasionally litigated; this is particularly true now, since fair use is regarded with such favor by judges. Copyright holders with good lawyers understand that any greater record of the usability of fair use may only encourage more fair use. Second, any particular lawsuit may be an outlier in any direction to a trend. Third, when you initiate a lawsuit, much can happen that confuses or changes the story, muddying the judgment you wanted to get. For instance, the artist Shepard Fairey seemed to have a very clear fair-use right to use a photograph of Barack Obama for a poster. But during preparations for the trial, he admitted lying about the photograph he used, creating great distrust and prejudicing his case. Far better than waiting for a definitive test case is establishing clear standards of interpretation. Such standards can be highly useful in any ensuing litigation.

MYTH: Fair use is too dangerous; even if you win a lawsuit, your life and finances could be ruined.
REALITY: This conclusion is drawn from two common but unfortunate practices: looking only at lawsuits, not at practice; and lumping together all kinds of intellectual property conflicts. If you only look at lawsuits, you will only see danger. If you look at lawsuits in context, you will see them as the very occasional and circumscribed circumstance in a wide sea of perfectly legal and uncontested practice. In reality, people are employing fair use casually and comfortably every single day across the nation, often without thinking about it, and they get into no trouble at all. They are in the safe-harbor areas of fair use. In the rare event of a copyright lawsuit, defendants have a solid phalanx of pro bono lawyers who are eager to litigate on fair use, including the Stanford Fair Use Project, the ACLU, EFF, and some intellectual property clinics. Courts strongly encourage settlement and discourage trials. Finally, anyone who proceeds with litigation has rejected plenty of opportunities to settle for relatively small costs. But the most important thing to remember is that lawsuits are extremely rare, the exception to the rule.

People frequently confuse one kind of danger with another. For instance, the RIAA has sued a clutch of average-citizen downloaders. By means of a few strategic lawsuits, the RIAA attempted to create publicity and public awareness about the illegality of downloading copyrighted material available for sale. These lawsuits did not significantly impede downloading, while racking up enormous legal bills for the RIAA and others. But the RIAA's case against downloaders addressed a different problem than most people face in applying fair use in creating new work.

Downloaders were simply accessing for free material that they could buy, typically to use in exactly the way it was being marketed. The music industry may be backward-looking, but its legal case was technically sound. It was not grounded in fair-use arguments. Fair users do not need to be frightened of RIAA lawsuits.

MYTH: Fair use is just a defense, not a right.

REALITY: Fair use is in fact a right that comes into play once someone accuses you of infringement. At that point, you would respond by saying that you had a right to use that material. Until then, everyone is simply going along minding their own business, creating culture. The right of defense occurs in other contexts as well. For instance, if you are physically attacked, you have the right of self-defense. This right never comes into play until you are both attacked and someone accuses you of hurting them. Then you will invoke your right of self-defense. The fact that fair use is a defense does not make it any less of a right.

MYTH: Fair use is just an interpretation, not part of the law.

REALITY: Fair use is neither new nor a mere interpretation. A 150-year-old feature of the law (and widely exercised before that, without being explicitly invoked), it is a key element of a policy dedicated to promoting culture. Fair use is an essential tool for us to be able to exercise our First Amendment rights.

MYTH: I can't use fair use, because the copyright holders would never agree to it.

REALITY: Fair use is a right that you employ simply by accessing material, copying it, and incorporating it into your project within an appropriate context. You do not need to get anyone's permission to do that, and you do not even need to let them know that you did it. Some legitimate and uncontested claims of fair use are even made after one or more attempts to license; the attempt to license may even increase one's case for fair use, if the material is vital to what you are trying to say. Some people like to alert the people whose work they took, as a gesture of respect or homage, and this act of politeness is very often deeply appreciated. Sometimes they may want to alert a vendor or archives holder of their fair use, because they have an ongoing business relationship that involves licensing, they may want to eliminate ambiguity about the use, and they may want to stay on the best terms possible.

Answers to Fair Use: You Be the Judge

PTA Flyer (p. xiii)

This will be an informational document, oriented to members of a non-profit organization, but it also is promoting a commercial activity (selling books). You won't be able simply to argue that this is noncommercial use; besides, that is never a sufficient reason for fair use. So apply the reasoning described on page 24. Ask yourself: why are you using those book covers? Is it merely to decorate the flyer? That is a weak answer. Do you intend to illustrate the kind of activity being described? That is a stronger answer, because you are showing how you are repurposing the original purpose of the book cover. Are you reproducing a range of covers, thus demonstrating a range of choice—for instance, age groups represented, hardcovers, board books, paperbacks in popular series? If so, that is a strong example of how you are repurposing, or transforming. Are you using rather small reproductions, for instance low-resolution thumbnails pulled from the Internet? If so, this demonstrates how you are using amounts of the material appropriate to the purpose. Asking yourself these questions, you can create a strong fair-use argument; it might be helpful to you, and save time in the future, to keep a note of your thinking. Once it is a fair use, it really doesn't matter what medium it is in. Could you be challenged with, say, a cease-and-desist letter? It is not impossible, but the likelihood is so remote that it should not trouble you. In the event anyone ever did challenge you or the PTA, you and the PTA would respond confidently with the answers you had created by asking yourself these questions.

Blogging (p. 6)

Bloggers routinely excerpt and share limited amounts of other bloggers' and other news sources' material. Not every reference to other people's information necessarily triggers fair use; for instance, you can always put in web links without worrying about copyright law. If you are embedding content, you'll apply fair-use reasoning. You will ask yourself, What new purpose am I putting this material to? How much do I need for that purpose? The material you want is designed to inform the public about food safety issues. If you want merely to share that information, you are safest providing a description in your own words and a link. After all, you are performing the same service—informing the public about topical food safety issues—as the original material. If the material is otherwise unavailable, you may have a stronger case, particularly if you add value to it in some way, for instance by commenting on it. If the material is not designed for this purpose (for instance, a scene in a TV program that demonstrates a common myth about food safety), you also have a stronger argument for using the appropriate amount within this changed context. If what you want to do is not merely to aggregate current news but to comment on or critique a particular kind of news coverage, then you may have an argument for employing more of the material, possibly even the entire broadcast segment or newspaper article. In any case, attribution is a polite and useful gesture (links are, effectively, attribution, but otherwise you would be wise to make sure your readers know where you got that material). And in all cases, there is no need to contact the original source, whether you are merely linking to them or quoting them in part or in whole. You may want to do so for other reasons—developing potential partnerships or exchanges, for example.

TV Program (p. 22)

You might want to start by consulting the *Documentary Filmmakers' Statement of Best Practices in Fair Use* (at http://centerforsocialmedia.org/fair-use). The understanding of fair use in documentary production described there is relevant whether the work is on television or in a theater or on DVD. Your use here is related to the statement's second category, of illustration. You have a clear new purpose that would "transform" your use of the old and new films, so you are in fair-use range. Now you just need to take a good look at how much you are using, whether you are using only what you need, and whether what you are using demonstrates the new point you are making. In that introductory montage, is the link between what you are quoting and the subject matter of your program clear, or is that material designed just to tickle the viewer's eye and keep him there past the commercial? Do the montages make the point you want to make? Have you made clear—perhaps in surrounding narration or setup—what point this montage is intended to make? You don't need to worry about contracting with celebrities for permission (or paying residuals), because when you fairly use material, you do not inherit any of the contractual obligations to the talent that the original maker entered into. To avoid any problems with rights of publicity, however, you should be sure not to use unlicensed celebrity images in the advertising and promotion of your program.

Fan Site (p. 29)

You might want to start by reading the *Code of Best Practices in Fair Use for Online Video*, which describes some common fair-use situations. Two of them are relevant to you: discussion and comment/critique. As a fan, you are making a commentary on *Lost*; don't forget, criticism can be positive as well as negative. Should you post the entire episode on your website? This is a big decision, not only because you want to obey the law, but also because there is corporate surveillance on the web and you may be challenged by *Lost*'s owner, ABC. You need a reason to use it, one that demonstrates how you are repurposing and justifies the amount you are using. You have a repurposing reason. As a fan, you selected this episode as uniquely significant. Now, you need to ask yourself: Do you need the whole episode to make your point? Could you achieve that goal by selecting relevant portions and commenting on them? If you can reach your goal with excerpts, that is the smart and safe approach. If not, you need a reason others can understand. In any case, it will be smart to integrate the reasons why you chose the material into the fan site—which likely you are intending to do anyway. By the way, if you were dealing with a very hard-to-come-by piece of work not in commercial distribution, instead of a series that is sold on all platforms, you might be able to make a fair-use case (as the code suggests) for archiving work on the web.

Public Radio News (p. 44)

Many gatekeepers believe that hard numbers govern decisions about fair use. Gatekeepers sometimes also say you can never use a work in its entirety under fair use. They are wrong on both counts, as the *Code of Best Practices in Fair Use for Media Literacy Education* explains. This is always a case-by-case decision based on the reasons for your reuse of the material and the amount you are choosing, as well as other considerations such as noncommerciality and the nature of what you are taking. In this case, you have been given bad information. There is no "10 percent" or "30 second" rule. You also don't get a special break, in this case, because you work in public radio, but you don't need one either. Although public broadcasting does have some special exemptions, this is a situation where you need to make up your own mind. To help your reasoning, you should refer to the questions on page 24. You are already comfortable, as most journalists are, employing fair use for quoting excerpts of copyrighted material. Your problem is with the whole amount. Ask yourself: Do you have a good reason for playing all of this commercial? Do you need for the listener to hear the entire thing to grasp the points you are making in the reporting? Will you make it easy for the listener to understand why they need to hear the whole thing? Your answers to these questions will determine your choice. You can then go back and help educate the person who gave you that misinformation. It won't hurt to make a note for yourself of your reasoning; if anyone within your station or beyond it ever challenges your choice, you'll be able to show them you thought about this, and had good reasons.

Orphaned Material (p. 59)

You are probably using copyrighted material, unless it is so old that it has fallen into the public domain (see p. 33). And you probably need to do more than a quick Google search to make a good-faith effort to find the owner. But after you have, you still may not be able to find the owner. Then you're dealing with an "orphan work," copyrighted material whose owner is missing. Current copyright law makes no special provision for using orphan works. You may, in that case, want to employ fair use, which is available for any kind of material, including orphan works. You might want to start by consulting the *Documentary Filmmakers' Statement of Best Practices in Fair Use* (appendix C of this book and at http://centerforsocial media.org/fair-use). You will find the second (illustrative) and fourth (archival) categories useful. You will want to ask what your reason is for employing this material. Are you using the photos and images of letters to further the explanation you are making in the documentary part of the film? Are they important to that explanation? Some of your film is fictional. While fair use has been employed in fiction films, many of the arguments for fair use in documentary would not apply. In the fiction part of this film, you probably have enough opportunity to create material that you do not need to consider using this material under fair use. It is also worth remembering that the law specifies the effect of the use on the market as one consideration that influences fair-use decision making. When a work is truly "orphaned," then—by definition—its owners aren't making a licensing market for its use. This could add additional punch to your argument for fair use.

Video Games (p. 66)

You have a clear fair-use argument for using screenshots in your book, as film scholars and communication scholars assert in their codes of best practices (available at http://centerforsocialmedia.org/fair-use). Similar uses for illustrative purposes, connected to the arguments of your book, on the website will be fair uses under the same logic. Please consult these codes for their principles and limitations, and then ask yourself questions about how you work within those terms. As for the machinima: Often, people who produce machinima produce it with a license from the video game maker. Then they are hostage to whatever conditions the video game maker imposes. In this case, though, you have impressively gained access to the material without such a license, so you can entertain the question of fair use. You have a clear transformative purpose. You are using this material both to illustrate the form and to further explore an argument you are making about the form. You need to ask yourself how much of this material you need for these two transformative purposes. For instance, you may have designed a narrative in machinima that explores or extends the argument within the form you are describing. In this case, you may have a strong argument for using video game characters in an extended sequence. The fact that you have tried to license this material does not alter your claim to fair use. Indeed, having asked and been turned down may actually improve your argument, since it means that you are not depriving the owner of licensing revenue, and at least suggests that that owner may have a noneconomic reason for rejecting your request. If the rejection is content-based, your argument is strengthened further.

YouTube Takedown (p. 71)

You need to revisit your arguments for your fair use of this material. You can get help by consulting the *Code of Best Practices in Fair Use for Online Video*. Then, if you are still confident that your uses were fair, you can find out what kind of removal it was. The Electronic Frontier Foundation has great online resources (for instance, http://www.eff.org/issues/intellectual -property/guide-to-youtube-removals) to help you figure it out. If you are confident that you have a good reason, depending on the kind of removal you can issue a dispute or a counternotice. A dispute is a simple explanation to YouTube of your fair-use reason for using the material, and it is usually resolved very quickly. In the case of a counternotice, you will have to provide information and agree to resolve the dispute in your local federal court as a jurisdiction should the copyright holder sue you—no matter how unlikely that may be. There was no evidence of a single lawsuit of a copyright holder against a typical YouTube user, as of 2010. If the copyright holder does not contest your claim, the video goes right back up.

Music in Curricula (p. 75)

You are concerned not about the performance (which you will record with written permission), but about the music. This music, since it's classical, could well be in the public domain, and you wouldn't even need fair use. But the orchestra might be using a recent arrangement of the music, which might still be under copyright. (Whether arrangements are actually copyright-protected is in some dispute.) So you need to find out the copyright status of the arrangement they are using. If it is under copyright, then you need to consider whether fair use could apply. The *Code of Best Practices in Fair Use for Media Literacy Education*, and especially its first and second categories, may give you some help with your fair-use reasoning, even though it wasn't designed for music teachers. You will ask yourself, Why are you excerpting the orchestra? What do you want your students to take away from this segment? How will you help them to understand what to get out of the segment? The answers to those questions will help you understand how you are repurposing the orchestra's performance, which we assume was executed in order to share with music-loving listeners a piece of music. They will also guide you as you ask yourself how much of the musical performance you need. Because you will be explaining your pedagogical purpose when you excerpt this material, the logic of your repurposing will be clear.

Checklists (p. 83)

No, the most helpful approach will be to help people understand the reasoning that governs a fair-use decision, summarized in the questions on page 24. People love checklists, because they hope that the lists will do their fair-use reasoning for them. But checklists tend to be more trouble than help. Sometimes a checklist simply discourages fair use in situations where the user might have an adequate rationale not captured by the list. More often, checklists simply lead to further confusion. Focused on the four factors, they treat the factors as if they had a concreteness that they do not. Those four factors have been widely interpreted by judges over the years. Professors are fully capable of making reasoned decisions about what to post to their own class sites. This is a particularly safe environment, too. These sites are typically passworded and limited only to students enrolled in the class. The professors should ask if the material selected is being repurposed, and if so what that repurpose is, associated with their teaching objective for the class. Then they will ask if the amount taken is appropriate to their need. Where they may need help is in knowing which of the materials they are using were designed specifically for the educational environment they are teaching in (for instance a text written for their subject), and if any of the media they use was licensed with terms that rule out fair use.

Curriculum (p. 111)

You may want to start by consulting the *Code of Best Practices in Fair Use for Media Literacy Education*, which wasn't designed for biology teachers but may help you with your reasoning. The first two sections, on employing copyrighted material in classes and curriculum, may give you some analogies. In regard to the quotations, you will ask yourself: What purpose do you have for aggregating these quotations in your slide show? You have a specific educational purpose, and you have harvested them from a variety of places. Do you need all of the material you are quoting? You will have selected certain parts of these quotes in order to demonstrate your purpose. If you have good answers to these questions, then you are in the fair-use zone. You probably want to make sure that somewhere in that slide show, maybe on the slides themselves or at the end, you provide a citation to the works you used. That will also model appropriate behavior in research for your students. If your fair-use reasoning is solid enough for the classroom, it will be just as durable for sharing with other teachers and students. If you are making it available to the general public, you need to make sure that the educational context of your use is crystal clear.

School Projects (p. 117)

You are in luck, because you can consult the *Code of Best Practices in Fair Use for Media Literacy Education*, designed specifically for your community of practice. You'll want to look at the fourth and fifth categories of the code, concerning student work and its distribution. The code notes, for instance, that "students may use copyrighted music for a variety of purposes, but cannot rely on fair use when their goal is simply to establish a mood or convey an emotional tone, or when they employ popular songs simply to exploit their appeal and popularity." You will want to design a policy that works both within and beyond the classroom, since you hope that your students will produce good enough work that it can be shared beyond the classroom, and also you know that they probably will share it in any case. If your students want to use entire songs and they can still make a strong fair-use argument for them (rather than just relying on their love of that music), they may be operating in a fair-use gray zone that is increasingly well-inhabited and may be close to the fair-use safe harbor zone of the codes.

Parody and Satire in Slideshows (p. 138)

Parody and satire are so closely related that it can be hard to tell the difference, but both are different from just being funny. When you parody, you need to be referring to a text, which can include a performance, because you're imitating it with a critical purpose related to the specific text. Satire is typically focused on behavior not necessarily contained in a specific text. Your project sounds like satire. In this case, you have a range of purposes. You are mocking politicians by developing ridiculous versions of their names. This does not involve copyright, and since they are public figures you are free to make fun of them. Regarding photographs, we're presuming you took those pictures and therefore own the copyright for them; and we're presuming you took pictures of a public event. So you have no issues; you are free to use that material. If you are using someone else's photograph—for instance, a picture off a newspaper's website—then you have copyright questions. You will need to ask what different purpose you are using it for, and whether your use conflicts with a reasonable after-market for a topical photograph. Your argument here is that you are incorporating it into a musical revue that is critical of election practices. Next you'll ask if your use is limited to what you need to make a point. So you might have an excellent rationale for one photograph or for a montage of photographs describing a range of, or pervasive, behavior. Or you might have only one point to make and need only one photo to make that point. Finally, you want to include cartoons. These too are copyrighted. Once again, will your use be different from the original purpose of the cartoons? If you just want to use them to make or reinforce your political point, it may be hard to justify fair use, because you are repeating the original purpose of the cartoon. But if you are using the cartoons, for example, to demonstrate that many different perspectives emerged about a particular political act, you would have a strong fair-use argument.

REFERENCE LIST

Aoki, K., J. Boyle, et al. 2008. *Bound by Law? Tales from the Public Domain*. Durham, NC: Duke University Press.

Aufderheide, P., and P. Jaszi. 2004. *Untold Stories: Creative Consequences of the Rights Clearance Culture for Documentary Filmmakers*. Washington, DC: Center for Social Media, American University.

———. 2007. *The Good, The Bad and the Confusing: User-Generated Video Creators on Copyright*. Washington, DC: Center for Social Media, School of Communication, American University.

———. 2008. *Recut, Reframe, Recycle: Quoting Copyrighted Material in User-Generated Video*. Washington, DC: Center for Social Media, School of Communication, American University.

Balkin, J. 2004. "Digital Speech and Democratic Culture: A Theory of Freedom of Expression for the Information Society." *New York University Law Review* 79: 1–58.

Band, J. 2008. *How Fair Use Prevailed in the Harry Potter Case*. Washington, DC: Association of Research Libraries.

Beebe, B. 2008. "An Empirical Study of U.S. Copyright Fair Use Opinions, 1978–2005," *University of Pennsylvania Law Review* 156 (3): 549–624.

Bielstein, S. M. 2006. *Permissions, A Survival Guide: Blunt Talk about Art as Intellectual Property*. Chicago: University of Chicago Press.

Bollier, D. 2001. *Public Assets, Private Profits: Reclaiming the American Commons in an Age of Market Enclosure*. Washington, DC: New America Foundation.

———. 2002. *Silent Theft: The Private Plunder of Our Common Wealth*. New York: Routledge.

———. 2008. *Viral Spiral: How the Commoners Built a Digital Republic of Their Own*. New York: New Press.

Bollier, D., and T. Watts. 2002. *Saving the Information Commons: A Public Interest Agenda in Digital Media*. Washington, DC: New America Foundation: Public Knowledge.

Bourdieu, P. 1984. *Distinction: A Social Critique of the Judgement of Taste*. Cambridge, MA: Harvard University Press.

Boyle, J. 1996. *Shamans, Software, and Spleens: Law and the Construction of the Information Society*. Cambridge, MA: Harvard University Press.

————. 2008. *The Public Domain: Enclosing the Commons of the Mind.* New Haven, CT: Yale University Press.

Burkart, P. 2009. *Music and Cyberliberties.* Middletown, CT: Wesleyan University Press.

Calabresi, G. 1961. "Some Thoughts on Risk Distribution and the Law of Torts." *Yale Law Journal* 70: 499–553.

Coase, R. H. 1960. "The Problem of Social Cost." *Journal of Law and Economics* 3 (1, 44): 1–44.

Coombe, R. J. 1998. *The Cultural Life of Intellectual Properties: Authorship, Appropriation, and the Law.* Durham, NC: Duke University Press.

Crews, K. 2001. "The Law of Fair Use and the Illusion of Fair-Use Guidelines." *Ohio State Law Journal* 62: 98.

Csikszentmihalyi, M. 1996. *Creativity: Flow and the Psychology of Discovery and Invention.* New York: HarperCollins Publishers.

Deazley, R. 2006. *Rethinking Copyright: History, Theory, Language.* Cheltenham, UK: Northampton, MA: Edward Elgar.

Decherney, P. 2005. *Hollywood and the Culture Elite: How the Movies Became American.* New York: Columbia University Press.

DiCola, P., and K. McLeod. 2011. *Creative License: The Law and Culture of Digital Sampling.* Durham, NC: Duke University Press.

Doctorow, C. 2008. *Content.* San Francisco: Tachyon.

Donaldson, M. C. 2008. *Clearance and Copyright: Eveything You Need to Know for Film and Television.* Los Angeles: Silman-James Press.

Elkin-Koren, N. 2005. "Intellectual and Public Values: What Contracts Cannot Do; The Limits of Private Ordering in Facilitating a Creative Commons." *Fordham Law Review* 74: 375–422.

Elkin-Koren, N., O. Fischman Afori, et al. 2011. "Fair Use Best Practices for Higher Education Institutions: The Israeli Experience." *Journal of the Copyright Society of U.S.A.* Forthcoming. Available at http://papers.ssrn.com/sol3/papers.cfm?abstract_id=1648408.

Fisher, W. W. 2004. *Promises to Keep: Technology, Law, and the Future of Entertainment.* Stanford, CA: Stanford Law and Politics.

Flynn, S., and P. Jaszi. [2009]. *Untold Stories in South Africa: Creative Consequences of the Rights Clearance Culture for Documentary Filmmakers.* Washington, DC: Program on Intellectual Property and the Public Interest, Washington College of Law, American University. (See p. 63.)

Gibson, J. 2007. "Risk Aversion and Rights Accretion in Intellectual Property Law" *Yale Law Journal* 116: 882–951.

Gillespie, T. 2007. *Wired Shut: Copyright and the Shape of Digital Culture.* Cambridge, MA: MIT Press.

————. 2009. "Characterizing Copyright in the Classroom: The Cultural Work of Antipiracy Campaigns." *Communication, Culture & Critique* 2 (3): 274–318.

Hauben, M., and R. Hauben. 1997. *Netizens: On the History and Impact of Usenet and the Internet.* Los Alamitos, CA: IEEE Computer Society Press.

Hobbes, R. 2010. *Conquering Copyright Confusion: How the Doctrine of Fair Use Supports 21st Century Learning.* Thousand Oaks, CA: Corwin.

Hobbs, R., P. Jaszi, et al. 2007. *The Cost of Copyright Confusion for Media Literacy.* Washington, DC: Center for Social Media, School of Communication, American University.

Hugenholtz, P. B., and R. L. Okediji. 2008. *Conceiving an International Instrument on Limitations and Exceptions to Copyright: Final Report.* Geneva, Switzerland: Open Society Institute.

Hyde, L. 2005. *Frames from the Framers: How America's Revolutionaries Imagined Intellectual Property.* Cambridge, MA: Berkman Center for Internet and Society. Research Publication 2005–08.

———. 2007. *The Gift: Creativity and the Artist in the Modern World.* New York: Vintage Books.

———. 2010. *Common as Air: Revolution, Art, and Ownership.* New York: Farrar, Straus & Giroux.

Kaplan, B. 2005. *An Unhurried View of Copyright, Republished (and with Contributions from Friends).* Newark, NJ: LexisNexis Matthew Bender.

Keller, B. P., and J. P. Cunard. 2001. *Copyright Law: A Practitioner's Guide.* New York: PLI Press.

Joyce, C., M. Leaffer, P. Jaszi, and T. Ochoa. 2010. *Copyright Law.* Newark, NJ: LexisNexis.

Jenkins, H. 2006. *Convergence Culture: Where Old and New Media Collide.* New York: New York University Press.

Judge, E. 2009. "Kidnapped and Counterfeit Characters: Eighteenth-Century Fan Fiction, Copyright Law, and Custody of Fictional Characters." In *Originality and Intellectual Property in the French and English Enlightenment,* ed. R. McGinnis, 22–68. Routledge, New York.

Larsen, L. O., and T. U. Naerland. 2010. "Documentary in a Culture of Clearance: A Study of Knowledge of and Attitudes toward Copyright and Fair Use among Norwegian Documentary Makers." *Popular Communication* 8(1): 46–60.

Latman, A. 1960. "Study No. 14: Fair Use of Copyrighted Works." In *Copyright Law Revision: Studies Prepared for the Subcommittee on Patents, Trademarks and Copyrights of the Committee on the Judiciary, U.S. Senate, 86th Congress, 2d Session pursuant to S. Res. 240.* Washington, DC: Government Printing Office.

Lessig, L. 1999. *Code and Other Laws of Cyberspace.* New York: Basic Books.

———. 2001. *The Future of Ideas: The Fate of the Commons in a Connected World.* New York: Random House.

———. 2004. *Free Culture: How Big Media Uses Technology and the Law to Lock Down Culture and Control Creativity.* New York: Penguin Press.

———. 2008. *Remix: Making Art and Commerce Thrive in the Hybrid Economy.* New York: Penguin Press.

Leval, P. N. 1990. "Toward a Fair Use Standard." *Harvard Law Review* 103: 1105–36.

Litman, J. 2006. *Digital Copyright.* Amherst, NY: Prometheus Books.

Logie, J. 2006. *Peers, Pirates, and Persuasion: Rhetoric in the Peer-to-Peer Debates.* West Lafayette, IN: Parlor Press.

Macpherson, C. B. 1962. *The Political Theory of Possessive Individualism: Hobbes to Locke.* Oxford: Clarendon Press.

Madison, M. J. 2004. "A Pattern-Oriented Approach to Fair Use." *William and Mary Law Review* 45: 1525.

Maxwell, T. A. 2009. Uncle Tom's Cabin in the Public Domain. Available at SSRN: http://ssrn.com/abstract=1481382.

McLeod, K. 2005. *Freedom of Expression: Overzealous Copyright Bozos and Other Enemies of Creativity.* New York: Doubleday.

Netanel, N. 2008. *Copyright's Paradox*. New York: Oxford University Press.

Patterson, L. R., and S. W. Lindberg. 1991. *The Nature of Copyright: A Law of Users' Rights*. Athens: University of Georgia Press.

Patry, W. 2009. *Moral Panics and the Copyright Wars*. New York: Oxford University Press.

Phillips, V. 2007. "Commodification, Intellectual Property and the Quilters of Gee's Bend." *American University Journal of Gender, Social Policy & the Law* 15: 359–76.

Rogers, T. & Szamosszegi. 2010. *Fair Use in the U.S. Economy*. Washington, DC: Computer & Communication Industry Association.

Procter, J. 2004. *Stuart Hall*. London; New York: Routledge.

Samuelson, P. 1996. "The Copyright Grab." *Wired* (January): http://www.wired.com/wired/archive/4.01/white.paper.

———. 2007. "Leary Lecture: Preliminary Thoughts on Copyright Reform." *Utah Law Review*: 551–71.

———. 2009. *Unbundling Fair Uses: Law and Technology Scholarship*. Berkeley, CA: Berkeley Center for Law and Technology, University of California, Berkeley.

Streeter, T. 2010. *The Net Effect: Romanticism, Capitalism, and the Internet*. New York: New York University Press.

Tushnet, R. 2009. "Economies of Desire: Fair Use and Marketplace Assumptions." *William and Mary Law Review* 51: 513–46.

Ward, T. B., S. M. Smith, et al. 1997. *Creative Thought: An Investigation of Conceptual Structures and Processes*. Washington, DC: American Psychological Association.

Woodmansee, M., and P. Jaszi. 1994. *The Construction of Authorship: Textual Appropriation in Law and Literature*. Durham, NC: Duke University Press.

Working Group on Intellectual Property Rights, Information Infrastructure Task Force. 1995. *Intellectual Property and the National Information Infrastructure: The Report of the Working Group on Intellectual Property Rights*. Bruce Lehmann, Chair. Washington, DC: US Patent and Trademark Office. Available at http://www.uspto.gov/web/offices/com/doc/ipnii/.

INDEX